OLD SOULS

Aged Women, Poverty, and the
Experience of God

OLD SOULS
Aged Women, Poverty, and the Experience of God

HELEN K. BLACK • ROBERT L. RUBINSTEIN

ALDINE DE GRUYTER

New York

About the Authors

Helen K. Black is currently conducting a study at the Philadelphia Geriatric Center.

Robert L. Rubinstein is Professor of Anthropology at the University of Maryland at Baltimore County.

ALDINE DE GRUYTER
A division of Walter de Gruyter, Inc.
200 Saw Mill River Road
Hawthorne, New York 10532

This publication is printed on acid free paper ∞

Library of Congress Cataloging-in-Publication Data

Black, Helen K., 1952-
    Old souls : aged women, poverty, and the experience of God / by Helen K. Black and Robert L. Rubinstein.
        p. cm.
    Includes bibliographical references and index.
    ISBN 0-202-30633-X (cloth : acid-free paper) — ISBN 0-202-30634-8 (paper : acid-free paper)
    1. Aged women—Pennsylvania—Philadelphia Metropolitan Area—Economic conditions—Case studies. 2. Aged women—New Jersey—Economic conditions—Case studies. 3. Aged women—Pennsylvania—Philadelphia Metropolitan Area—Social conditions—Case studies. 4. Aged women—New Jersey—Social conditions—Case studies. 5. Poor aged—Pennsylvania—Philadelphia Metropolitan Area—Case studies. 6. Poor aged—New Jersey—Case studies. 7. Aged women—Pennsylvania—Philadelphia Metropolitan Area—Religious life—Case studies. 8 Aged women—New Jersey—Religious life—Case studies. I. Rubinstein, Robert L. II. Title.

HQ1064.U6 P424 2000
305.26'09748'11—dc21

                                                                99-054971

Manufactured in the United States of America

10 9 8 7 6 5 4 3 2 1

This book is dedicated to
Helen A. Black
who showed me how to love;
Professor Leonid D. Rudnytzky
who taught me that confidence is humility;
and
Bob
who gave me the opportunity to use what I learned.

Table of Contents

Preface   ix

1 Introduction and Theoretical Description   1

    Methods   3
    Issues of Narrative   6
    Issues of Class, Gender, and Race   7
    The Experience of God   9
    Background   10
    Explanation of Further Chapters   12

2 Subjective and Objective Poverty   19

    Summary   45

3 Expectations   47

    Expectations Shaped by the Legacy of Family   47
    Expectations Shaped by Gender   57
    Expectations Shaped by Social Class   60
    Expectations Shaped by Perceived Limitations   62
    Accomplishments in Light of Expectations 64
    Summary   70

4 Self-Presentation   73

    The Life Story   74
    Themes   83
    The Theme of Independence   86
    Temporal Focus of Presentation   89
    Summary   96

5 Strategies and Techniques of Coping with Poverty   97

    Generativity Used as a Coping Strategy   97
    Spirituality Used as a Coping Strategy   107
    Accomplishments Used as a Coping Strategy 113
    Summary   118

6 Class and Self-Concept   **121**

   Perception of Privilege   122
   Perception of Poverty   131
   Class Awareness   135
   Social Forces   139
   The Interview   144
   Summary   148

7 Thoughts of the Future   **151**

   Issues of Spirituality   155
   The Afterlife   161
   Paranormal Experiences   166
   Issues of Dying and Death   171
   Expectations for Future Generations   176
   Summary   183

8 Poverty as a Moral Issue   **185**

   Summary   206

9 The Value of Retrospection   **209**

   Self as Package   215
   Characters in the Story   221
   Metaphors   228
   Summary   232

10   Conclusion   **233**

   Subjective and Objective Poverty   234
   Future Research   235

References   **237**

Index   **241**

PREFACE

WHAT THIS BOOK IS ABOUT

This is a book about older women and their subjective experience of chronic poverty. The case studies used in this book came from a research study entitled, "Chronic Poverty and the Self in Later Life." The National Institute of Aging (5 RO1 AG11233) funded our research. Data were collected through in-depth, qualitative interviews that began by asking respondents to tell their life story. The interviews took place between 1993 and 1997 in Philadelphia and its surrounding suburbs, and in southern New Jersey. After obtaining the life history, interviewers asked respondents to talk about their financial histories and other aspects of their lives. This book is the result of the wealth of information that women shared about their pasts, their presents, and their thoughts about the future, especially in light of living in poverty.

Although this book provides a myriad of details about the lives of older women who are poor, three important points emerged in the analysis of our data. First, poor women of all backgrounds rarely saw themselves as victims of oppression, but interpreted their experience of hardship through the small lens of everyday life and especially their personal relationships. Second, as they aged, many women grew increasingly proactive, making day-by-day choices in their lives that are authentically the stuff of independence. Finally, many of these women spoke of the role of God in their lives in response either to specific questions or otherwise. For the authors, the women's emphasis on God was striking, and thus it is recalled in the title of this book.

INTERVIEWERS

Interviews were conducted by a research team that altered during the course of the 4-year project. Two full-time interviewers (one is the first author) are Caucasian women who conducted most of the interviews and worked the duration of the project. Of the two part-time interviewers, one is an African-American woman who worked for the first year of the project and the other is a Caucasian woman who worked approximately 6 months of the project. The second author, who was the project's Principal Investigator, also conducted interviews.

RESPONDENTS

The respondents for our study were 50 Caucasian and 50 African-American women, who were over 70 years of age, and were either divorced, separated, or widowed. This group of 100 women fell under our "objective" measure of poverty, i.e., they were poor according to 1992 Federal income standards. A contrast group of 50 Caucasian and 12 African-American nonpoor women were also recruited for the study.

WHO WE ARE

Helen K. Black was a full time researcher in the study of Chronic Poverty. She is currently conducting a study at the Philadelphia Geriatric Center on elders' personal definitions of suffering under the rubrics of health and spirituality. Robert L. Rubinstein was the Principal Investigator of the Chronic Poverty study. Formerly Director of Research for the Philadelphia Geriatric Center, he is currently Professor of Anthropology at the University of Maryland at Baltimore County and continues to do research at the Philadelphia Geriatric Center. Helen K. Black wrote the majority of this manuscript, including the case studies and their analysis, and developed the overall structure and analytical plan. Rubinstein provided additional material.

ACKNOWLEDGMENTS

It is difficult to adequately express our thanks to the women who shared their life stories with us. Without their interest in our research, their willingness to talk about their lives and their financial histories, and their ability to articulate their thoughts and feelings within their narratives, we could neither have engaged in our research nor have written this book. Since respondents' narratives usually included other characters, we protect the privacy of both our informants and their significant others by using pseudonyms, initials, or fictitious place names in this book.

We also acknowledge the support of the National Institute on Aging (NIA). The stories that follow offer a slice of history that has largely been ignored—how women living in poverty experienced their "smaller" world of home and workplace as framed by the "larger" world of historical realities, such as the Depression and World War II. This "other" history might not have been told without the funding of the NIA.

The project itself could not have been completed without the talent of the research team. We wish to thank Dr. Marcene Goodman, formerly senior research scientist at the Philadelphia Geriatric Center. She was a consummate recruiter, interviewer, and creative thinker on matters relating to this study; Dr. Anne R. Bower, senior research scientist at the Philadelphia Geriatric Center, gave her invaluable skills as a linguist and interviewer to this project; Dr. Felicia Hill, formerly a clinical psychologist at the Philadelphia Geriatric Center, offered her interviewing and analytical expertise to the study because of her personal interest in this research.

The first author also wishes to thank her colleagues, especially Anita Garber, Christine Hoffman, and Mary McCaffrey, at the Philadelphia Geriatric Center. They provided unfailing camaraderie, encouragement, good humor, and wisdom during the construction of this book.

1

&

Introduction and Theoretical Description

This book springs from a research project entitled "Chronic Poverty and the Self in Later Life." The project explored the experiences of older women who have lived in poverty throughout their lives. The major specific aim of our research was to explore the relationship of poverty to notions of self and personal and cultural identity in later life. The main question asked was: How do elders who have been poor most or all of their lives face the personal, developmental, and cultural tasks associated with old age?

Our research was an anthropological, qualitative study concerned with the personal meaning of poverty. Personal meaning may be defined as each person's interpretation or version of her own life, abstracted from shared, cultural meanings and individual experience (Rubinstein, 1992). The "activity" of personal meaning is interpretation. In this case, our research examined the effects of a single "objective" stimulus, lifelong and current poverty, on subjectively held notions of "meaning" and "purpose" in later life. In other words, our research engaged "objectively" poor informants, and members of a comparison group, and asked them to reflect on, interpret, and make subjective "sense" of the objective state of poverty.

It is important to note that we, as authors, situate ourselves not as students of poverty but as gerontologists. Our accountability is to the community of aging research—to those who study the cognitive, emotional, and spiritual development of elders. In this case, we ask particularly how chronic poverty affects the development and self-concept of women in later life. It is surprising how rarely lifetime, chronic poverty—a reality for many people—is viewed as a developmental issue outside of childhood. Certainly poverty in childhood and youth is a tragedy whose deleterious effects last a lifetime. We asked those elders who were poor as children and adolescents a "follow-up" question. What happens when prior patterns of poverty continue into adulthood and later life? The meaning of poverty in older age is qualitatively different from the meaning of poverty experienced earlier

1

in life (Townsend, 1970). In youth, expectations for an "improved" life may remain strong despite poverty. In older age, past experience of hardship and the sheer work of survival allow little time or hope that your financial status will improve. Through our research, we explored the link between the important tasks of aging, such as finding meaning in life and granting cohesion to the life story, and chronic poverty. Are the assaults against an integrated aging self, such as illness and loss, unmanageable when poverty is added to this mix? Is the Eriksonian concept of generativity significant to a person struggling simply to survive? In sum, we asked how women in our study dealt with the "work" of aging while coping with the hardship of poverty.

Therefore, the focus of our study was on women who are now poor and have always been poor—the chronically poor—rather than those who became poor for the first time in later life. Our particular interest was in studying mainstream poor women, the so-called working poor—those who have spent most of their working lives in poorly paying jobs—and the marginally employed poor—those whose income histories have been erratic or who have been homemakers in poor families. It is important to note that almost no recent work has examined the personal or cultural meaning of lifelong poverty among mainstream elders and the subjectively perceived effects of poverty on their lives, on their notions of who they are, or on their lifetime development. Our research was directed to this subjective experience of lifelong poverty among these women.

One important aspect of our book is to examine the tension between subjective and objective notions of poverty. To reiterate, the focus of this book is on subjective or personal meaning. We focus on the subjective experience of poverty for the women interviewed, recognizing that poverty, as a concept, is as fluid as the context in which it is used.

In the context of elderly women, poverty as a financial status intermingles with the effects of racism, social status, educational level, and health care. Because of this intertwining, "the word [poverty] has no absolute meaning which can be applied in all societies at all times" (Abel-Smith & Townsend, 1972). We recall some of the questions that we asked in our research proposal:

What is the experience of lifelong and current poverty?

What is it like to have been poor all your life and now be old?

Has chronic poverty affected or shaped personal and cultural identity in later life and if so in what ways?

How do poor elders compare themselves to other elders?

How do notions of the life course as a sociocultural construct differ for elders who are chronically poor and for those who are not?

Do poor elders see themselves as poor?

How do poor elders evaluate their lives retrospectively?

What is the status of developmental notions including generativity, integrity, and lifetime accomplishments among chronically poor elders?

What strategies or techniques do poor older women use to ameliorate what they perceive to be the negative effects of poverty, including interpersonal relations or religious techniques?

The chapters that follow develop material and analysis that treats these questions.

METHODS

Conceptual Framework

To reiterate, we are not attempting to provide a sociological, conceptual, or theoretical framework for the study of poverty. Neither are we offering a definition of poverty, even as a relative concept, that would speak to the copula of gender, race, and social status of our elderly respondents. We view ourselves as gerontologists who have studied a particular group of elderly women that has lived its life in "objective" poverty, as determined by income standards of the United States government. However, we looked to our informants to provide a definition of what poverty is, and whether they are, indeed, poor. Therefore, the conceptual framework of our research is based on a model of the person derived from work in cultural anthropology and gerontology (Rubinstein, 1989, 1992). This model sees the older person as the active constructor, interpreter, and creator of meaning and focuses on the personal meaning systems of older people as part of the larger system of cultural and social meaning. This model is particularly relevant to the subjective experience of the person—in this case to elderly impoverished women—and how the person views herself and her world in light of her age and her poverty.

We engaged the meaning systems of our respondents through a carefully crafted interview schedule that included requests to hear women's (1) life story, (2) financial history, and (3) answers to questions concerning past dreams, memories, daily experiences, and thoughts about the future. The interview schedule consisted of open-ended questions designed to evoke extensive life and financial histories as well as narratives about past expectations, present concerns, and future plans. This methodology of qualitative interviewing enabled researchers to validate initial informant statements (including statements concerning income) through the development of trust and rapport, and by reintroducing initial comments for reflexive discussion in ongoing interviews and various information contexts. The interview focused particularly on respondents' feelings about their poverty and its effects on their past, present, and perceived future quality of life.

Respondents

The participants in our study were 50 Caucasian and 50 African-American widowed, divorced, or separated women ($n=100$), aged 70 or over, whose monthly income was $766 or below if they lived alone. This figure adheres to the 1992 Federal standard for poverty in a one-person household. If the woman interviewed shared her household, the poverty level of her household size and income was used to determine eligibility for the project.

The average age of poor Caucasian respondents was 80. The oldest respondent in this category was 96 and the youngest respondent was 70. The average monthly income for this group was $586; the average years of education was 9.8. When asked, "What religion are you?" 22 women in this group answered Catholic, 13 Protestant, 11 Jewish, 1 Ukrainian Catholic, 1 Pentecostal Interdenominational, 1 Reformed Baptist, and 1 woman answered "none."

The average age of the poor African-American respondents was 76. The oldest respondent was 88 and the youngest respondent was 70. The average monthly income for this group was $574; the average years of education was 9.5. In this group 33 women indicated that they were Baptist, 5 Catholic, 4 Methodist, 3 Holiness, 2 Protestant, 2 Pentecostal, and 1 Episcopalian.

Also interviewed for our initial study was a contrast group of women subject to a different set of income criteria. Income criteria for the nonpoor comparison groups was set at four times the 1992 official poverty line, and ranged from $2200 to $4166 a month (an amount construed to represent a "middle-class" level of subsistence).

The intention in selecting the income range was to see the "gap" between the incomes of the poor and the comparison group, and to tap into the stories of those "middle-class" women who shared in reaping the benefits of the "American dream." The authors realize that the monthly income of the latter groups did not determine their "real" income or class status. Indeed, the assets of women in the nonpoor groups had a wide range. Many women in the contrast groups, while receiving a fluid monthly income that adhered to our "objective" income criteria, held other assets, such as certificates, stocks, mutual funds, and real estate, that raised their level of income. For this reason we designated our comparison group "nonpoor" rather than "middle class" to reflect their broad scope of assets. Sixty-two

women (50 Caucasian, 12 African-American) were interviewed in this latter, nonpoor financial category.

The average age of the nonpoor Caucasian women was 81. The oldest
respondent was 96 and the youngest respondent was 71. The average
monthly income for this group was $3700; the average years of education
was 15.5. In this group 28 women indicated that they were Protestant, 11 Jewish, 3 Catholic, 3 Quaker, 2 Methodist, 1 Unitarian, and 2 women answered
"none."

The average age of the nonpoor African-American women was 76. The
oldest respondent in this group was 87 and the youngest respondent was
70. Their average monthly income was $2283; their average years of edu-
cation was 14.3. Nine women described themselves as Protestant and 3 as
Catholic.

Procedure

The poor respondents in our study were actively recruited through senior centers, subsidized housing and community outreach programs (home
repair, energy, and legal assistance), newsletters from senior organizations,
and housing project flyers.

Nonpoor women interviewed in the study were actively recruited
through senior centers, retired women's professional groups, the alumni
of local universities, and members of church groups.

Data for the study were collected in Philadelphia and its suburbs and in
southern New Jersey between 1993 and 1997. Private interviews were conducted in the respondents' homes for intimacy and comfort and lasted
from 1 to 3 hours in each of two to three sessions.

Format

The interview began with the interviewer asking the respondent to tell
her life story. We emphasize that the use of the life story question at the
beginning of the interview is a respectful, creative, and effective way of
accessing subjectively significant experiences. We have used, and continue to use this format in many studies of sensitive topics with elderly
informants.

After obtaining the life story, we explored the women's financial histories, focusing on their financial pasts during childhood and young adulthood, their economic situation during marriage, and how their financial
circumstances changed when they became widowed, separated, or divorced.
After providing their life stories and financial histories, respondents were
asked questions about their personal achievements and sense of self, such
as whether they held youthful dreams, hold goals for the future, their opinions on current events, and their thoughts about daily life experiences,

particularly in light of poverty. Answers to most questions were probed with tailor-made follow-up questions.

ISSUES OF NARRATIVE

The ethnographic narration of qualitative interviewing is appropriate for the framework used in our research—the model of the person as active interpreter and constructor of life's meaning. The method used in our research follows studies that used the life story to tease out the personal meaning of complex concepts, such as old age, quality of life, or, in this case, poverty (Kaufman, 1986; Gubrium, 1993). Although "poverty" as a concept may be too abstract to be incorporated into a personal identity, recounting one's life inclusive of episodes of "having it hard" or "just getting by" concretizes poverty and elucidates its subjective meaning. Thus, the life story is the juncture at which an individual life lived in specific circumstances at a particular period in history comes together (Josselson, 1993).

Although women of this cohort may feel removed from actually creating or developing historical events, a woman's self-image was fostered, in part, by her social place in the larger world. She took the meaning and purpose of her role in society and adapted it into the smaller context of everyday life. Since a people's history is a history of individuals, women both created a personal and social history and lived within a history that created them, their expectations, limitations, and possibilities (Funkenstein, 1993). Women rarely talked about the "larger" world under such a heading (Rosenthal, 1993); they simply shaped individual ambitions, dreams, and talents into the narrow mold of acceptable roles for women of their cohort. Within their narratives, women interpreted and reenacted their lives; they explicitly "spelled out" for themselves as well as the interviewer its implicit meaning. The meaning of life, explicated through the life story, is constructed along with a self who becomes interpreter of a personal and historical past and predictor of the future (Funkenstein, 1993).

The interview process may be seen to construct reality as much as describe it. However, starting with a request to hear the life story invites respondents to "be first" in selecting where to begin (in childhood, youth, or adulthood) and how to begin (with an event, issue, or feeling that is significant). Although the questions that follow (concerning finances and day-to-day life) are semistructured, the interview's open-endedness provides informants with a voice to describe the world from alternate vantage points (Gubrium & Holstein, 1997). The interview process remains a social interaction whose outcome is uncertain; it is dependent on the intention as well as on the conversational give and take of both interviewer and respondent (Facio, 1993).

In our study, women were comfortable with story telling; most respondents enjoyed recounting their life. Quite a few informants began their life story with a comment such as, "You'll never hear a story like mine," or ended the interview with a question like, "Did you ever hear of such a life?" In the act of emplotting their life story, respondents created a narrative identity, i.e., a sense of an integrated self articulating their life's personal and public events and adhering their smaller world to the larger world (Widdershoven, 1993). This idea of women's smaller and larger worlds will be developed throughout the book.

It is important to note that respondents were asked to remember feelings and reproduce incidents that took place up to 75 or more years ago. This retrospective view creates a past that becomes true with the present telling. In this sense our book mirrors the women's retrospective reconstruction. Although we used the "real" notes and transcripts from the original tape recordings from the women's interviews, we are rebuilding them according to our subjective experience of the women, their homes, the ease or tension of the interview, and our own biases. Ethnographic writings are fictions only in the sense that we create another story out of the "real" dialogue with respondents (Geertz, 1973). Because the interview is indeed a dialogue, what results is the unique outcome of an interaction between two people. If someone other than the particular interviewer spoke with a particular respondent, a different story would have been told.

ISSUES OF AGE, CLASS, GENDER, AND RACE

Salient issues that interconnect with the subjective experience of poverty are those of age, class, gender, and race. Since female identity is deeply linked to a physical form, gender and age impose particular experiences of personhood (Gergen & Gergen, 1993). To be an elderly woman in Western society is to be both subject and object—you objectify yourself according to the value society places on being female and elderly, then you conform to a set of behaviors that is consonant with each (Rubinstein, 1996). Your self-concept is forged, diminished, or enhanced by critiquing this objectified self.

Adding a class status based on finances to this identity pot imposes yet another set of expectations about life that informs your sense of self (Bower, 1996). An elderly nonpoor woman assumes and displays an identity that is qualitatively different from those assumed and displayed by women in other financial situations, such as poverty (Fraser, 1997). For example, women's presentation in the interview, such as clothes worn or refreshments offered, as well as what is considered "suitable" discourse for the interview, has much to do with women's perceived class status. Some theorists state that class status is easily identified; it is as apparent as your age, gender, and race (Cannon, 1997).

Color adds another facet to the structure of identity. Although all elderly African-American women face the problem of "triple jeopardy" (King, 1988), that is, being aged, female, and of minority status, poor African-American respondents were the most vulnerable group in our sample concerning health, income, and lack of social support. Despite enduring lifelong hardship, most of the poor African-American women interviewed displayed positive self-esteem. For this group, personal spirituality was used most often to deflect and cope with long-term adversity (Grant, 1989; Jackson et al., 1993).

Although both Caucasian and African-American women from the poverty groups and Caucasian women from the nonpoor group were easily accessed, recruited, and interviewed, women from the African-American nonpoor sample were more difficult to access. Despite extensive recruiting, only 12 nonpoor African-American women participated in the study.

The cognitive dissonance of middle-class African-Americans has been well documented (Frazier, 1962). Despite reaching the American dream, i.e., climbing the ladder built of particular cultural and social values toward material success, they learned that induction into middle-class life, such as welcome into middle-class neighborhoods, was fraught with color barriers (Black, 1997a).

Twelve nonpoor African-American women requested to be interviewed. However, some of their interview answers reflect Cannon's (1997) belief that although poor African-American women may accept the "descending hand of whites," nonpoor African-American women need not. They have a different vantage point from poor women of any color. They became aware early in life that they and their families, particularly fathers and husbands, had as much or more talent than Caucasian counterparts, yet were forced to work harder for similar or lesser rewards. They protected themselves against "let[ting] a white person, particularly a lower class white person, know anything about them." Witness this response from a nonpoor African-American respondent when asked if she considered herself a religious or spiritual person.

> What does that have to do with anything? For a white person to talk about African-American spirituality, oh no. It seems to me that this is something that goes back to slavery, back to the secrecy that we had, that we had to have. This is hallowed ground. It has to remain between us.

Our awareness that race and class together are significant issues to be further explored in the context of cross-interviewing engendered further questions. Why did poor and nonpoor Caucasian women request to be interviewed? In the case of nonpoor Caucasian women, sharing their life story reaped a two-fold benefit. Although they enjoyed the interaction of the interview, they also seemed gratified to participate in an endeavor that would "help others." Many were knowledgeable about and approved of the goals of research.

Success with recruitment of poor women was no doubt aided by the $100 honorarium we gave to each informant as a "thank you" for her time. Nonpoor informants received a $50 honorarium. Perhaps our ability to "pay for" personal information forced poor women into becoming a captive group for study (Roach & Roach, 1972; Zimmerman, 1997). Indeed, people who have experienced severe economic and social problems often "need" to discuss their hardship with perceived "powerful" others (Bentz, 1997). This leads to questions for researchers, such as: How much of "reality" can interviewers see? How are informant narratives edited for presentation to interviewers? What are alternative purposes for presentation of narrative accounts? Our best response to these questions is to deliver informants' answers, and their conditions of creation, as completely as possible.

We are convinced that our description and interpretation of respondents' stories result in the dissemination of a cultural and historical knowledge that would not have been accessed other than through our research. We believe, from respondents' comments, telephone calls, and cards written to interviewers after the interview, that the women interviewed had found a welcome and coactive environment for talking about the significance of their lives.

THE EXPERIENCE OF GOD

Women's personal and collective histories shaped their experience of God. Their history of poverty as well as their belief in God as personal, concrete, and this-worldly are mirrored in their prayers and in their self-concept. Respondents conversed with God about everyday issues—of illness, financial hardship, family worries, and fears of dying alone. When one respondent was a destitute young mother, she prayed for and received the miracle of "getting milk money" for her infant son.

> I got that milk. But I had the faith. You have to have faith because I don't think—. If you don't have faith, I don't think that the incident or whatever will never happen. It will never happen if you don't have the faith. Part of what happens is your believing it will happen.

The above comment shows that she took an active stance before God, and believed that the onus of responsibility for the miracle's occurrence rested on her faith. This sense of responsibility led her to (1) a relationship of perceived reciprocity with God and (2) self-esteem in being the "other" partner in this alliance of reciprocal power. Women's active faith ensured God's corresponding gifts, particularly when they were most needed (Mitchell, 1975; Blank, 1992).

Although most poor women used their faith both as a way of viewing themselves and others and as a way of adapting to the harshness of the world, they did *not* use it as an opiate for passivity and submission (Pargament, 1997). Women did not construe their relationship with God as an entitlement to an easier life, but as a route toward heightened independence and self-reliance. They often cast God in the role of a long time, loving, and powerful friend who is empathetically aware of the details of their lives. They perceived themselves as knowledgeable about the ways of God; they spoke easily about God's purposeful instantiation in their everyday affairs. They believed, therefore, that the intimacy of shared experiences prompted God's hand to heal physically, comfort emotionally, and help financially.

BACKGROUND

Poverty as a concept is certainly complex and there is dispute over how to define or evaluate it. The breadth and intricacy of poverty as a concept are shown in the absolute and relative definitions of poverty that connect to the definer's culture (Mencher, 1972). For example, Ruggles and Moon (1986) calculate the 1984 poverty rate for six measures of poverty that range from earnings only, to all cash income, to cash plus food stamps and all medical benefits. Despite disparate figures, the general consensus is that some 42% of elderly Americans are poor, near poor, or economically vulnerable (Villiers Foundation, 1987).

Despite this, there have been strides made in the economic well-being of the elderly in the past decades. The good news about the general decrease in the poverty rate and an overall increase in the incomes of many elders is offset by a number of counterbalancing trends. In fact, whereas the percentage of aged poor has decreased from 15% in 1976 to 12.2% in 1987, the percentage of poor and near poor (between 100 and 125% of the poverty line) has fallen from 25 to 20.3% in the same period but has been unchanged since about 1983 (Smeeding, 1990). Also, particular subpopulations of elders are particularly vulnerable to poverty: minorities, women (Davis et al., 1992), the unmarried, urban dwellers (Ford et al., 1992), and the old old (Hess, 1987). Although the economic status of elders as a group has improved through the past two decades, the economic status of older couples and single older men has improved more than single women. As a result, the income gap between married and unmarried elderly women has increased. In fact, the problems facing elderly poor people are said to be largely a reflection of single women's poverty, including women who are divorced, separated, or widowed (Brubaker, 1994; Dodge, 1996).

Gerontological research has examined the occurrence and nature of poverty among elders. In contrast to the assumption that poverty in later life is entirely stable, recent studies have demonstrated that, objectively, such poverty can in part be dynamic (Bound et al., 1991; Coe, 1988; Moon, 1988; Holden et al., 1986). These studies demonstrate that some senior adults can move in and out of poverty, particularly around life events such as retirement (Burkhauser & Duncan, 1988), widowhood (cited in Moon, 1988; Bound et al., 1991; Crystal & Beck, 1992), and through illness (Smeeding, 1990; Clark, 1988). However, it is also true that previous poverty in life tends to predict current poverty (Ruggles, 1987).

Antecedent conditions to lifelong poverty have also been examined. Most clearly (and germane to this research) is the list of predisposing factors: previous poverty, employment history, greater age, low educational attainment (Crystal et al., 1992), uninsured catastrophic health expenses (Coughlin et al., 1992), urban residence, gender, and racial status are all predictive of later life economic status (Schiller, 1989). Besides those who have always been poor, there are those who may move into poverty at retirement or widowhood. In part these are the so-called tweeners: elderly lower and middle-income persons (20% of all elders and 40% of elders living alone) with income between 100 and 200% of the poverty line, who are particularly vulnerable to the effects of catastrophic life events and are largely dependent on income from Social Security (Smeeding, 1986). The poverty rate for older unmarried women is about 21% (Moon, 1988). African-American widows are among the poorest and most vulnerable elders (Chatters & Jackson, 1989).

Michael Harrington's (1965) "rediscovery" of American poverty in the early 1960s highlighted its prevalence after the Depression years. Despite a remarkable improvement in the material welfare of many Americans after World War II, over 25 million Americans remained "poor" (The President's Commission in Income Maintenance Programs, 1972). This "Paradox of Poverty" underscored poverty's link to personal value, i.e., that the poor were the marginal in society—African-Americans, unmarried women, and the elderly (King, 1964; Roach & Roach, 1972; Lloyd, 1994). The notion that poverty is related to a fluid economic standard of living *and* to a normative idea of the "person" gives a moral, political, and social meaning to the word poverty (Jones, 1990; Jordan, 1996).

Thus, of central interest as an objective stimulus state for this subjectively oriented research were older chronically poor women. The unmarried women we interviewed (1) were full-time homemakers, with current income now largely contingent on former husband's earnings, (2) have full-time work histories in low paying jobs, or (3) have histories of partial, seasonal, interrupted, or marginal work.

Distinct from research that studied the poor for "pathological" behavior or as a contrast group in surveys on the interests of the middle class (Roach & Roach, 1972), our research placed poor women as the bases of comparison in qualitative ethnographic research, with nonpoor women acting as the group of comparison. For that reason, the majority of case studies used in this book are gleaned from the poverty sample of our respondents. Nonpoor case studies were used mainly to compare or contrast analyses of case studies of poor women.

EXPLANATION OF FURTHER CHAPTERS

We have divided this book into 10 chapters with various subheadings. Within each chapter we use case studies to illustrate the analysis of our data. Because the study on which this book is based is a qualitative study, we present little in the way of statistical data. Rather, the format we use is the case narrative. To illustrate the main topic or issue of each chapter, we introduce a number of case presentations of informants. These rely heavily on interview notes and on verbatim transcripts of tape-recorded interviews. Each case is used to highlight a salient issue or theme that emerged in many of the women's narratives, and to flesh out an interpretation or conclusion we make concerning those issues or themes. This is handled in a descriptive rather than a statistical way. Methodologically, as well as in our narrative reports, our goal was to illuminate informants' qualities of experiences and their interpretations.

The first chapter, Introduction and Theoretical Description, presents the purpose and goals of our initial research. This chapter examines the major questions asked in the study, the methods used to gather data, and the conceptual framework on which the study was constructed. In Chapter 1 we look at the importance of qualitative interviewing and narrative as methodological tools to gather data. We also examine issues of age, class, gender, and race and their significance to the findings of the study. We offer a commentary on the salience of women's experience of God in our analysis of data. We provide a brief background concerning old age and poverty and offer a summary of the nine chapters that follow.

In the second chapter, entitled Subjective and Objective Poverty, we explore the intertwining of subjective experience with objective phenomena and reiterate our focus on the subjective experience of poverty. We recognize that any concept of poverty is dependent on the context in which it is used and acknowledge that only in pinning life experience to its cultural and historical context can the experience (in this case, of poverty) be described and interpreted. We negate the idea that there can be an objective notion of poverty without a story that defines it. In this chapter we also explore the subjective experience of reliving an objective past (in poverty) through narrative. Through analysis of our data and its presentation through case studies, we present a new concept of the paradox of poverty, the fact that the subjective experience of poverty has so little to do with objective criteria.

The third chapter is entitled Expectations. It became clear to us that women's expectations for their lives were important to their experiences of poverty. This chapter focuses on women's retrospective views of what they expected from life as adolescents or young adults. Reviewing past expectations often became a springboard for respondents to describe their life course, particularly for what they achieved in light of what they expected. Chapter 3 demonstrates that expectations about life are tacitly embedded within the life story. Past expectations are both revealed as well as constructed in light of present day achievements and concerns. Some respondents admitted that "just surviving day by day" during the Depression years of childhood and young adulthood precluded having goals or making plans for life. Some women recalled earlier expectations that either "came true" or failed to materialize. Other women built or reconstructed their youthful expectations by focusing on what they achieved.

Expectations were shaped for respondents in at least four ways: (1) by the legacy of family, (2) by gender, (3) by social class, and, (4) by perceived limitations. Examining women's expectations is one point of departure for understanding how respondents came to explain, interpret, or deny their poverty. Past expectations placed alongside present achievements lent a balance to life stories. The women whose case studies are used in Chapter 3 showed expectations about their lives that were both unique to themselves and common to their age, gender, race, and the era in which they lived.

The fourth chapter, Self-Presentation, deals with how women presented themselves in the interview. We focus on this interview question: "Would you describe your life for me; whatever comes to your mind about what happened along the way. Start where you like and take as much time as you need." We examine the way women began their life stories, described their relationships with significant others, offered a newly constructed or pervading life theme, and where they temporally focused their narrative. The request to hear a life story allows respondents to see themselves as the agent of what happened along the life course. It also permits their life story to emerge from the vantage of older age and the standpoint of late life development. The requested story lets the past be told over against the present, i.e., to list expectations in light of achievements and to name limitations in light of accomplishments.

In Chapter 4 we also examine the themes that pervade women's narratives. Because the theme of independence was salient in most respondents' life stories, we devote a special section to that theme. Women's independence is connected to their ability to choose. Making choices within the boundaries of poverty was the cornerstone of independence. If going without or getting into debt were the perceived alternatives, depriving yourself of a pleasure seemed not only the sensible choice, but one that gave women control over their lives. Presenting yourself through the life story is like describing a journey. You are both observer of and participant in what happened along the way. Although each narrative has time gaps and conversational meanderings, the notion of a journey allows the narrator to see a beginning, middle, and perceived end, not only to their narrative, but to their life. You "try out" a future that coheres with your past and present. This grants integrity to the life story by anticipating closure.

The fifth chapter, Strategies and Techniques of Coping with Poverty, examines the various methods that women employed to cope with emotional or financial impoverishment. By exploring these methods, we determine that women usually did not equate poverty with lack of money. Issues of emotional, relational, and spiritual impoverishment emerged as an important predictor of self-defined poverty.

We examined their coping methods by viewing three general strategies: (1) through the generativity of raising, nurturing, and having hope for future generations, representing an essential faith in the continuity of the self through time, (2) through the comfort received by religious and spiritual beliefs, and (3) through the pride of personal accomplishment and the achievement of independence posed as contrasts to financial poverty.

For various reasons, the women interviewed did not necessarily look to their children and grandchildren as sources of support. Many relied on their religion and spirituality to cope with hardship. They also focused on their perceived accomplishments as a means of "playing down" economic poverty. For example, a story highlighting personal achievement, family harmony, or friendship often followed a mention of financial lack.

We posed one question to poor respondents: "All in all, financially what was the worst time of your life?" Answers to this question were significant to the findings of our study. Women often answered this question by detailing an event or time period that spoke to an *emotionally* trying time. We named this the paradox of poverty, i.e., women in this study did not experience poverty as primarily financial. Rather, deprivation was often equated with an emotional, relational, or spiritual lack. Also, it is critical to note that women did not define themselves through their impoverishment. Rather they described themselves (1) in relation to their accomplishments in the face of adversity: "I know how to make soup from one onion," (2) their parental achievements: "I raised good, decent citizens," or (3) through their positive personality traits: "I have a smile for everybody; everybody likes me."

The sixth chapter, Class and Self-Concept, explores women's awareness of social and financial status. It examines whether the women perceived themselves to be poor or privileged and why. In this chapter we attempt to answer one of the major questions asked in our study of women living in chronic poverty: Do poor women see themselves as poor? We also explore our respondents' reaction to the interview in light of their social and financial status. Some women questioned why their life story would be important, interesting, or the focus of a research study.

Although the notion of class can have two constructs that intertwine, i.e., financial and social, women in our study saw the weaving of social and financial class less clearly. Some women determined to be objectively poor according to 1992 Federal income standards described themselves as "rich" or "upper" class socially. Situating yourself in a certain class implies awareness of other classes. Implicit then in a perception of poverty or privilege is seeing yourself in relation to others. In the case of many poor women, cognizance of other individuals who had "more problems" or "even less than I do" led them to definitively name themselves as *not* poor. Some women used the term poverty to describe negative character traits, such as "I think of a person as poor if they are always depressed or in trouble," or even a lack of faith, such as "poor is when you don't believe in God." Poverty, for women in our study, was not a single concept. It has cultural, emotional, financial, historical, relational, and spiritual components that do not stand alone, but are complexly intertwined. Women used the term poverty to describe aspects of the self through time rather than a financial state.

Chapter 6 also examines the role of society in creating and sustaining poverty. We witness the destructive effects of poverty across generations through a case study. The narrator is a woman whose marginal placement in American society bequeathed a legacy of poverty and despair to her children and grandchildren.

The seventh chapter, Thoughts of the Future, is devoted to issues that women think about as impacting their personal future: the opportunities and problems of subsequent generations, death and dying, and issues of the paranormal, spirituality, and the afterlife. We specifically requested women's responses about their personal future and those of subsequent generations. Although respondents saw succeeding generations as having more and better options than *they* had to succeed in life, women also saw their children and grandchildren as failing to take advantage of these opportunities. Integral to their disappointment was that respondents perceived a lack of similar religious or moral values in their kin.

Eriksonian concepts of integrity and despair emerged in women's responses to questions about the future. Women constructed thoughts about the future based on their personal pasts. Their conception of the future might balance earlier or present hardship with the belief in a joyful afterlife, tie up unresolved issues in this life, or promise an answer to existential mysteries. Generating an end that logically follows the beginning and middle of your life course grants integrity to the narrative. Likewise, reactions to death and dying (your own or significant others) were built on women's personal histories. For example, the narratives of poor African-American women spoke to the random violence that was commonplace in their neighborhoods. "I want to die a natural death," one respondent said. "I don't want no one coming in the house hurting me. But you know, a bullet don't have no name on it." Personal spirituality and thoughts about the afterlife were often a syncretization of traditional religious beliefs and personal experiences.

The eighth chapter, Poverty as a Moral Issue, is linked to our second chapter, Subjective and Objective Poverty, through its emphasis on how women internalized society's standard, not only of poverty, but of moral worth in the face of poverty. A link between "high" moral standards or "strong" family values and success is a legacy of the "spirit of capitalism" [Weber, 1996 (1930)]. We examine this connection through a case study analyzed in this chapter.

In Chapter 8 we further explore our concept of the paradox of poverty and its tie to the American dream. We acknowledge that some respondents were surprised by their present poverty. They had expected in youth that their lives would improve by the time they reached adulthood. However, the moral sting of poverty was sometimes salved by listing "other" accomplishments in life, such as being a good wife, mother, or worker.

We also explore the issue of shame in relation to poverty. For women interviewed, shame had little connection with financial poverty, but with regret over past behaviors, such as drinking, smoking, or having love affairs. This highlights the fact that while women may have internalized society's moral definition of poverty, many disputed it, and created new definitions not only of poverty, but of moral worth and shame.

The ninth chapter, The Value of Retrospection, explores the manifold value of looking back at your life. The format of the life story lends testimonial flavor to the recounting of life, and displays life as a package that crystallizes in older age. Imbuing the past with meaning and cohering it to the present and future are cognitive, emotional, and spiritual acts. The value of retrospection also reveals the value of narrative, of making explicit the implicit meaning of life (Widdershoven, 1993). Choices made of "what to tell" in the life story weave the disparate events and feelings of life into a meaningful whole, and create a "new" narrative identity. A person's self-concept is revealed by the decisions of what to include or exclude in the life story.

There were vast differences in how respondents valued this retrospective view. Although many poor African-American women enjoyed the vantage of "looking back from a mighty long ways," poor Caucasians, as a group, preferred "living in the present, one day, one hour at a time." The different expectations that women held for their lives influenced this positive or negative take on retrospection. Stirring up the memory of unmet dreams often carried disillusionment or regret in its wake.

Our tenth chapter, the Conclusion, offers a summary of our findings. We also discuss the value of using case studies as a research tool and a means to disseminate knowledge. We explore whether our data can be generalized to a larger population and what, in general, we have learned about older women in poverty. Although our focus is on the subjective accounts of women's lives, it is critical to the amelioration of poverty to understand its objective conditions, such as discrimination, lack of opportunity and education, social and family instability, marginalization, crime, drugs, and despair. What is remarkable about these women's narratives is the frequency with which these topics are taken up within the context of the subjective account. Particularly striking in these narratives, as well, is the degree of marital disruption and spousal abuse.

The chapter divisions allow us to use a rubric under which to offer women's stories. However, the women who shared their narratives with us did not divide their lives neatly into the chapters or subheadings under which we placed them. The life history and open-ended questions of the qualitative interview invite respondents to be whole. Answers are spontaneous and unique, springing from an individual psyche and a personal and communal history, and embedded in a cultural context.

2

❧

Subjective and Objective Poverty

The difficulty of dealing with objective phenomena vs. subjective experience has been extensively explored in social science literature. States of being vs. what is immediate and true for the individual may not be dichotomous categories. A particular subject names a state of being as "objective." This naming depends on the gender, race, and sexual orientation of the definer and the culture-laden space in which he or she stands. Despite this, certain "objective" facts have been garnered from our research. For example, by using the Federal income standards of the 1990s, we determined who was eligible to be included in a study on poverty. Although this objective measure helped us to categorize respondents as "poor," it did not determine their subjective experience, i.e., that they "felt" or "were" poor.

In this chapter, we intend to continue the exploration of objectivity and subjectivity by transposing the objectified state of poverty, as delineated by income figures, into a subjective experience of poverty as described by our respondents. It is the women who become the experts in these two categories of subjectivity and objectivity. For the women who are the subjects of their own stories, the past is alive. It is something that is reworked as respondents reenter its parameters, which extend into the present. As an object, the past is closed. It can be investigated, manipulated, created, and recreated.

As researchers, we named the poor women in our sample "objectively" poor. For the most part, they refused to define themselves as such or to place themselves into an objective category (if there could be such a thing) called "poverty." As researchers, we created this category by excluding certain people under this "objective" rubric. Within the scope of our study we did not include the homeless poor, poor men, poor younger women, or poor children, for whom the experience of poverty is almost certainly different from the elderly women we interviewed.

We hold that the objective meaning of poverty for our study (such as being eligible for subsidized housing, utility reimbursements, or food stamps, or having enough money to pay bills and to purchase the necessities of life but to forego most small and all large luxuries) forms a certain mold that shapes the way life is lived. Informants were included only if their household income was within 125% of the poverty line, they had no more than a few thousand dollars of assets, and agreed that they were poor or near poor most of their lives. We also acknowledge that some women fit themselves into this mold without a great deal of thought. They lived, and in most cases thrived as individuals, within the space permitted by the tacit rules and sanctions of society regarding the financial or social class of its members. Many women interviewed appeared unaware of the boundaries that society had placed around them: what they were permitted or denied in terms of education, or what doors were quietly closed or opened before them regarding jobs. This is no less true for ourselves and our readers than for our respondents.

However, we also hold that for most women, the mold of poverty was both strong and loose, i.e., respondents often changed the configuration of the strong mold to fit their own expectations about life. By struggling against the strong grip of poverty they created a looser fit that accommodated *their* definition of poverty.

It is what the women do within these strong templates of poverty, the choices made within its "objective" boundaries, that makes it a subjective experience. We attempt to bring the subjective and objective notions of poverty together by describing the circumstances in which the women lived, by recording their thoughts and feelings about their circumstances, and by interpreting the women's discussion of their internal and external states.

This format of this chapter sets the stage for how our material will be presented. We will use case studies, which include demographics, a brief background of the women's lives, quotes from respondents' interviews, and the author's interpretation of the women's narratives, as the vehicle to show the objective facts and subjective vantage of poverty.

In this chapter we will examine dimensions of similarity and dimensions of difference in relation to the subjective experience of poverty. We emphasize the contrasts of poverty, i.e., that two women who live within similar parameters of poverty, such as receiving a similar income or living in subsidized housing, will experience poverty differently. Indeed, as we hope to show throughout the book, most "poor" women in our sample did not see themselves as poor in relation to material goods or social status. However, this is not to say that they did not experience impoverishment. For example, issues of estrangement, particularly from children, or poor health, were uppermost in many respondents' minds. Indeed, the fact that many of our informants lived in subsidized housing and received Supplemental Security Income, food stamps, and Medicaid, often caused them to see the present as "the best financial time in their lives." The present positively contrasted with the past, when these services were unavailable to them. Freed from securing the basic necessities of life, they were also able to recognize and define poverty in a multitude of ways, such as a lack of health, lack of closeness with significant others, or lack of faith.

We introduce Mrs. Sheck, a 74-year-old poor Caucasian widow and mother of four children who lives in a small apartment in a suburban subsidized housing community. She collects $565 monthly from Social Security. She has no assets.

She excused the disarray of her apartment by assuring the interviewer, "Nothing's dirty, understand. It's just newspapers and books." Mrs. Sheck speaks loudly and often punctuates an anecdote with a guffaw. When asked to tell the story of her life, she described an argument with her oldest son Gary that occurred 3 years previously. Thus emerged the theme of her narrative—her anger, confusion, and hurt due to her unsatisfactory relationships with her children.

> That last day, on Christmas, when they were bringing me home, she [daughter-in-law] said to me, 'You embarrassed me on my wedding day.' Gary [son] said, 'Get out of my car, and don't come up here no more.'

Mrs. Sheck remains mystified by the charges hurled against her and does not know the "real" reason her son and daughter-in-law are displeased with her. Mrs. Sheck also has no communication with her second daughter, Rosa, and is uncertain of her whereabouts. When asked what caused the rift between Rosa and herself, she admitted that Rosa "had always been a problem." When Rosa was 19 she spent a weekend away from home without revealing where, or with whom, she stayed. She explains her feelings about this incident.

> That's what turned me off about her. How are you supposed to feel about your children when they act like that?

Mrs. Sheck's relationship with her other children, eldest daughter Kristin and youngest son Jake, is "okay." She sees Kristin, who lives nearby, at least once a week, and she often "stays over" in Jake's Pocono home to baby-sit his two young children.

Mrs. Sheck was the oldest of five children born and raised in Brewerytown, a community of row homes in Philadelphia whose residents worked in the surrounding breweries. When asked to describe her life at home, she shrugged and returned to the theme of her narrative—her lack of closeness with her own children.

It was sociable, I guess [life at home]. The only thing is my mother had me to do all the work. See, my mother wasn't close to us. My mother had no mother. She lived in boarding homes. She had a lousy father and four lousy brothers, and a lousy husband [laughter]. She had to work. So, it was a very abusive home life and it showed onto me. I wasn't close to my children. [Pause] I never gave them a kiss or a hug. But I couldn't be any different.

Mrs. Sheck rationalizes her lack of affection with her children by comparing it to her mother's way of relating to her—she showed her love by making her do "all the work." Mrs. Sheck confided that at her mother's funeral a family friend whispered, "she [mother] loved you the most." Mrs. Sheck takes solace from this; she connects her mother's "tough" love with her behavior toward Kristin. However, Mrs. Sheck worries about her role in forming Kristin's "abnormal" lifestyle.

I wonder if I treated her [Kristin] the way I was treated. Now I feel something's wrong with her. She's fifty and not married. That's not normal. When I was 50 I expected to be married. I often feel bad because maybe I kept her back from meeting fellas. After her dad died, she wanted to take care of me all the time. She left her life go.

Mrs. Sheck is relieved that Kristin "finally met somebody." She enjoys a live-in relationship with a "fella who's nothing to brag about, but he's sociable and they get along."

Mrs. Sheck met her husband, a neighborhood boy who was home on leave from the army, at a USO dance in 1941. They corresponded when he returned overseas and finally married when Mrs. Sheck was 19. She admitted that although she "liked him," her "real" reason for marrying was "because I was tired of working and I wanted to get out of my household." Mrs. Sheck had difficulty describing her husband when asked.

Eehhh. He was a fella. He liked to go down the shore. He didn't care for company.

The Shecks set up housekeeping in a small apartment near their respective families, where they raised their four children. Because Mrs. Sheck's parents were ailing, she often "ran home to take care of them." Mrs. Sheck's childhood and adolescence were financially "hard"; the financial tone of her marriage fared no better.

It was hard because he was out of work a lot. Either the jobs weren't there, or he got thick-headed and quit.

The family was forced to go on welfare because of Mr. Sheck's inability to either find or hold a job. Mrs. Sheck believes that her husband's talent and diligence as a first rate machinist, as well as his stubbornness, cost him his life.

> While he was eating his supper he'd try to figure out a job he was working on, that's what caused the stroke. He never concentrated on eating.

Mr. Sheck went on disability after his first stroke; Mrs. Sheck took physical care of her husband for seven and a half years, until his death from a second stroke. She named the period of her husband's illness as the hardest time financially in her life. Although she knew that he would never work again, she was anxious to move away from their "changing" Brewerytown neighborhood to a "predominantly German parish." She scrimped and saved money earned from cafeteria and factory work for a down payment on a home in a "better" neighborhood. Her husband was too ill to discuss the move; she relates how she told him they had just purchased their first home.

> I came back and said, 'Well, get packed. We got a house on L. Street.' He was laying on the sofa. He said, 'Where'd you get the money?' 'None of your damn business. It's for me to know and you to find out.'

Despite the couple's lack of discussion over major events in their lives, such as the purchase of a home, and their harsh and shallow method of communication, Mrs. Sheck's vivid storytelling paints a more complex portrait of their marriage. When asked how she adjusted to widowhood after 18 years of marriage, she related an incident that occurred shortly before her husbands' death. It graphically depicts his increasing dependence on her and their abiding concern for each other.

Mrs. Sheck was disturbed to learn that her husband called a cab to their apartment early one summer morning.

> He didn't say nothing to me. I heard the front door go, and I thought, where's he going? He couldn't walk that good. He had to have somebody hold his hand when he went up and down the steps. This morning he went down with no bother at all. You goddamn louse you, I said to myself, I worry about you and here you're getting down the steps yourself. I see the cab and I knocked on the window. I said, 'Don't you take that man away; he's not a well man.' And I said to myself, you son of a bitch, where the hell you going? Later in the afternoon I heard a key in the lock. That son of a bitch, where the hell was he? This was 2:30 in the afternoon, from 7 o'clock in the morning.

He came in and he yelled, 'Yo, Bette.' I didn't answer. 'You goddamn f—, where you at,' he called again. 'Yeah, what?' I said. 'Did it rain up here?' I said, 'No.' 'It rained down where I was.' I said, 'Why, where did you go?' 'Down Atlantic City.' He said, 'I went to the place where we used to get our ham sandwiches and beers and had my lunch. Rain didn't let up so I came the hell home.' I said, 'You son of a bitch, every time the phone rang I thought it was the cops telling me they found your body in the Schuylkill.' He didn't say nothing to that, but when I helped him get undressed, he said, 'Can I go down next week again?' I said, 'Yeah, if you tell me where you're going.' A week after that he died.

Mr. Sheck returned, with extreme physical difficulty, to a place where the couple had made memories. Both knew his death was imminent. It is interesting that Mr. Sheck went alone—perhaps the place they ate ham sandwiches is the shrine and his going was a pilgrimage celebrating their lives together. Perhaps it is an anticipatory grieving for his own death, a way of releasing her, a practice for traveling alone on his final journey.

The description of her husband made earlier in the interview, "Eehh, he was a fella, he liked to go down the shore," foreshadows the above narrative. Her story allows a window into her worldview; the clarity of long ago memories suggests that she replays them in her mind. The narrative is filled with the emotions of the long-married—annoyance, silence, spite, and an abiding concern. It is a narrative rich in communication—both in what the couple do and do not say. Although Mr. Sheck is ill, he leaves home without telling his wife. When they do speak, their language seems harsh and uncommunicative—gruff phrases, feelings couched in silence, concerns cloaked by curses.

The incident of which she spoke occurred 30 years previously; Mrs. Sheck related it as though it happened the day before. She did not pause. She gazed out of her living room window as though she could see, in her mind's eye, her frail husband getting into the cab, her own face by the window, and her unmentioned relief when he returned home.

Unfortunately, the couple never moved into the house on L. Street. Her husband's death caused Mrs. Sheck to reconsider the move. She continued to raise the children in their Brewerytown apartment. At the time of Mr. Sheck's death her youngest child, Jake, was six, her eldest, Kristin, was in high school. Although Mrs. Sheck had once attended a trade school for dress-making and "had a talent" for sewing, she took the jobs that were offered to her: salad girl, cafeteria cook, and factory piece-worker. Although she was "so tired of working," and thought remarriage might give her a better income; she decided that she "didn't want no strange man over the children."

Three of her children eventually left home to marry; Kristin stayed with her mother until Mrs. Sheck was eligible to reside in senior subsidized housing. She contrasts the financial hardship of her earlier years with her relatively secure present.

> It was pitching pennies then. I'm in heaven now. I can do what I want and I always have a few pennies. I can buy food that I wasn't able to do then. I can buy shoes. I have no bosses.

Mrs. Sheck's "heavenly" situation is aided by her feelings of independence. She likes living alone because she is free to "come and go, cook when I want, and don't answer to nobody."

The ease of her current financial situation is marred only by her thoughts concerning her children, particularly her estranged son. She goes over their Christmas day argument continuously. Her only solace is that "God will take care of it."

> He breaks my heart every holiday. I just hope I live long enough that he gets it paid back to him in one way or another. Either his children will do something to him and he'll wonder why they're doing it to him. Or—. See, he's a sheet metal worker. He's out of work. Since him and I ain't on talking terms he's been out of work more than I can remember. I said that God's punishment. [Pause] Sorry to say it. But she [daughter-in-law] works as a social worker. So she's making the dough-re-me.

Mrs. Sheck's idiosyncratic religious beliefs allow her to hope that God will resolve this family situation. Helpless to avenge her anger by herself, she includes revenge as one of God's attributes, and wonders why *she* is being punished. Despite her anger and her sorrow, she admits that she prays for a reunion with Gary.

> I pray about it. I say, 'Why's it happening to me? Why is this happening with my son? Bring him back to me. Inspire him one way or another to give me a call.'

Mrs. Sheck believes that her prayers regarding Gary have been answered. Her belief permits her a modicum of control in a situation in which she feels helpless to effect a reconciliation.

> I often think he does try to call me because I pick up the phone and I hear somebody on the other line. I'll say hello and all of a sudden it will go down. One night it got me so mad I said, 'If you got that extra money to call me and you can't talk to me then you go to hell.'

Mrs. Sheck identified her life as "tough." It is possible to see how her mother's economic and psychological hardship contributed to Mrs. Sheck's troubled relationships with her children. However, Mrs. Sheck no longer thinks of herself as poor financially; her personal sense of poverty now concerns her disconnection from her children. When she shared her thoughts about an afterlife, perhaps she was referring to all times and aspects of her life. Hearty laughter punctuated the following exchange.

Mrs. Sheck: I was taught in grammar school that there was heaven and hell and purgatory.
Interviewer: What do you believe?
Mrs. Sheck: Oh, I believe it.
Interviewer: Where do you think you'll go?
Mrs. Sheck: I could go to heaven.
Interviewer: What do you think it's going to be like?
Mrs. Sheck: Like heaven. Happy, parties [laughter].
Interviewer: Is this hard for you to believe as something real?
Mrs. Sheck: To a certain extent yes. But you have to go somewheres. And you're supposed to see God at least once.
Interviewer: Do you think you'll see God?
Mrs. Sheck: I'm hoping to. I'd like it very much. I'd like to thank him personally for my tough life [laughter].

Mrs. Sheck's present sense of poverty is rooted in her strained relationships with her children and her inability to discuss her feelings with them. Despite this, Mrs. Sheck has not been defeated by her "tough" life. Memories of a "good" marriage, present relative financial contentment in subsidized housing, a sense of independence, unfailing humor, and trust in God's justice keep despair at bay, and allow Mrs. Sheck to hope for improved family communication, particularly with her son.

Mrs. Butcher is a 70-year-old African-American woman who was divorced over 30 years ago and is the mother of one daughter, aged 54. She receives slightly more than $500 a month from Supplemental Security Income and a small pension garnered from factory work. She has no other income. She lives in a subsidized facility for seniors located near Center City. Her twelfth floor apartment is small and bright, with yellow-painted living room walls. The crest of her gold floral sofa is lined with small stuffed bears that she sews and gives as presents when she visits the sick in a nearby hospital. Mrs. Butcher told her life story in a few brief sentences.

I was raised in Atlantic City. It was a friend of my mother's. She raised me for a while. I went to school down there for a little bit. And I came back up here. I lived in South Philly mostly all my life. Went to Catholic school up here to the eighth grade. Came out, went to junior high to the tenth grade and that's when I got pregnant. And I came out, had the baby, messed around for a while, got a job. And I been working ever since.

Mrs. Butcher did not name the lady who raised her and admitted that she "never saw her again" after she returned to Philadelphia and her mother's home. She described her mother only as "nice and friendly." When asked why she did not live with her mother during her childhood, Mrs. Butcher answered:

> There was a couple more kids so she just, you know, let the lady raise me for a while. She [the lady who raised her] only had one son. So, she let the lady raise me so she could get back on her feet or something like that. But I was kind of young then, I don't tend to recollect too much. She [the lady who raised her] was nice.

Mrs. Butcher did not flesh out this painful story. She was one of eight children born to her mother. She named her one remaining sibling, a sister who lives nearby, as "close to [her] and important in [her] life." Although she never knew her other siblings, she learned as an adult that "a couple of them" died in childhood.

> My sister's the only one I can remember. Most of them died by the time I got back up here. I never met none of them.

When asked about her father, Mrs. Butcher considered.

> You might as well say I don't remember him. I think the first time I seen him I was about 11 years old. We was at my aunt's house in West Philadelphia one Sunday and me and my sister was laying across the bed and my mother called us in the kitchen and said, 'I want you to meet somebody.' I said, 'Yeah, who?' She said, 'Your father.' I just looked at him and said, 'Oh, hello.' That's about all. He said, 'Hello and you all look nice and you growed up nice,' something like that. He took us to meet his madam or girlfriend or wife, whoever it was. We came back to mom's house and that's the last time I seen him. Next time I heard about him he was dead.

When asked, Mrs. Butcher had difficulty either articulating, recalling, or sharing her feelings about her mother's difficult life, being raised by "a friend of her mother's," or her estrangement from her father. When the interviewer commented on her mother's heartbreak over her children's deaths, Mrs. Butcher shrugged and said simply. "I guess so." When asked how she felt about meeting her father for the first time at age 11, she began to laugh.

> To tell you the truth I can't say [what I feel]. I didn't know the man, so . . . .
> At least you can say I met him one time anyhow.

Mrs. Butcher became pregnant when she was in the tenth grade of a South Philadelphia high school. She left school to raise her child in her mother's home. She did not marry her daughter's father, but encouraged her daughter to keep in touch with him. She also sees him "every now and then."

> I was 15 when I was getting her [daughter]. Me and her father never got married. But he took care of her though. He was a nice jolly person. But marriage just never came up between us. My mother was a good help in raising her. His family was a help too.

Mrs. Butcher was well into her thirties, raising her teenage daughter in her mother's home, and working in a factory when she met her husband. Mrs. Butcher dated her husband, a truck driver, for 2 years before they married. Her daughter was a "good size" by then and decided to remain with Mrs. Butcher's mother when the couple moved to a South Philadelphia apartment. Although Mrs. Butcher left factory work after she married, she continued to do "days' work now and then" during her marriage. Although the Butchers both worked and were financially "okay" during their short marriage, they never talked about buying a home.

> We always had apartments. But he give me so much for the house and stuff like that. And he kept a little bit for himself like for cigarettes or whatever, maybe drinks. He gave me my money, that was for sure. We had no problem moneywise.

The marriage ended abruptly after 5 years. Mrs. Butcher had no inkling that her husband was unhappy; she learned from a neighbor the reason for his departure. When asked to recall the tone of their marriage and why it ended, Mrs. Butcher answered:

> He was tall, slim, a friendly-like fellow. He was very nice with the family and my friends. Everybody liked him. [Pause] So, it wasn't no rough stuff or argument or something like that. He just went one time and didn't even come back. Somebody told me he was living with another woman and she was raising his son. I didn't know he had a son. So I said, 'Well, if he won't bother me I won't bother him and that's it. I can't let it worry me; I can't let it get me down.' It was a little hard but I finally got over it. I had to keep on getting up.

Mrs. Butcher often used phrases such as "I had to keep on" or "keep moving," or keep getting up." These cliches reveal a personal "truth"—she could not and did not allow herself time to dwell on her hardship. They also show either her minimalist reaction to life's heartaches or her disinclination to share her feelings with the interviewer.

Mrs. Butcher actually tried and failed "a couple times" to find Mr. Butcher. She never saw her husband again, and has no knowledge of where he is living or even if he is alive. Mrs. Butcher does not speak ill of him, nor does she care to think about this period of her life.

> He sent me money a couple of times. After that it just stopped, so I just went on with my business. Sometimes I remember him, it all comes into focus, then I think of something jolly and then you just laugh at yourself. I don't let things worry me. You got to keep moving.

Mrs. Butcher described the period after her husband left as the worst time of her life financially. Because days' work was "too uncertain," she found permanent domestic work in a doctor's home in the suburbs. She was employed by this family for over 20 years.

> I worked for a doctor for about twenty-five years. They took me as a member of their family. They was very nice.

Despite taking her "as a member of the family," Mrs. Butcher was forced to fend for herself when "they went away for summer vacations." During this time, Mrs. Butcher took whatever work she could find until the family returned. Although she believed that remarriage might have made her life easier financially, she consciously and adamantly chose to remain single. When asked if she ever considered marrying again, she laughed heartily.

> No, no, no, no, no. One time around was enough. You go your way; I'll go my way. That's it. Oh, I had some nice gentlemen friends through the years, but I never thought about no more marrying. I got somebody now, for twenty-some years now. We go out to dinner, to the movies, stuff like that, go to friends' houses, play cards. He's very nice. But no marriage, oh no!

When the interviewer commented that Mrs. Butcher lived most of her life as a single woman depending only on herself, she agreed. "Yeah, beside my mother, there was no one to depend on." Mrs. Butcher added that her faith also sustained her during the worst emotional and economic periods of her life.Talking to God continues to "lift" her.

> Like I would say, 'Dear God, please help me and pray for me.' So like if I'm down or something, I just close my eyes and say a prayer and that sort of lifts me up a whole lot. Just talking to God.

Mrs. Butcher considers the present to be the best time in her life—both materially and relationally. She enjoys the company of her gentleman friend and neighbors who live in the apartment building. She described one of her neighbors as her closest confidant. She named her daughter and 33-year-old granddaughter, both of whom live nearby, as "the people closest to me." Like Mrs. Sheck, Mrs. Butcher's description of her day-to-day life was similar to her description of heaven. She portrayed heaven as follows:

> It's jolly all the time. It's where you make everybody happy and laugh and have a good time all the time.

When asked to sum up her life presently, she laughed.

> I enjoy it, honey, really enjoy it. Make no mistake, I really enjoy it. I'm happy to be here. I can go and come as I please. I have plenty to eat and so-das to drink. If I want to cook, I cook, if I don't, I go get me a hoagie. I got television and radio. Sometimes company come on up and we sit down and have a few drinks and play the music. And maybe I get up a little and act like I can dance or something like that. I know how to have a good time!

In this, Mrs. Butcher takes responsibility for "making" her good time. She believes that she has the know-how to reap pleasure and satisfaction from life. Mrs. Butcher lists present contentment as one of her greatest life achievements. When asked to name her accomplishments in life, she considered:

> *Mrs. Butcher:* What have I accomplished? Hmm. To keep a roof over my head and food in my stomach. I enjoy my grandkids and my family and my friends. So, I would say I accomplished that much. And it feels good to me. Life has been pretty good.
> *Interviewer:* Why do you say that?
> *Mrs. Butcher:* Because of the way I feel, healthwise, and I'm happy. I'm happy most of the time. That's how I feel. And the way I carry myself.
> *Interviewer:* What do you mean, the way you carry yourself?
> *Mrs. Butcher:* The way I am. Real neat-like.

Mrs. Butcher is satisfied with her life as a whole because she focuses on her present state of good health, companionship, independence, and relative financial security due to a regular, modest monthly income. Although she acknowledges that she held youthful dreams, she differentiated them from her "real" expectations.

I had dreams. That's about all it was, dreams [laughter]. I'd like to have money; I'd like to have a nice house. One or two kids, maybe a nice husband or job or a car or something like that. I figured it wasn't going to happen so why think about it.

Mrs. Butcher changed her former expectations to accommodate the circumstances in which she found herself. This psychological restructuring helps her to believe not that her dreams failed, but that "real" life either met or exceeded "real" expectations. Perhaps Mrs. Butcher presents more acceptance than she "truly" feels. Most importantly, however, *she* chooses how to see herself, review her past, experience her present, and decide how much of that information she will share with the interviewer.

I like my life just the way it is. It feels good to me.

Mrs. Butcher's worldview and expectations about life allow her to add her age—70—to her list of accomplishments.

I used to say, God, will I ever make it? I'm glad I hit that spot. And I think I'm wise. I say to others. Keep on getting up. Don't be sitting in a chair. Get up and get out! Get yourself dressed! Take a walk into town; visit a sick person!

Mrs. Butcher's self-proclaimed wisdom and inner strength permit her to focus outward, and proudly share her prescription for happiness. When asked what she considers the main purpose in life, Mrs. Butcher acknowledged that financial security is only one item in the prize of personal contentment.

Probably to help somebody maybe less fortunate than me. Or to try to help others that have more than me. See, they may have more than me but they don't seem to be happy. So, don't sit on it; get up off your butt and go. Get out of the dumps. That's what I do. I just keep a roof over my head and food in my stomach. I'm very self-satisfied.

Mrs. Butcher kept much of her life story to herself, particularly feelings about her family of origin and facts about her daughter. She presented herself as living well despite poverty. Indeed, she carefully distinguished between herself and those who "have more but don't seem to be happy." The lack of a necessary link between money and happiness demonstrates her distinction between subjective and objective notions of poverty.

For our respondents, scarcity and want had several faces. Perhaps the most devastating notion of poverty is the lack of good health. We now present Mrs. Thorne, an 81-year-old poor Caucasian widow who lives in the home that she bought and shares with her 65-year-old sister, Mickey. Since Mrs. Thorne receives only $450 a month from social security, she is unable to own a home and manage its upkeep without financial help. Mrs. Thorne is also physically incapable of keeping house; Mickey is her sister's full-time caretaker.

The twin home in the northeast section of the city is small, clean, and simply decorated. Mickey sat in on the interview and often interjected names and places to jog her sister's memory. Mickey also supplied her sister's opinion on a subject if Mrs. Thorne hesitated or seemed confused by a question. A portion of interview time was taken up by Mrs. Thorne and Mickey debating the exact dates of significant events in Mrs. Thorne's life.

Mrs. Thorne walks with difficulty, suffers from shortness of breath, and presents a depressed affect. Mickey told the interviewer that her sister also has heart, bowel, and lung problems. Mrs. Thorne's daily life is comprised of making and keeping health care appointments and taking medication. Consequently, her poor health provides the major theme in her narrative. She explained sadly, "If I didn't have these health problems I would have been the strongest woman in the world." When asked to tell the story of her life, she sighed.

> I was married at 19 and had a daughter at 20. I had a cesarean birth. I started work at [. . .], that's a factory. Just before my husband passed away I came down with a fibrous tumor of the uterus. They didn't operate on me, they just inserted radium.

Mrs. Thorne's quick compilation of her marriage, her daughter's birth, and her husband's death was a short preamble for the main topic of her narrative—her illnesses. She believes that receiving radium created life-long health problems. Mickey concurs.

> Everything that she has today is from the radium from 40 years ago. She lost her kidney, the use of her bladder. Her bowels are all messed up. Actually the fibrous tumor wasn't as bad as they thought but they gave her too much radium.

Mrs. Thorne grew up in East Germantown, the oldest of 13 children, six of whom survived to adulthood. She described her childhood as harsh; she resents that she was forced to leave school after the sixth grade to care for younger siblings.

> That's why I had to leave school so early. I had to take care of each one that was born. I was not allowed to have any friends; I was not allowed to

associate with anybody. I was just home to do whatever had to be done. I took care of the kids. Everything was dumped on me.

Mrs. Thorne seems passively embittered by her memories. Her bland demeanor suggests that she is not really surprised, at least in retrospect, that her life turned out so badly; she hadn't really expected better.

Mrs. Thorne's longing to leave her unhappy home matched a neighborhood boy's desire to get married.

Bunky only lived two or three doors away from us. We actually grew up together. He was the only boyfriend I ever had. I wanted to get away from home. So we eloped. They [mother and father] were very upset. My oldest brother was out looking for me with a gun.

When asked to describe her husband and their marriage, Mrs. Thorne explained why she chose her husband and listed the reasons the marriage failed.

See, I wasn't in enough company to find different people, different men, you know. And he was Irish to begin with; I'm Italian. He just had that fault that he liked to drink. And it [drinking] did keep us battling all the time. I even had to go after him in the taproom. I had to keep after him for every dollar that I could take from him. We never had anything. I found a little home on H. Street. We never bought it. He couldn't keep a job long enough. Then he even tapped Addie [their only daughter] to try to get money for drink.

Mickey added her opinion of her brother-in-law: "When Bunky wasn't drunk he was a good man."

Mrs. Thorne's mother became pregnant soon after the young couple married. Mrs. Thorne ran home every week day to help her mother with the younger children. Her caretaking skill smoothed family tension over her unexpected marriage.

The Thornes had one daughter, Addie. They settled in Germantown, renting a home around the corner from Mrs. Thorne's parents. Although Mr. Thorne was an accomplished carpenter, nightly drinking kept him from getting up for work in the morning, and he lost several jobs due to absenteeism. Mrs. Thorne was forced to take a job at a nearby factory.

At the time I was married, that was the worst [financially]. I managed though to have a couple extra dollars unknown to him. Of course I lived very cheaply. I lived poorly. I done with the least little thing. I had no good time financially with him.

Mrs. Thorne admitted that her present financial circumstances, because of Mickey, are "the best."

Mr. Thorne was 49 when he suffered a fatal heart attack. Mrs. Thorne, then 42, moved into an apartment with 22-year-old Addie. Despite persistent ill health, she continued to do factory work. Although she did not like her job, its proximity to home kept her there for the next 30 years. Mrs. Thorne sums up her three decades of factory work:

> I got along with the workers. Those were the fun times when I got in with a crowd of girls and we used to get together and we'd make plans to go to a show. Those were the happy times I had. As sick as I was, I enjoyed work. Outside of that, I never got nowhere.

Mrs. Thorne's experience with Bunky, as well as her ill health, convinced her to reject remarriage.

> I had a bad marriage to begin with. I was sick in the hospital and he was out drinking. And you couldn't save with Bunky. Things were no good financially until he passed away. No more men in my life. They all seem to be fine, then after you marry them their faults seem to come out. Then I had so many things wrong, what man would want me? To lug me back and forth to doctors and operations and hospitals?

This bleak view of herself as an eligible woman fits neatly into Mrs. Thorne's worldview. From early on, Mrs. Thorne expected little, if any, happiness in life. By early middle age her prophecy of sickness and sorrow had actualized. Mrs. Thorne decided to take no more risks and to eliminate further disappointment.

Mickey, who had been her parents' caretaker, moved to an apartment from the family home after their death. When Addie married and moved away Mickey invited Mrs. Thorne to share her apartment. The sisters eventually bought a "handyman special," which is the small home they now share. Although their home still carries a mortgage, Mrs. Thorne feels unencumbered financially because she and Mickey share all expenses.

When Mrs. Thorne was asked about the hardship of raising Addie alone in light of her many health problems, Mickey answered.

> Addie was pretty capable. She had a sick mother and she took care of herself. And I was always around.

When Mrs. Thorne was asked if she thought of herself as an independent person, Mickey again replied, "She did at one time." Mrs. Thorne continued the thought, "Now I have to depend on whatever, anybody." Although

Mickey thought that a person needed money to feel independent, Mrs. Thorne disagreed. "No, having money wouldn't help me." When Mrs. Thorne was asked to describe herself, it was Mickey who spoke up. "Spunky and courageous." Mrs. Thorne nodded in agreement.

> Yes, I would say that is true. I had to fight for whatever I wanted, whatever I done. At work, anywhere anybody tried to give me any guff, I'd fight. I used to be outspoken. Now I just don't want to get in an argument. I don't want to get involved.

Allowing Mickey to answer questions that were put to her parallels Mrs. Thorne's waning desire to "get involved" in life. Perhaps she feels that her former strengths—fortitude and feistiness—are no match against the brute strength of her illnesses.

Mrs. Thorne's daughter, now 61, suffers from a significant depression. Addie and her husband visit the sisters two to three times a week, bringing food and household supplies. When asked to describe her daughter, Mrs. Thorne replied:

> Addie was a good person. The only thing is after she got married she came down with this depression and it affected her in different ways. She married and she had her child. Up until now she's still not right. I look at Addie and I say, that's not my daughter. She's wasting away. She's so thin. She doesn't care if she lives or dies. And she's always hiding behind sunglasses.

Addie's depression forced Mrs. Thorne and Mickey to raise Addie's only child, Sandy. Mrs. Thorne names the time spent with Sandy as

> a happy time in my life. My Addie was never a well girl herself so we tried to take some responsibilities away from her. We used to take her [Sandy] everywhere with us. [Pause] Now, she's 35 years old. She's got her own life. I see her maybe once in a while.

Mrs. Throne is disappointed that her granddaughter's busy life allows little time for visits or phone calls. She is also disappointed with the way Addie reacts to the hardships life dealt her. She thinks that Addie's excessive concern with her husband, who has a heart condition, is the cause of her depression and supersedes Addie's ability to be a more loving daughter.

> She would rather die than see her husband sick. She never worked. What would she do? Her husband even comes before her daughter.

Although Mrs. Thorne described Addie as "dutiful," she sees herself at the end of the list of her daughter's concerns. She feels uncomfortable telling Addie how she feels, but will eventually let her daughter "see" her hurt feelings in a monetary way.

> She won't even allow her husband to come over and run me out to the doctor. Those are the things that hurt me. I have been good to them when I was still able to but they haven't come back to help me out in any way. [Pause] If I have a dollar I'll leave it to Mickey, not my daughter.

Mrs. Thorne dwells in a prison of untapped abilities and unrealized dreams. This prison, constructed long ago from her self-perceptions and her illnesses, is now fortified by painful memories. When asked if she had a plan or vision for her life, she answered:

> My dreams never came true. If the sickness hadn't struck me, I would have left my husband, made my own money, and I'd have taken off away from him. But I had no where to go. He was no help. My parents were elderly.

Bunky's lack of ambition, her parents' advanced ages, and her own sickness all caused her dreams to wither. Her memories are shadowed by her own ill health; her future is darkened by worry about the health of her family. When asked what she would do differently in her life, she said:

> I'd never marry. That's when I would live independently. I'd work, I'd make my own money. If I had been blessed with good health, everything else would be different. I always think of the past, the hard times, of unhappiness, of disappointments. Now, Addie is sick, her husband is sick. Mickey was just diagnosed with cancer. It's rough all the way around.

Only one hope penetrates Mrs. Thorne's gloomy worldview—to die before her loved ones pass away.

> Why couldn't I go rather than wait and see my daughter sick; my sister sick. Why couldn't God have taken me and relieved me of all this? I don't want to stay around to see this.

When asked about her accomplishments in life, Mrs. Thorne saw her past, present, and future as knitted solely by illness and despair. Her answer seems sadly predictable.

> What did I accomplish in this life? Nothing. Just like I said my whole life was full of problems, sickness, heartaches. I don't think I accomplished much of anything. And now, my next move will be the cemetery. That's what my future holds.

Mrs. Thorne's illnesses and those of her family also frame her thoughts about religion, belief in God, and concept of an afterlife. She is disappointed that, thus far, she has received little if any reward for her faith. Since her concept of an afterlife reflects her experiences in this life, she is disinclined to hope for any good thing after death.

> I like my Catholic religion. It's just that I'm disappointed in what it handed me. Because I always feel we never harmed anybody. Why was all this thrown on us? I do believe in God. I pray a lot. But I feel as though I am not heard. I feel I was struck, but why was my family struck? He had enough to give to me, but let my girls alone. My mother and father, they know they left us and we're suffering. Why don't they appear to us and help us. Why don't they come to us? Because they can't. When you're dead, you're dead!

When Mrs. Thorne was asked what she believed was the main purpose or task in life, she paused, then answered with a sigh:

> I don't know. The only answer I can think of is I wish I had never been born.

Mrs. Thorne sees herself as impoverished in emotional, physical, and spiritual ways. The duration, extent, and intensity of Mrs. Thorne's anguish threaten the core of her beliefs concerning what kind of suffering is acceptable and deserved—*some* mental and physical pains. Conversely, the kind of suffering that she endures—the life-threatening illnesses of her "girls," the inability of her deceased mother and father to "help" her, and her own enduring and pervasive physical problems—casts doubt on the meaning of life, the purpose of her existence, and the possibility of an afterlife.

We now present Mrs. Winter, who tells the story of devastating poverty, both emotional and financial. Mrs. Winter is a 78-year-old poor African-American woman who lives in a subsidized housing facility in center city. Her one room apartment has uncovered cement floors, tan walls, and a tiny balcony. Although she sees only other high-rises from this outlook, and the noise from cars and workday business is deafening, she has placed a straight back chair next to the open glass door in order to sit and "look out." Propped on her single bed is a black plastic baby doll; atop her sofa rests a studio photograph of her husband, Duke. The picture of Duke and the baby doll are the only visible personal items in Mrs. Winter's apartment. They symbolize Mrs. Winter's desires, dreams, and disappointments. The picture of Duke, particularly, looms large in Mrs. Winter's small apartment, in her narrative, and in her life, still frightening Mrs. Winter with his ability to grant or withhold his love.

Physically, Mrs. Winter is frail; she suffers from emphysema, arthritis, and diabetes. She has trouble rising from a chair and must use a cane to walk. She occasionally leaves her apartment to visit a neighbor down the hall. She leaves the building only to attend a nearby Baptist church on Sundays.

When asked, Mrs. Winter described herself as "separated but still married—been married over 60 years." When asked what kind of work she did throughout her life, she replied, "a cleaner."

Mrs. Winter was confused when asked to tell the story of her life. "How far do you want me to go back?" she asked. She recalled that she was born in Maryland and brought to Philadelphia by a couple unrelated to her, Miss Dee and Mr. Cam, but was uncertain how they "got her." She is not even sure of her "real" name.

> I didn't know my name. My name was Elena. My mother named me Elena. I found that on my birth certificate later. But she [Miss Dee] called me Olga. My nickname was Gigi. Because I reminded somebody of something on the radio. I don't know. Anyway, Miss Dee was a woman in my mother's uncle's house. He had a big house in Maryland and they rented out the rooms.
>
> Miss Dee and Mr. Cam—he was her common-law, they weren't married. Now, Miss Dee told me that my mother was nothing but a little gyp and a whore and she went out and had a man and then by having the man, I was born out of that union. See, my mother's mother put her out, threw her out on the streets because she was disgraced. So this lets me know that I came from a pretty good background, that my grandmother wouldn't tolerate no kind of, what you call it, fishy things?

Mrs. Winter begged Miss Dee to tell her where she "came from." She accepts Miss Dee's assessment of her mother's character. However, she considers her grandmother's shame over her mother's pregnancy as a testimony to her own "good background." She puts together the bits of information made available to her throughout her childhood to present a personal legacy left to her by both her mother and grandmother.

Mrs. Winter painted a portrait of Miss Dee as a selfish, grasping woman who saw other people as a means to make money. She rented rooms in her South Philadelphia home and took in foster children for profit. According to Mrs. Winter, Miss Dee's interest in her young charges was purely monetary. Mrs. Winter remembers sorely wanting affection as a child. She recalled, with a laugh at her own naiveté, asking Miss Dee why she never touched her.

> I said to her one time, 'How come you never give me a hug or a pat or a kiss or something?' Because I'm not no kissing kind of person. Don't I let you

go to the movies? I said, 'Yes, ma'am. But in the movies, the girls, the mama and the girls, they kiss them and hug them.' See, the first bad experience I had with Miss Dee . . . . We had a long black stove, put the fire in there, charcoal and wood and make a fire. She put the tin tub on top of the stove and the clothes and the bleach and the soap and let them boil. And my job, I stood on a little stool or something like that and I stand on the stool and stir, you know, and this one day, I was standing and stirring and that tub of boiling hot soapy water fell over on me and I screamed, oh, how I screamed, that was my first hurt from Miss Dee. She had no business letting me stand. I wasn't tall enough. So she said, 'What good are you? What good are you? You ain't no good to me, you owe me the rest of your life. You'll never be able to pay me for what I done for you.' She would remind me of that all the time. 'Your mother was nothing but a whore; you're a little gyp.'

Mrs. Winter remembers being beaten by Miss Dee with a "cat-o'-nine-tails." Throughout her childhood years she was also verbally threatened with being "thrown out," and emotionally abused by being called "stupid" and "ugly." Mr. Cam stands as a silent partner to Miss Dee in Mrs. Winter's narrative. Mrs. Winter described him as a "nice man, dead now, God rest his soul."

Miss Dee finally found a use for Mrs. Winter; she supplemented her income by prostituting the child at age 8.

You ask your mother or grandmother, in the olden days, after the Depression, men would be out with sheets, oil cloth for the floor, rugs, all kinds of things, and they ring your doorbell and they would ask you, lady, want to buy? Dresses, different things. We call them peddlers. Anyhow, they used to come in to Miss Dee. I don't know what they would say to her or what she say to them, but she would march me back in the other room and have me strip off, strip stark naked. And them men would come in there and look at me and they said, 'Can I kiss her?' She say, 'Yeah, go ahead and kiss her.' It was the breadman and the milkman too, or anybody. See, because she'd get free bread or free milk. She would stand there and look and watch. And then she said, 'Okay, that's long enough. Now you got to give me another week on that book.'

Miss Dee's desire for favors extended beyond bread and milk. She made friends with a city magistrate who often "gave her a few dollars" in exchange for sex with her young charge. Mrs. Winter figuratively and literally "looked up" to Magistrate Jackson. He became an important figure in her childhood; a measure of manhood that she used as a benchmark of masculine attractiveness as she grew older.

Mrs. Winter:	Magistrate Jackson was an old man and he liked young girls. Now, Miss Dee would write notes and give them to me and tell me to go down to Magistrate Jackson's office and give them to him. I'd go to that office and sit outside until my time. When the office got kind of clear, he'd tell his secretary to send me on in. Now I go back in there in the room and I give him the note that Miss Dee give me to give to him and he tell me to sit down in the chair and he'd get up on the desk and take his privates out and put them down in between my bosoms because I was a big girl.
Interviewer:	How old were you at this time?
Mrs. Winter:	Eight years old. Eight going on nine.
Interviewer:	What did you think about all this?
Mrs. Winter:	I was afraid to tell anybody. [Pause] Besides, I kind of liked him. I respected him. He was a big, fine-looking man, smelled nice, fingernails polished, clean and what he was doing, I didn't know what the hell he was doing. I didn't know nothing about no sex. I couldn't read nor write and nobody told me nothing about it.

Because Mrs. Winter was always "big" for her age, she was encouraged by Miss Dee to look for "grown-up" work. She was 11 years old when she took a job as a waitress in a speakeasy.

When prohibition come, and they had open-up bars, what they call speakeasies and they wanted girls to serve the beer. There was one on T. Street. And they had signs, waitress wanted and I went in and ask for a job. And a man says to me, 'How old are you?' So I says, 'Oh, I'm 17.' You don't look to be 17 to me. Bring your mother back here and then if she says okay, then you can work. So I went and told Miss Dee. She said, 'Yeah, and I'll come.' When you going to pay her? He said, 'Every Saturday night.' She said, 'I'll come down here and collect the money.' That's agreeable. So they give me a little yellow uniform with a little white cap sit on my head. And the people liked me. I used to get tips, quarter, dime, nickels, and I used to come home from the job and sometimes Miss Dee'd be there and sometimes not. And I'd put my nightgown on, whatever she had me sleep in and I put my change underneath my pillow. You know that hussy would steal my change when I was asleep at night.

Mrs. Winter often fell asleep during the school day because she worked at night. She finally left school, with Miss Dee's approval, after the second grade. Although Mrs. Winter now regrets her lack of education, she was happy to "be done with all that school stuff." She recalled the cruelty of her classmates because she was "such a size" and was forced by Miss Dee to wear unusual, grown-up clothes.

> See, because of working, I started to go to sleep in the classroom. And the kids used to call me all kind of names, Knots, because my hair wasn't combed. Here come Knots. And I was big and fat. See I was so fat, and that's how in my later years, diabetes. It was not because somebody was giving me candy. It was because of that starch. It was for breakfast, lunch, dinner and supper. During the day Sunday she put on a pot of lima beans and pig tails. And that's what we ate, Monday, breakfast, Tuesday, Wednesday, Thursday, Friday, Saturday, Sunday until every bean was gone out of that pot. Starch. And the way I looked! If you give Miss Dee a dress for me it would fit, you know, only it would hang down way low. And Miss Dee would just take it and sew it on the outside. One time somebody give me a red chinchilla coat and she just took and folded that coat up and made a rip across there. And another lady give me a pair of high heel boots. So Mr. Cam took the hatchet and cut that heel down and that made the front part of the shoe turn up. And me with that big red coat on and them high topped shoes and the kids would say, 'Here comes the devil! Here comes the devil!'

Mrs. Winter draws a graphic portrait of Miss Dee's abuse, classmates' cruelty, and her own self-perceived freakishness. When the interviewer commented on the horror of her young life Mrs. Winter disagreed. She said that she had not known she was abused until recently, when she began to watch television talk shows.

> My life wasn't horrible. Geraldo, Montel, and some of them things started hitting me about what was going on. And I said, well I went through the same thing and I didn't think it was nothing.

Mrs. Winter believes that loneliness and "never being hugged or kissed" were far worse forms of abuse than beatings or forced sexual acts. Mrs. Winter admitted that as a child she "loved anybody who was kind to [her]" because she was "starved for love." She and her closest childhood friend, Lupie, who was Mr. Cam's only daughter, slept together in a makeshift bed until Lupie died of consumption at age 12. Mrs. Winter admitted that she "never got over" that loss. She often tried to make friends with the young women who roomed for short periods of time in Miss Dee's home. She became friendly with Celia, an "older girl" who had dreams of becoming a singer in New York. Mrs. Winter, then 13 years old and anxious to get out from "under Miss Dee's thumb," followed Celia to New York.

She [Celia] was so pretty. Pretty skin; long wavy hair. And this agent done got her a job in New York City. She says, 'I'm going to New York.' She said, 'Oh, come on.' So I went.

It was in New York that Mrs. Winter met and fell in love with Duke. She was attracted to Duke because of his uncanny resemblance to Magistrate Jackson.

Mrs. Winter: One day me and Celia go down Seventh Avenue and low
                 and behold here comes the fellow they call Clark Gable.
Interviewer: You mean Clark Gable the actor?
Mrs. Winter: [Laughter] No, I mean Clark Gable the black fellow. But
                 we called him that, that was his nickname. So now Celia
                 knows all about Clark Gable because he was like a
                 slicker. A con-man. And his buddy, Duke, he was with
                 him. I don't know if he was teaching Duke or what. See,
                 I had a hot for that rascal [Duke] because he reminded
                 me of Magistrate Jackson. And he was big and tall and
                 he was real quiet. I said, 'Oh, I like him.' So they sug-
                 gested to Celia going to the Woodside Hotel. You hear
                 that song, Jumping at the Woodside? They told her to go
                 up there and she would get a room up there. And I went
                 there with her. Now she had a boyfriend. They were go-
                 ing to have an affair. So she said to me, 'Baby, now you go
                 down to Clark Gable's place or upstairs to Duke's place
                 and wait for me.' So I went up to Duke's and the door
                 was opened. So I went on in there and I sat down on the
                 side of the bed. So Duke comes on over. Oh, he was hand-
                 some. He said to me, 'Want to get high?' I said, 'Yeah.' I
                 didn't know what high meant. So he give me a reefer.
                 And I smoke some and he smoke some and eventually I
                 said, 'Oh, I'm going to lay down.' So he said, 'Here's a
                 pair of pajamas.' I put them on and I got into his bed.
                 And he said, 'You don't mind if I get in my own bed, do
                 you?' So he got in and you know what happened.

Celia eventually found a job in a nightclub and informed her 13-year-old companion that she must find work in order to stay in New York and share the expenses of room and board. Celia suggested that her friend work as a prostitute.

See, Celia knew all about what Miss Dee was doing with the breadman and the milkman and all that. So she says, 'Ain't nothing much so different in what you was doing with Miss Dee. Only it'll be you that gets the money.'

Mrs. Winter prospered financially. Duke thought that she needed "protection," and suggested that they live together. In exchange for his protection, she would turn all her earnings over to him. Mrs. Winter was "crazy about Duke." Besides his resemblance to Magistrate Jackson, he was the first person who ever gave her "new" things, such as new dresses, shoes, and sheets for their bed. She did not mention that Duke's presents to her were bought with money that she had earned by prostituting herself.

Mrs. Winter: In the beginning he treated me nice. He bought me silk stockings. See, he didn't start to hurting me until I started getting older and he started with other ladies besides me. But he did marry me.

Interviewer: When?

Mrs. Winter: I guess I was 17. Yeah, he did marry me and then he met an educated lady, a lawyer, through his brother and then he asked me for a divorce. See, he wanted to get rid of me. And I said, 'Oh no.' I said, 'I ain't giving you no divorce.' I said, 'You can have as many women as you want sexually,' I said, 'but I didn't get anything out of this deal but I become a lady. I got a husband of my own from City Hall.' We're still married but I don't live with him.

Interviewer: How long did you actually live with him?

Mrs. Winter: I don't know. He started getting out when I started getting smart.

Duke began to "hurt her" as she "got older"—at least 15. He often beat her so badly that she would flee to Philadelphia and Miss Dee, who in turn forced her to return to Duke. Mrs. Winter often laughed when she told stories of Duke's cruelty, a sad commentary on the commonplace of violence in her life. She now recognizes that her love for him was never reciprocated.

Oh, I loved him. Yeah. But I was just another prostitute as far as he was concerned because he told me so one day. It was after we was married. See, he had a woman named Eliza. And he tell me to break Eliza in, you know, to show her where if she got a john, where to take him. So I got mad, I got jealous. Oh, I'm so jealous. I thought he was all mine. Everything I did to please him, just like I tried to please Miss Dee. Anything she said do, I did because I wanted to be loved. I longed to be loved. I was hungry for it. And if you disappoint me you just break my heart.

Mrs. Winter's mix of the past and present tense in the above account reflects her self-awareness. She did "everything" to be loved by Duke and Miss Dee, but came away from both relationships still "hungry" for connection.

Although she recognizes that neither Miss Dee nor Duke respected or loved her, she also admits that the starved place within her still longs to be filled.

By the time Mrs. Winter reached her twenties, New York police began to recognize her and arrest her "on sight" for prostitution. Duke, needing more gainful and less recognizable apprentices, found younger girls to "protect."

Mrs. Winter's story fades after the early period of her life. She eventually left Duke in New York, returned to Philadelphia, worked as a "cleaner," and joined a union for domestic workers. She found a small apartment and since then, has always lived alone. She is exceedingly proud that she "retired" from domestic work, and "became a lady" by marrying Duke. She said that she had "no more boyfriends" after Duke. Ill health forced her to retire at age 65 and made her eligible for food stamps, medical assistance, and subsidized housing.

Toward the end of the interview, Mrs. Winter reached under her daybed and produced a photo album filled with pictures of women whose names she could not remember, whom she met "somewhere," who were "like family" to her, but who were now "probably dead." She also took a picture from her purse that showed Duke currently. The picture displays an aging, still suave man smiling from an easy chair, being attended to by a male nurse. Mrs. Winter looked at the picture with a smile. When the interviewer asked how she felt looking at Duke's picture, she shrugged. Mrs. Winter admitted that she sees him occasionally, but only if she visits him in his New York apartment. She admitted with a laugh that he "turned mean, like a snake."

Mrs. Winter: Now that he's done got old and half sick, oh, he's so bitter.
Interviewer: Why is he bitter?
Mrs. Winter: Because he's sick. He got a bad heart and legs all swelled up and turn black.
Interviewer: Do you ever talk about the past?
Mrs. Winter: Not really. Every time something happens to him, he calls me up and tells me all his downfalls. [Pause] But he got a lovely bedroom apartment down in the Village. He got a nice little kitty cat. He adores him [the cat]. That gentleman there [showing the picture] with the blond hair, that's his caretaker. [Mrs. Winter reaches for the baby doll on the bed and hands it to the interviewer.] Last time I seen him, he says, 'You're always talking about how you wanted a baby. Here, here's a baby for you.'

Mrs. Winter laughed about this incident, then took the doll from the interviewer and held it close to her for the rest of the interview. Miss Dee passed away from some "terrible ailment—worms come out of her stools" over 30 years ago. When the interviewer asked Mrs. Winter how she remembers Miss Dee, she considered.

> She was only nice to me when I had money. The last thing she did before she died, I was forty years old and she sent for me. She invited me and Duke to come and spend a day and a night with her. So I says, 'What should I do?' He says, 'Yeah, I'll treat her to a bottle of gin and she'll be happy. I'll give her a couple of bucks and she'll be happy.' See, if I had a nice new dress and would go down dressed up, she'd say to me, 'Give me that dress!' So the last time, I was careful what I wore [laughter].

Mrs. Winter's continuing search for love and acceptance brought her, in the latter stage of her life, a plastic doll and memories of abuse from those closest to her. It also brought her a "comfortable" subsidized apartment and the respectability of belonging, for the first time in her life, to a church. Her comments about Duke and Miss Dee show that she holds no delusions concerning their feelings toward her. Perhaps her ability to focus on those things that she did gain—retirement from a "legitimate" job and a marriage certificate—met some of her expectations about life. The fact that she did not think her life was "horrible" is perhaps a tender mercy *and* an indictment of a society that ignored its neediest members and applauded their silence.

SUMMARY

In this chapter we brought forth an idea we hope to elucidate in following chapters—the paradox of poverty. That is, women often defined poverty in other than financial terms. For Mrs. Sheck, estrangement from her children occupied her thoughts and caused her feelings of deprivation. Mrs. Thorne defined impoverishment in terms of her own poor health and the illnesses of loved ones. Mrs. Butcher, on the other hand, did not consider herself poor and was pleased with the unfolding of her life. She saw her present relationships as satisfactory, her physical needs as being met, and her lifestyle as comfortable.

All three women earned similar amounts of money and were considered "poor" objectively. However, their subjective definition of poverty varied. Both Mrs. Sheck and Mrs. Butcher lived in senior subsidized housing and used the word "heaven" to describe their present financial circumstances. Mrs. Thorne, helped financially by her sister, but in poor health, admitted "more money wouldn't help me."

Mrs. Winter embodies the devastation of poverty, both emotional and financial. She displays the intricate interweaving of subjective and objective notions of poverty. For Mrs. Winter, poverty, as a concept, is both linear and circular. In a linear way, the poverty of her past has influenced her present quality of life. Her unfulfilled longing for love as a child, physical and sexual abuse, lack of education, her work as a prostitute—all manifestations of different types of poverty—continue to affect her life presently. Physically, she is ill. An unhealthy diet and heavy drinking and smoking in youth have taken their toll. Emotionally she is volatile. She admits that only her minister knows about her past, and she is afraid that either her neighbors or her "church sisters" will one day find out.

As a circular concept, Mrs. Winter is locked into a cycle of poverty that started in her childhood, hurling her onto a life course from which she could not free herself. This cycle of poverty created her worldview. Trapped within the cycle she could imagine no better life and was forced to fear those she was "supposed to" trust—"authority" figures—God, Miss Dee, Magistrate Jackson, Duke, even the interviewer. During the second meeting with the interviewer, Mrs. Winter admitted that she had lied during the first interview—she hadn't given Duke's "real" name." After the interviewer left, Mrs. Winter's television "blew." She took that as a sign of God's punishment for lying. By telling the "truth" at the start of the second interview, she appeased God and the interviewer as an instrument of God's power. It also allowed her to retain an image of herself, garnered late in life, as an honest person who "never lies no more."

Mrs. Winter's poverty also affects her beliefs about the future. She is afraid of dying alone and hopes that "the Lord will forgive me my past."

Although no excuses are made for the cruelty that Mrs. Winter's "family and friends" inflicted on her, society itself constructed the social mores of her era. The clear connection between racism, poverty, and the "permitted" physical and sexual abuse of children and women are witnessed in Mrs. Winter's narrative.

Poverty, as a cultural and social construct, cannot be understood without mooring it in the story of a life, and to a person who gives the experience of poverty a reality. The women whose case studies are presented in this chapter superimposed themselves onto the template of poverty, creating not only their own loose fit within the construct but actually creating another unique, personal pattern of poverty. In this, there can be no "objective" poverty without linking it to a subjective definition and a lived experience.

In Chapter 3 our respondents take a backward glance over their lives to recall early expectations and decide, in older age, whether those expectations had been met, exceeded, or failed.

3

𝒮

Expectations

The personal meaning of lifelong poverty can be examined through the lens of expectations. To define yourself as poor implicitly suggests the possibility of imagining yourself to be nonpoor. When the women in our study were young, how did they imagine their lives would unfold?

Some respondents had a clear recollection of earlier expectations. Goals forged in childhood and adolescence were recounted and checked off if achieved. Some women acknowledged that dreams were forgotten, suspended, or canceled through the years and unrealized hopes became a source of continuing regret. For other women, expectations were a retrospective projection of the present, that is, they built or reconstructed their expectations by focusing on what they achieved. For them, thinking *in the present* about their past caused them to retroactively construct expectations about life. This retrospective view requires careful juggling. Balancing the scales between expectations and accomplishments may demand either limiting expectations or broadening definitions of achievement.

We found that respondents constructed their expectations about life in at least four ways: through the legacy of family, through gender, through social class, and through perceived limitations, that is, a conviction that their lack of skill, talent, or self-esteem was an insuperable obstacle in pursuing a life path different from the one already begun. We will discuss what women perceived they accomplished in light of their expectations. We begin this chapter by examining how the legacy of family shaped women's expectations about their lives.

EXPECTATIONS SHAPED BY THE LEGACY OF FAMILY

Mrs. Quill is a 73-year-old nonpoor Caucasian widow whose looks and demeanor suggest middle rather than older age. She is tall, slender, and wears her blond hair in a loose, girlish style.

Mrs. Quill, the eldest of two children, was born and raised in Northeast Philadelphia. Both siblings learned in childhood to weigh the consequences of their actions carefully.

My brother and I were very cautious. There was always the fear of getting in trouble and we didn't want that. You did what your parents wanted you to do then. You didn't argue as much. You didn't want something to happen bad.

As Mrs. Quill grew into adolescence, her own expectations about career and marriage were modeled on her parents' financially stable lives. After graduating from business college, she worked in several firms throughout the city, viewing her various bosses as prospective husbands.

I especially liked it when I went to [. . .] Company. I liked it because the men that I worked for were all college graduates and gentlemanly and intelligent. Before that the men were okay but they were more like the sales type.

Mrs. Quill met her husband, who hailed from Indiana, at a Lutheran church group. Although she knew he would be "special" in her life, she "put off marriage" until she visited his family home in Indiana.

I would never have gotten serious if I didn't see where he came from and meet his family. You have to marry somebody that comes from a similar background or has similar feelings about what they want in life. His [Mr. Quill's] family had a very lovely home, but everybody worked in the steel mills. I happened to visit one time when they had a strike. It lasted for 13 weeks. We rode around and I saw all these people standing around. Everybody was out of work and it was depressing to see it. I said to him, 'I wouldn't want to live where your job would depend on this because that's scary.' See, my father was a man who worked in an office, went to work dressed up. He worked all through the Depression.

Fortunately, Mr. Quill agreed with this concept of a working man. Before their engagement he decided to "build a home in suburban Philadelphia and find a job in a good company." During their engagement, they planned their lives—they would have four children and she would not work outside the home. According to Mrs. Quill, planning and organizing one's life, as well as assuming traditional gender roles, contribute to life's success.

We knew that we would like to have four children. My husband didn't want me to work. I was a Girl Scout leader. I used to help at the Sunday school. My husband and I were presidents of the PTA.

Mrs. Quill described her four daughters as "intelligent and successful girls" who hold "good" jobs. She attributes their achievement to careful monitoring in childhood: "I always knew what they were doing."

Mrs. Quill is not surprised that her life unfolded according to plan. Indeed, her own sense of achievement is seen as the culmination of her past vision. "As a girl, you envisioned what you saw would be possible for yourself."

Mrs. Quill fulfilled her expectations of having four "good" children and achieving financial security within her marriage. She elaborated on her husband's "excellence—He was such a good provider." Her marital satisfaction was intricately linked to the economic stability her husband provided. Her husband, like her father, tended emotionally and financially to the women in their lives.

At the end of the interview, Mrs. Quill said, "When I look in the mirror I see my mother and father." She clearly reflects her parents' vision for her life. She internalized, throughout her life span, their consistent signals for how to proceed successfully through life. Her current satisfaction is her reward for observing those signs.

Mrs. Potts, a 75-year-old nonpoor African-American woman, described her life as "simple and happy." Like Mrs. Quill, she constructed her personal expectations in childhood and modeled them on her parents' lives. Her parents' affection toward each other and their two daughters, their emphasis on education, and her trust that her parents' "knew what was best" were the foundations for Mrs. Potts' expectation about her own life.

Mrs. Potts: I grew up in a small town in West Virginia. In school, I went to a boarding high school and then college. High school, college, working.

Interviewer: Why did you go to a boarding school?

Mrs. Potts: If my mother said it was good, I didn't question her. Looking back, well I just thought if she said it—it was good for you. And it *was* a good experience. Of course my sister couldn't do it. She didn't want to be away from Mama.

Mrs. Potts denied that any personal strength allowed her to live away from home at the tender age of 13. Rather, faith in her mother's decisions about her life determined her reaction to leaving home.

Interviewer: What was it about you, what strength did you have that allowed you to stay after your sister left [the boarding school]?

Mrs. Potts: I didn't think of it as a strength to tell you the truth. I knew because my mother said it would be—it was a good

school. You get an excellent education. So I said, I didn't
question it.

After graduating from boarding school and teacher's college, Mrs. Potts
never returned to the family home in West Virginia. She boarded with "nice"
families throughout the South, teaching English and History in black elementary schools. She maintained a "terrific" closeness with her mother
and sister after her father died.

> When I think of it, it was really remarkable. My mother and I had a ter-
> rific bond. She expected us to be close even though we were not together. She
> used to say we were the three musketeers, and she talked to us from very
> young children about so many things. I shared everything with her. Silly
> little things that I did, good and bad, to big things.

Mrs. Potts met her husband while working in Washington as a school-
teacher. She described their meeting, as well as their lives together, as
"nothing spectacular."

Mrs. Potts: We met through a friend. We dated a couple of years, decided to get married. Our meeting was coincidental. A
girlfriend told me about him. Jimmy [husband] and his
friend used to go to football games. She [the girlfriend]
arranged for us to be dates. We went to the game, had
dinner, and he came back by the house. It was pleasant.

Interviewer: Can you tell me a little bit about Mr. Potts as a person?

Mrs. Potts: Quiet. Pleasant. I wasn't interested in forming a deep relationship so I started dating him because I thought it
was going to be a casual relationship. It wasn't anything
spectacular. He dropped out of school. He never got a degree. He had gone to a college in Washington. So he never
got around to going back and getting his degree which
of course he didn't [get the degree] after he came here
[Philadelphia]. There's nothing really spectacular to tell
about it.

Interviewer: Did you know that you wanted to marry him?

Mrs. Potts: [Pause] It more or less happened gradually. We spent
more time together. Let's get married. I mean it wasn't
anything spectacular.

Unfortunately, the life that unfolded with Mr. Potts did not correspond
to Mrs. Potts' model of marriage and family, which was based on her parents' "household where there was communication and love."

When he [husband] went to college, he was majoring in architecture and engineering and he had not followed through. He had the chance but for some reason he didn't have the courage. Courage is important. I think that the inferiority because of that (pause)—must have—I really feel that was one of the things. Also, he was an only child. He was not able to share. I had come from a home where everybody shared. My father and mother both were educated. So I came up in a home where everything was discussed. And I loved it. It was difficult for him to share. I couldn't get him to share, and over the years I got to the point where I said, this isn't working.

Mrs. Potts eventually ended her marriage and "had no desire" to marry again. Although Mrs. Potts showed disappointment about marriage in general, she negated the importance of being part of a couple in order to feel content. She did explain, however, how her idea of marriage had been implicitly formed in childhood.

Mrs. Potts: Those things that I don't have, my childhood dreams, they weren't dreams that you harbor—. I just assumed I would live in a big house, have a loving husband and children. I guess I based the relationship on my mother and father. My husband wasn't an affectionate man. I can remember once when I was little, my mother and father standing up in the kitchen, hugging and kissing. I was on one side pushing, and my sister was on the other side, 'Kiss me, too.' I can remember mommy and daddy bent down and they kissed us and went back to kissing. Now my husband never had that warmth.

Interviewer: And you had hoped for that?

Mrs. Potts: I had assumed that was part of life—like sharing.

Mrs. Potts repeated the words affection and sharing throughout the interview. Taking cues from her family of origin, she divorced her husband when she realized that he did not "share" her concept of family. Rather than give up those expectations about family life, she said she "worked hard" to ensure that her two children achieved the model of family that had given her own young life structure. Although her children are separated by 11 years in age and live in different states, Mrs. Potts described their relationship:

The children are extremely close. That was something I worked hard at. I mean I was aware of it. My son, I used to let him go in the summers with my sister, who had children. But after my daughter was born, I wanted them—. My sister and I were very close even though we had not been together, we were extremely close. My sister, mother and I had a tight bond and I wanted my children to have that support because mom and sister were my support. So I was very aware of it. And something must have been done right in all of the wrong because they are extremely close. He [son] has a very protective attitude toward her [daughter]. Because his father was gone when she was about four and a half. But they are extremely close and share confidences. I've been fortunate.

Although Mrs. Potts' expectation about a warm and sharing marriage had not been realized, she impressed her children with the picture of a family that supported her in the past *and* present. In this, her expectation about family found fruition in her children, particularly in the way they mirror her past relationship with her mother and sister.

A "negative" legacy of family also shaped women's expectations about their lives. Mrs. McKenna, a 77-year-old poor Caucasian widow, is the mother of one son, age 54, who, she reports, has "mental problems" and cannot work. Although he did not live with his mother since he was 2 years old, he now spends most of his time at Mrs. McKenna's small, subsidized, center city apartment.

When asked to tell the story of her life, Mrs. McKenna began by revealing her illegitimacy. Her conviction that she was unwanted by her mother and "the man who only gave me a name" (stepfather) framed her narrative. Mrs. McKenna's life story attested to the fact of "not belonging."

Born in Austria, Mrs. McKenna resented that her biological father's identity was "kept secret" by her mother's sister, Paula. Mrs. McKenna remained in Austria with her grandmother when her mother and stepfather came to the United States. After her grandmother fell ill, she was forced to join her mother and the man who adopted her, but who acted as "no real father at all." She was 14 years old.

The fact that her mother and stepfather had a child "together" emphasized Mrs. McKenna's feelings of marginality. The child was treated "like a prince" because he was their own. After their mother died in 1981, Mrs. McKenna lost contact with her half-brother.

Mrs. McKenna: You know people say you shouldn't have abortions. I think instead of my mother treating me the way she did, you know, she should have had it. It would have been better for me and her.

Interviewer: You think that even now?

Mrs. McKenna: Yeah, I do. Because I really had no real life, nothing but work, work, work. The first stupid mistake I made was to come to this country because I had nothing but trouble. It was like going from heaven to hell.

Interviewer:	You mean your life would have been different if you stayed in Austria.
Mrs. McKenna:	I don't know. Not long after I left Hitler came into power and took over Austria. I guess I would have been in the Hitler youth group. Maybe I would have gotten smarter.
Interviewer:	What do you mean?
Mrs. McKenna:	Well, he taught a lot of things that weren't any good but I bet he taught things that you could use, in other words, to be smart in the wrong way. That's what he taught.
Interviewer:	Is that what you want, to be smart in the wrong way?
Mrs. McKenna:	[After a pause] It's not worth it to get to be 76 and live in all this mess. It's just not right. I just wonder if it's all worth it at this stage of the game.

Mrs. McKenna's negative expectations about life were cemented at age 14 by her first "stupid mistake"—coming to the United States. Although she finished high school, she was unable to find a "good" job and began a lifelong career in "food services," and "doing domestic work on weekends." Mrs. McKenna met her husband during one of her stints in food services. She blames this "sad affair" on her stupidity.

I was stupid. My idea of marriage was to do what I didn't have—make a home. It didn't turn out that way. I was stupid. I didn't know he was an alcoholic. I don't think I was with him for more than about two years. When I was depending on him, or what he was supposed to bring home, he didn't. The very first time ever that I was on welfare he got hold of the check and spent it and they blamed me for it. How can you live like that?

Mrs. McKenna left her husband before their third anniversary. She and her only child, Douglas, then 2 years old, lived a life on the run, moving from "room to room" in other people's houses.

He [husband] always seemed to know where I'm at. At night, when I got out of work, he used to be there, waiting for me. He always wanted a dollar or two.

Mrs. McKenna placed Douglas in a foster home when he was 3 years old. She did so because she was "always afraid" that Mr. McKenna might "take Douglas and leave him in a saloon for a drink because they take everything that they can grab and convert it into money." Douglas stayed with the

Griffins (foster family) for the next 30 years, until the death of his foster mother in the early 1980s. After the interviewer commented on the heartache she must have experienced in giving up her son, Mrs. McKenna half smiled and shrugged. "I went there on weekends. He called both of us mom." When asked if she intended to take Douglas out of the foster home, she hesitated.

> Well I don't know. If I would have gotten a place, sooner or later his father would have found out. Then he would have been there and forget it! Also, for 14 years I worked two jobs, so it was 7 days a week I worked.

Mrs. McKenna described herself in negatives, such as "not very sociable" and "not a lady." When asked to elaborate, she answered: "I never went out. I always worked and I didn't have time to do anything." In Mrs. McKenna's words, her work kept her from "sociability," from friendships, and even from being Douglas' mother, perhaps because she thought so little of her ability to manage that role. Indeed, Mrs. McKenna believed that she fell far short of what a woman should be. When asked what principles guided her life, she answered:

Mrs. McKenna: I learned a lot from Mrs. Griffin [Douglas' foster mother]. How good and how patient she was and how she conducted herself. And never, never angry and stuff like that. Aunt Paula the same way. These two women—helped me.

Interviewer: What do you mean?

Mrs. McKenna: They showed me what I *should* be. They were both ladies.

When asked how a lady is defined, Mrs. McKenna said, "ladies are discreet." When the interviewer commented that Aunt Paula's "discretion" concerning her father's identity caused her unhappiness as a child, she hesitated. "Well, at least they don't curse, and I curse all the time."

This interchange highlights Mrs. McKenna's willingness to compare herself unfavorably to those women she admired. It also emphasizes her expectations that her present lot in life—unhappiness and impoverishment—is deserved since she did not quite make the grade in any of life's arenas—work, marriage, or motherhood. Mrs. Griffin, as a lady, became Douglas' mom. Aunt Paula, as a lady, found a good husband, bought a beautiful home, and gave birth to a healthy daughter. If Mrs. McKenna embodied these qualities, would her life have turned out differently? She believed that her early lack of legitimacy denied her the "rights" to any good things in this life. Her family legacy framed her emotional as well as her financial poverty.

Conversely, for Mrs. Cleveland, an 89-year-old poor African-American divorcee, family legacy bequeathed a powerful sense of self-esteem that negated "feelings" of poverty. Her self-concept included the belief that she deserved and therefore expected the best from life. Interestingly, "the best" in life was not equated with possessing money, but with holding a healthy vanity, a compassionate view toward others, and a refusal to let herself "go down shabby."

Mrs. Cleveland was raised in a small town in South Carolina by grandparents and uncles who "loved [her] to death." She is convinced that her upbringing effected a life-pervading optimism, and an injunction to treat others *and* oneself with kindness and respect.

> I guess I got that from my mother. I don't have anything to do with how you treat me. But I have something to do with how I treat you. Still, I had a friend who said, 'Gert, you ain't going to let nobody make a fool out of you.' I said, 'No, my mother's life gave me a lesson.' Out of all the troubles and ups and downs I have had, I kept my head up. I didn't get in the gutter. I didn't let nobody put me in the gutter. That's how I came along.

Like Mrs. McKenna, Mrs. Cleveland felt compelled to give up her only child, Ellen, when she was 2 years old. For Mrs. Cleveland 1925 was a "bad" year. She "got in trouble" and her mother died shortly afterward. She married Mr. Cleveland after their daughter's birth and moved to Philadelphia. Since, she reported, Mr. Cleveland was "on the lazy side," she was forced to find days' work with several families. While rooming in her cousin's West Philadelphia home, a neighbor woman "took" Ellen. Mrs. Cleveland's cousin argued that since Mrs. Cleveland had to work, she couldn't take care of Ellen. She described this episode as how "my daughter got away from me for a while." Although she tried repeatedly to get her daughter back,

> She [Ellen] had been whitewashed. She cried so I had to take her back [to the other woman]. When I saw her again she was 12 years old. I used to visit her, though.

Mrs. Cleveland ended her marriage soon after her daughter was "taken." Once she became aware of Mr. Cleveland's "pedigree," she "quit" him.

> You know, an ignorant person is terrible to deal with. I had to quit him. When I found out he didn't want nothing but to sleep and eat and worry the devil out of me, I told him, 'You don't want nothing, I don't want you. If I ain't going to have nothing, I ain't going to have nothing by myself.' He wasn't a man what a man should be, so I quit him.

Mrs. Cleveland held a clear expectation about how her husband should provide for her. This deservedness was linked to her early life—her grandfather and uncles "worked hard" and lavished her with affection. A fierce independence grounds her self-concept. Although she cannot remember a "good" time financially, she believes that the deprivation of her past contributed to her present strength and self-reliance.

> My background was a pip. But hard times made a woman out of me. It make me look out for myself and don't let no man pull me down. Because some men will do it. What some of these women take I wouldn't take it because this is a big world. I always said I'm not going to let nobody abuse me. And I meant that. I ain't never let myself go down shabby. I didn't make no lot of money but I went to work anyhow, sick or well. If I didn't have 5 cents, nobody didn't know but me and God.

Mrs. Cleveland lives in subsidized housing and receives about $600 a month from her husband's pension and her own social security. She considers the present as the best financial time in her life.

> It seems that now since I'm up in my 80s, it seems like I'm more financial fixed right now than I ever been in my life. Because see, I worked all my life. I didn't make much, I worked anyhow. And it looked like, in fact it *is* coming together and paying off right now. That's a blessing. [respondent's emphasis]

Mrs. Cleveland believes that she is now reaping the harvest for her life of hard work. She is not surprised by her present "good fortune," which consists of a "comfortable" apartment, a devoted granddaughter-in-law, and the confidence that God "continues to bless [her]." Her conviction that she was loved and protected by her family nurtured her self-regard and the expectation that life would ultimately reward her. The spirits of her ancestors continue to guide her.

> Some people say that the old people watches over you when they pass. And I say, well my grandmom and grandpop still watching over me then.

Although expectations shaped by the legacy of family were personally formulated for each woman, each of the four groups shows how expectations are formed within a particular racial and income sector.

In general, expectations for financial and emotional security conflated for the nonpoor Caucasian women we interviewed. They studied the model and worldview of their parents' lives and vision. They watched their parents' lives unfold according to plan and likewise plotted a life that held few surprises. For example, Mrs. Quill did not deviate from the emotional and financial path on which her parents placed her in childhood. Her own diligence in finding a mate with a similar background and values ensured a straight and secure route through life.

The larger society offered little to African-Americans of any financial status during their youth and young adulthood. Although they lived within the overarching mores of the "white" world, they forged their self-concept within their own tradition. For example, Mrs. Potts expected from life what she could garner from the "smaller" society of African-American schools and employment that was open to her. However, the legacy of her family bequeathed an expectation of marital sharing that sadly failed to materialize.

The legacy from the families of poor Caucasians was idiosyncratic. Respondents' financial expectations often reflected the poverty in their family of origin and their mother's hardship in raising children alone. In other words, poor Caucasian respondents held scant expectations in childhood and adolescence for financial improvement in adulthood. Although some poor Caucasian women harbored dreams that husbands would bring economic betterment, disappointing or truncated marriages often dashed those dreams. Unemployed, underemployed, or profligate husbands led the way to emotional as well as financial poverty.

Although poor African-American women were the most disenfranchised group financially, their self-concept appeared to be determined more by their perception of positive personal traits than their limited finances. Like Mrs. Cleveland, women in this group often interpreted their strength as an antidote to poverty. Although admitting to "having it hard," they countered hardship with personal strength.

EXPECTATIONS SHAPED BY GENDER

For the women interviewed, awareness that gender shaped their expectations was often linked to the need to work. Although some nonpoor Caucasian women anticipated this eventuality by obtaining an education or had access to jobs through their familial or social network, most poor Caucasian women in our sample did not. Insufficient skills for jobs forced poor Caucasian women to remain, in young and middle adulthood, in the cycle of simply making ends meet. Financial poverty, due to early widowhood or divorce, was salient in their stories. Husbands who could not find steady work through lack of skill or addiction to liquor or gambling were named as factors in present and past hardship. Following this, many poor Caucasian women spoke as if they "fell into" the work they did *and* the lives they lived.

Both poor and nonpoor African-American women usually worked "all their lives." In regard to the kind of work they did, expectations shaped by gender conflated with an awareness of what jobs were open to African-American women, whether the women were skilled or not. Death or divorce of a spouse did not appear to appreciably change the financial status of African-American groups.

Although many nonpoor Caucasian women had worked for pay before marriage, motherhood and active involvement with their children's activities or with civic or religious organizations consumed their time, talents, and energies. Below, we examine women's attitudes to the work they found through circumstances and gender.

Ms. Coles is a 74-year-old poor African-American woman who lives in a small row home in the heart of North Philadelphia. The home is owned solely by her sister-in-law since her brother's recent death. Her relationship with her sister-in-law is "good. We're company for each other, and we go half [for expenses]." Ms. Coles was one of nine children born and raised in a "nice little town" in North Carolina. She returns every year for family reunions. Ms. Coles' two sons were born in North Carolina. She decided not to marry either of the men who fathered her children. She explained:

> The father of the oldest one, we were talking about marriage, but after he went into the service, it was different. The father of the youngest son, no, that was just a couple of times, you know.

Although the children "remained close" to their fathers, neither man supported the boys. Ms. Coles chose to look for work in Philadelphia because her brother was living there. She was 20 years old when she found work in a laundry in North Philadelphia, where she remained for the next 30 years.

> Coming to Philadelphia was work-related. Because at home they only had season jobs. So the most thing I did was laundry work because then you could always depend on having a job. See, there aren't too many white women in the laundry. White people just didn't go in for it. Besides it was never hard. It's never hard if you enjoy your job. And they were happy to have me. I was a presser. And I was fortunate to have something I always liked.

Although Ms. Coles liked her job and was proud to raise her children "without too much help," she described her early years in Philadelphia as the hardest financially.

> It weren't easy when they [sons] were small. My family was supportive of me. But it was hard, I couldn't save; it took every penny I was making. You didn't make a whole lot then.

Ms. Coles did manage, however, to save enough money to buy a home of her own in North Philadelphia where "the boys grew up." She "loved" the small brick row house, took pride in ownership, and lived there for over 30 years. She explained the circumstances that forced her to leave.

The inside was fixed up, but the front of it, the bricks and things fell out of it. It cost so much to fix it. After my house was condemned, that's when I moved here.

Ms. Coles was grateful that she could return to her brother's home, 50 years after she had first moved to Philadelphia. She named "having a nice place to live right now" as one of her accomplishments in life.

Ms. Coles made choices in her life within a limited framework of options. Although she believed that "men have more choices than a woman do," she took pride in and "enjoyed" a job that "white women didn't want." However, she held a retrospective vision of what life might have been if she had either married or "made more money myself."

If I had made more [money] I probably would have made better choices. I probably would have did more for myself, maybe taking up some kind of trade, like beautician. When you don't have the money it's hard. If I could go back I would try to do more like saving more money. Then now I would be in a position that—one thing, you would have more to look forward to, and in emergencies not depend on anybody else.

Ms. Coles' expectations were limited by her class, gender, and race. This triple jeopardy clearly influenced her choice of jobs and places to live. Although Ms. Coles understands the limitations imposed on her by the social and historical forces of her era, *she* takes responsibility for her past; she believes that *she* should have, somehow, saved more money to ensure a financially secure older age. In this, the paradox of poverty emerges clearly: given Ms. Coles' gender and race, past chances for Ms. Coles' financial success seem slim. Yet, society succeeded in placing the onus of individual responsibility for success on Ms. Coles—making her feel accountable for past and present hardship. Society firmly imprinted Ms. Coles with its badge of individualism. Yet, Ms. Coles' rules her "small" world by how she chooses to perceive herself, react to life events, and interact with others, despite her embeddedness in a "larger" world that closed many of its doors to her. When asked what she believed to be the main purpose in life, she answered:

You have to be thankful it was as well as it was, because it could have been worse. So, the main purpose is the way I carry myself and what I have done, the good things I did. So it's just the way you do, and carry yourself and treat people.

EXPECTATIONS SHAPED BY SOCIAL CLASS

Women of all groups formed their expectations and their self-concepts within the framework of a singular life. Being born into a particular financial status often predicted a similar status throughout life.

For the poor Caucasians in our sample, minimum education usually permitted few perceived choices concerning husbands and work. If women in this group aimed to "better" themselves and acquire "more" financially, they usually hoped to do so through marriage, rather than entry into their own career. If a "bad" marriage or widowhood dashed dreams of financial betterment, poverty at the end of life resulted in a bewildering disappointment.

African-Americans of both economic groups were aware that their race and their class limited their opportunities in the larger world. The melding of race and class was a powerful predictor of poverty in late life for poor African-American women. African-Americans in the nonpoor group struggled to attain and maintain a "middle-class" status.

However, nonpoor Caucasian women sometimes described their childhood as "poor." They became aware, while growing up, that the Depression negatively affected their family's income. However, help from extended family and well-placed friends permitted life plans to develop according to expectations despite the interim of "poverty." This grants a window into how the women formed subjective definitions of poverty.

It is important to note that the concept of class may be placed under at least two rubrics: finances and social status. Like nonpoor women who thought of themselves as poor in the past, women who were considered financially "poor" sometimes rated themselves as middle, upper-middle, or upper class socially. This also speaks to women's social expectations about their lives, that is, despite having little money, they considered themselves as coming from "good" families and sought companions from similarly "refined" backgrounds.

We present the case of Mrs. Corner, a 73-year-old nonpoor African-American widow who struggled throughout her life to achieve and maintain her middle-class status. Mrs. Corner lives in a large row home in Northwest Philadelphia. Her only son, now divorced, lives "temporarily" with her. Awards received from church, community, and civic organizations are displayed on the gold-sparkled walls of her living room. Mrs. Corner placed photographs and records of family achievement on the dining table. During the course of the interview she pointed to a picture or document that described a particular event in her life.

Mrs. Corner stated that education was stressed during her childhood, although her mother "wasn't even a high school graduate." When the interviewer commented on her mother's vision despite the struggle to raise five children alone, Mrs. Corner bristled.

> It isn't unique to have a single family home and emphasize education. The motivation came from within. It doesn't seem unique to me in reading biographical sketches of giants where the parents didn't have education. It doesn't really enter into the picture except you have a strong parent who wants you to do well.

Mrs. Corner described her family of origin as "unreal, phenomenal" in their talent. She explained that although her family's characteristics were superior, they were also normative in relation to other "giants."

Mrs. Corner added her talent—music—to the family trove. Teachers discovered her skill for playing the flute when she was in the sixth grade of a Harrisburg public school.

> I didn't really choose the flute. There was a need because the flute is a unique instrument. It was an instrument that needed to be pursued. It just happened. But I had a talent. Because they can tell. So I was very fortunate. I had excellent teachers.

Mrs. Corner received a music scholarship to a Virginia college where she majored in psychology and excelled in athletics. She met her future husband in her sophomore year and left school when they married. When asked what attracted her to her husband, she considered:

> What we had in common was where we met on the college campus. I do think that I wanted to meet someone on my level. That should be a requirement. You shouldn't get someone beneath your level. We had an educational background, very strongly, in common. And then we had his athletic abilities and so forth. And he was really brilliant. He could have been a scientist. But he went into sports. I saw that he was elevated, absolutely. I wanted that level.

After marriage, Mrs. Corner worked full time as a city clerk, chaired several civic organizations, and sought outlets for her musical talent. Her commitments influenced the couple's decision to conceive only one child. After their son was born, Mrs. Corner's self-description as a perfectionist cemented their resolve to have no more children.

> When I saw what was involved [in having children] and going back into the system [to work] I didn't feel that I was interested in coping with the second [child]. I hired someone to take care of him but by the time I told her what had to be done and how I wanted it to be done, I was exhausted.

Mrs. Corner remains a "doer." When the interviewer arrived, Mrs. Corner was in the midst of organizing a writing campaign against a popular television hostess whose show she "disapproved of." She was also "doing a mailing" for an upcoming church event. She worries that she doesn't allow herself enough "alone time" because constant requests for advice and assistance dot her day.

> When I'm involved in a life such as this I'm constantly getting telephone calls and people are requesting things from you, they're constantly asking this and that. I'm a committee woman, too. And people will call and ask your opinion about the political arena. And because I'm into gardening, I'm constantly helping this one and that one. Because there are different levels.

When asked to describe herself, Mrs. Corner answered with a smile.

> Well, people ask me, where do you get the energy? Your energy level, and so forth. Wherever I go I make sure I have this kind of strength. See, there are white people who feel surprised that African-Americans live on such a high level. Yes, there are some of them that are that high.

Mrs. Corner repeated words such as "deep, unique," and "level" throughout the interview. They telegraphically describe her internal characteristics and the external plateaus that she sought. The words also string together recognition of her talent and advancement despite the obstacles she encountered because of her race. Mrs. Corner struggles to maintain this level of superiority in her own neighborhood.

> The newcomers [in the neighborhood], we talk to. Because if you don't they might not realize that you have a concern for maintaining the level of the neighborhood.

Mrs. Corner realized early in life that despite "phenomenal" talent and advanced education, her race would be the primary criterion on which she and members of her family were judged. This double impetus of proving her talent and combating racism caused Mrs. Corner to expect as much from others as from herself, to describe herself as a "perfectionist," and to demonstrate to anyone looking that she had indeed "made it" to an advanced level.

EXPECTATIONS SHAPED BY PERCEIVED LIMITATIONS

Limitations were often constructed from the idiosyncratic circumstances of a particular life. Perceived limitations emerged from the individual pasts and self-concepts of the women interviewed, as well as from internalizing the gender and racial roles that society allowed.

Personally perceived limitations were most salient in the discourse of poor Caucasian women. However, actual limitations of gender and race modified what women in all groups sought and achieved.

Mrs. Clarkson is a 72-year-old poor Caucasian widow who lives in a subsidized housing facility. The brightness of Mrs. Clarkson's apartment—purple placemats and yellow silk flowers on her dinette table—contrasted her aura of sadness. Mrs. Clarkson is one of 15 children who grew up in a suburb of Philadelphia. Her younger brother, who lives nearby, is the only sibling left. Mrs. Clarkson began her life story this way:

> It [my childhood] was very nice. I saw my husband for the first time when I was 10 years old. He was my brother-in-law's nephew. I started writing to him when he went in the Navy. After I saw him, I never looked at another man.

The above comments signal that Mrs. Clarkson's husband and marriage are uppermost in her mind. However, Mr. Clarkson died over 25 years ago, when he was 52 years old. When the interviewer commented on his early death, Mrs. Clarkson began to cry.

> It was a very bad shock. I don't know if I can tell you about it. See, my husband committed suicide.

Although Mrs. Clarkson continues to question why her husband took his life, she remembers early signs of emotional instability. She recalls his extreme possessiveness, his "need to have [her] complete attention all the time," and his inability to "take rejection." She admits that while raising their two daughters she often "walked on egg shells" because "the girls got in the way as far as he was concerned." She complained that Mr. Clark's mother acted "distant" toward him, and related instances of her cruelty. She pondered whether unresolved anger concerning his mother caused him "to act the way he did."

> She went to visit her other children all the time, but never him. I know he cried about that. All he ever talked about was how his mother neglected him.

Although she believes that unhealed childhood wounds caused his depression and resulted in his suicide, she questions *her* role in his final act.

> I thought that he and I were too close for him to do something like that. The only thing I wonder—Why I wasn't enough, you know? Because he was everything for me. What did I do wrong? I tried to make up for what happened.

Mrs. Clarkson is convinced that her inability to supply her husband with what had been emotionally denied him in childhood ultimately caused his death. This all or nothing mindset is reflected in her self-evaluation. When asked to describe herself, Mrs. Clarkson related how her daughters think about her.

> The girls say with Mother it's black or white, there's no gray areas. It's right or wrong. There's no middle road. Middle roads are excuses.

As the person who "should have loved him best," Mrs. Clarkson blames herself for her husband's death; failure to do so would seem like an excuse. Most of her responses to the interview questions related to her husband's suicide. When asked what she believed was the main purpose or task in life, she replied:

Mrs. Clarkson: We're here to learn something and if we don't get it right we'll be back again.
Interviewer: Do you think you'll be back again?
Mrs. Clarkson: Sure. I'd like to come back again and meet the same man and know what I know now and I'd be different.
Interviewer: How would you be different?
Mrs. Clarkson: Well, I guess I'd spoil him.
Interviewer: Do you think you didn't spoil him?
Mrs. Clarkson: Well, I guess I'd spoil him even worse.

Mr. Clarkson's suicide is the climax and vantage point of Mrs. Clarkson's life. Her self-regard, memories, and hopes are filtered through his shocking and untimely death. Her previous worldview disintegrated with his suicide; his passing forced her to reconstruct her thoughts about herself, life's meaning, and her purpose for existence. Into her new self-view she places her first sure fact—"why was I not enough?" Mrs. Clarkson's limitations were borne of the unfortunate circumstances of her husband's suicide and her inability to move beyond this tragic event.

ACCOMPLISHMENTS IN LIGHT OF EXPECTATIONS

To discuss your expectations about life is to acknowledge, either tacitly or explicitly, what you have accomplished in light of those expectations.

A continuing life plan pervaded the narratives of most nonpoor women in our sample. In this, there was an overt link between expectations and achievement. A less well-defined connection between expectations and accomplishments appeared in the poor groups. Although poor women spoke proudly of their personal accomplishments, such as raising children or being a "hard" worker," they also related how simply reaching older age was a major accomplishment. This highlights the "day-by-day" construction of their lives, and their surprise in having grasped the unimagined plateau of later life.

Women were asked in the interview about the dreams or visions of their youth. We cannot know whether their answers sprang from expectations remembered from childhood and adolescence or their retrospective projection of dreams onto a life that already unfolded. The interview questions may have prompted a revisionist balancing between dreams and accomplishments. Although we will say more about women's accomplishments in Chapter 5, under Strategies and Techniques of Coping with Poverty, we present the case of Mrs. Quaid, who, in her narrative, revealed her past expectations in light of her accomplishments.

Mrs. Quaid is a 71-year-old poor African-American widow who lives in a subsidized apartment with her cat, Butch. At first, Mrs. Quaid seemed hesitant to talk about herself, but instead revealed that Butch had been abused as a kitten. The interviewer knelt by Butch, stroked him, and commented on the charm of Mrs. Quaid's apartment. Mrs. Quaid smiled and replied, "You should have seen my home on S. Street." She thus began a series of stories in which she reveals personal traits that are important to her, such as kindness to animals and maintaining a cozy home. Her first remarks also show a continuing feature of her narrative—she overcame life's disappointments by focusing on her personal strengths and perceived blessings.

> I was born and raised in South Philadelphia. My mother died when I was about 4 or 5 years old. She died from cancer from having too many pregnancies. But my father kept us until I was about 13. Then I went to stay with my aunt, then another aunt—different ones. They say my mother had 11 children but only 9 survived. My mother was very young, they were from Virginia. My father came up and got a home up here for her. My father was about 22 years older than my mother. My father was a very hard working man. After my mother died he said he would never marry again. He took care of all his children. Even though it was during the Depression, we didn't know nothing about the Depression because my father had a lifetime job at the river front. He lived to be 100.

When asked about her place in the family line, Mrs. Quaid answered:

> I'm the seventh child of a seventh child. I have visions and dreams. About two years before my first job, every night I was dreaming I was pulling these threads, pulling these threads. It was a little short dream. And sure enough I got that job in a carpet factory. That was during the war years. My father

and brothers wanted me to go to college. I had a chance. But I wanted to get me a job. Now was my opportunity. I was going to get me my own house because like I said I was from one place to another since I was a child.

Despite her father's wish to keep his children together, financial circumstances separated the family. Because of Mrs. Quaid's rootlessness in adolescence, the picture of a stable home and family loomed large in her dreams. She believed that "working hard" throughout her life was one way to achieve her goals. She also thought that her dreams would find fruition when she married because her husband's dreams were similar. Besides, Mrs. Quaid thought that it was "about time" she "settle down."

I met him in the church. He was the organist there. He was interested in me first. I always sang on the choir, and everybody was talking about the new organist and this one liked him and that one liked him. He started asking me out. See at that time I was an unwed mother. I had the one boy, Jason. I kept putting it [marriage] off. Then along came Nathan [her second son]. And I said I'm not going to make the same mistake with him.

Although the couple divorced after 10 years of marriage, Mrs. Quaid described her husband and their marriage in glowing terms.

We had a beautiful marriage. He was a very hard working man. We worked hard together. He was a teacher of the organ. He was a professional musician. Then he played the organ at churches. He had students all around the city. He could sing. We only separated because at that time there was too much of a push for me. I had just buried my sister, my father, my aunt, all of them within about seven years. And then for 18 years I just had taken care of the sick, the sick, the sick.

Later in the interview Mrs. Quaid revealed that reasons other than extended caretaking precipitated her divorce. She vividly recalls the moment she knew her marriage was over.

See the reason why he got that divorce—He kept on saying, I'm going to get me an apartment; I'm going to get me a place. So I got tired of hearing this. But that's because he wanted to do his little thing outside. In other words, and see, I understood what had happened. You know these men, when they get 45, they're changing life. And he couldn't do anything. So you know some girls out there they'll do things the wife won't. So he met this girl, the girl was right there in the church, and they were running around together. I couldn't cope with it. What really broke the camel's back—we had a back way, he was going out the driveway. By this time people was talking, it was going around about his stuff. He always kissed me at the door and I'd turn my cheek. It must have come to him; he got half way to the step and he come back and said, 'What's the matter, you don't want to kiss me on my mouth any more?' So I said no. And that's when it was. Right then.

Mrs. Quaid's poignant story provides a glimpse into the couple's lives. Traveling different ways, meeting needs through other people, the devastation of infidelity—all come to a climax on an ordinary weekday morning. The moment becomes extraordinary because Mrs. Quaid captures it as a flash of honesty and insight by both of the couple. After the divorce, Mrs. Quaid was physically and financially unable to keep her beloved home. Disappointed that neither of her grown sons wanted to "move in and pay half and do some of the work," she reluctantly moved into her present apartment. Mr. Quaid died a year after their divorce. Despite the divorce and evidence that he had remarried, Mrs. Quaid considers herself the "widow."

We were still friends. Even when he had his heart attack, I went to the hospital and everything to see him. His girlfriend claims that they had gotten married, but it didn't make any difference to me. Everybody sent *me* the cards, everything came to the house. She's [the girlfriend] upset to this day. [Respondent's emphasis]

Mrs. Quaid admits that many of her dreams died when her husband left—such as plans to expand and beautify their home and an intention to travel after their retirement.

He was teaching a lot, so we didn't go out much. But we used to say after the kids are grown we're going to get a mobile home and travel all around the country.

Despite the fact that divorce, the loss of her home, and ultimately her husband's death crushed many of her expectations about life, Mrs. Quaid makes the most of the present. Frequent telephone calls and knocks at the door interrupted the flow of the interview. Mrs. Quaid explained. "I'm the assistant floor captain. It really is nice here. Everybody is nice."

Mrs. Quaid spoke often about Nathan, her younger son, an accomplished musician. Pictures of Nathan are displayed throughout her apartment— Nathan playing an instrument, Nathan with his girlfriend, Nathan as a child, a current Nathan.

Nathan plays jazz and he just played at the big church in town. He played the Christmas and Easter contada. I am very proud of him. And he's very, very, very devoted.

Tucked inside Mrs. Quaid's huge entertainment center was a small solitary picture of Jason, her older son. The black and white photograph showed a young Jason leaning against the wall of their former home.

> Now Jason, he's lovable and stuff but he's distant. I mean he's there, but I think he kind of regrets now that he's at a standstill. When he told me he wasn't graduating high school, I told him then you're going to work. After he went into the service he got in with the wrong crowd. He has this hurt now because of Viet Nam. When he came back he was going to be a cop but things didn't work out for him. That same little job that I got him when he was a teenager, he still on that same job today.

Mrs. Quaid identifies strongly with Nathan. She also sees in Nathan the musical talent that originally attracted her to his father. Likewise, it is Nathan, but not Jason who exhibits the values that Mrs. Quaid believes she inherited from her father, such as hard work, ambition, and independence. She attributes her father's lack of gender bias to her own choice of seeking and finding "male" jobs. Her favorite job was operating a power machine during the Second World War.

> I always liked to have my own money. We were brought up that way. My father didn't believe in just women's work and men's work. You learned both things. I can paint; I can do anything. My father was a man ahead of his time. That's the way he raised his children; that's the way I raised mine. He was a longshoreman. But he did all the cooking. All his people were like that. And my sons, too, they can make beds, wash dishes, scrub floors, anything. And I let them know that's not a sissy job. I opened the way for them to be independent. And I've always been an independent person. When it got so that I wanted something I'd go to do days' work. I scrubbed floors. No matter how hard or dirty the work I would do it to get the something I wanted.

Mrs. Quaid sees her desire to succeed not only as the means to acquire "things," but as an exemplary way to live. When asked what she believed was the main purpose in life, she answered:

Mrs. Quaid: Well, whatever it is you set out to accomplish, you accomplish that. Obtain whatever it is you have worked for.

Interviewer: Have you accomplished what you set out to do?

Mrs. Quaid: I think so. And like I say I pass on the same philosophy to my children. And I am blessed. I have two boys—both are independent and no drugs, nothing like that.

Mrs. Quaid chooses how she will view the circumstances of her life—as blessings rather than disappointments. She does not see unmet dreams as failed expectations, but as an actualization of the higher purpose that was intended through those unrealized goals. When asked about her current aims in life, Mrs. Quaid explained:

Mrs. Quaid: I always wanted to go on a cruise but it look like God don't intend for me to go on no cruise.

Interviewer: Where does God fit into that disappointment?

Mrs. Quaid: Well I feel like this here, there's always a reason why. Like I have a saying that I don't know what's around the bend, but you know, Lord. So when I get to the bend, please be right there for me.

Interviewer: And is God there?

Mrs. Quaid: Yes. I'll give you an example and maybe that will clear it up completely. When we were coming out of junior high I wanted to be a nurse. I passed all the tests as far as the written tests. But the physical part I couldn't finish because I couldn't stand the smell of blood. So then I wanted to be a hairdresser. Well at that time the only place they had for teaching blacks was J. High School. I went there. I passed everything but the physical. Because standing over, you know on black people's hair they use hot combs and stuff. I would inhale, oooh, that was out. When you go down for your counseling and stuff the only thing for blacks is home economics, that's what got me into sewing. So I couldn't get the things that I wanted. Well, as I grew up with the different ones passing on, each one of my family, I took care of them, although I'm the youngest one. Now like they say at 12 or 13 I'm supposed to have died [of rheumatic fever]. All right, so each one, even with my aunts, I was the one, even my older sisters, I took care of them. Now this is the sickliest one in the family doing this. Now this is God's work. He didn't let me be a nurse otherwise, but I was a nurse for the family. I give you that thing to show you. When something comes up in my life, then I look back and I say oh, now that's why God didn't intend for me to do this.

Mrs. Quaid detailed her dreams and showed how they *had* come to pass, however circuitously. In this way, she chooses to recast untaken paths as veiled blessings—with an ultimate purpose that will eventually be revealed to her. She does not seem to question the social forces, such as high school restrictions about what African-American female students *could* study, that prohibited her from making other life plans. Thus, her life seems carefully orchestrated in retrospect. Also, Mrs. Quaid is able to rename her regrets as blessings for at least two reasons: (1) because she believes that her greatest treasures, her two sons, are doing relatively well, particularly when compared with friends' and neighbors' children, and (2) because she retrospectively recolors the dark moments in her life with a brighter hue. She actively decides to view past sorrows as blessings that are revealed as such as her life unfolds.

SUMMARY

The question of expectations about life is tacitly embedded within the life story. Past expectations are revealed as well as constructed in light of present day achievements and issues.

The women presented in the case studies in this chapter showed expectations about their lives that were both unique to themselves and common to their race, gender, age cohort, social class, and the era in which they lived.

For example, both Mrs. Quill and Mrs. Corner grew up with expectations concerning their class status that were based on money and education. Although Mrs. Quill's education came as a matter of course, she also planned to marry a man who would provide financially for his family. Her focus was centered on her own and her family's achievement. Mrs. Corner's sense of achievement was individually *and* community oriented. She pursued an education with a mind set on finding a husband on a similar "level." By elevating herself she believed she also elevated the status of African-Americans, and acted as a representative of them.

It is important to remember that the rubrics under which important pieces of women's stories fall, such as expectations, themes, or accomplishments, are interwoven. Expectations are bonded to limitations; the start of a woman's narrative is often the point of departure for a life theme, and accomplishments are acknowledged or denied in light of expectations held.

For example, Mrs. McKenna's major theme, illegitimacy, informs the substance of her life story and the fact that she had scant expectations about life and few perceived accomplishments. Because she believed that her life was denied at its start, she also believed that she was destined to remain that way throughout her life course. Negation of the right to a good life came from her "illegitimate" beginning.

Conversely, Mrs. Quaid perceived that many of her "dreams" came true by carefully formulating why others failed to materialize. Her past expectations and present self-concept are intertwined. Despite enduring major disappointments, she maintains her self-esteem by thinking of herself as "blessed." She believes that God transformed the frustrations of her life into the "greater" purpose planned for her.

From women's revelations about what they expected in life, and what they achieved, we turn to Chapter 4, which deals with how women presented themselves during the interview.

4

❧

Self-Presentation

In this chapter we examine how women in our study presented themselves in the interview, focusing particularly on how they responded to the question, "Would you describe your life for me—whatever comes to your mind about what happened along the way. Start where you like and take as much time as you need." From this point of departure, we will explore how they began their life stories, described their relationships with significant others, offered a newly constructed or pervading life theme, and focused their narratives temporally.

We will discuss ways in which women defined themselves, i.e., whether they saw themselves as the agents or recipients, actors or reactors to what happened along the life course. We will report on how the women told their life stories from the vantage of older age and the standpoint of late life development, i.e., whether the past was interpreted in light of their expectations, limitations, and accomplishments. We will examine whether the Eriksonian concepts of integrity and despair resonate in the women's narratives.

In this chapter, we explore the themes that pervade women's narratives, acknowledging that themes play a consistent role in the life story. Themes (1) anchor the self with an image that explains, validates, and links a self-concept with the circumstances of life and (2) impose a consistent and continuing personal meaning onto life's joys and sorrows. Since all of the women in our study spoke of "independence" as a pervasive theme—significant to their past, present, and future selves—we will give that theme special attention in this chapter.

Another issue central to this chapter is the temporal focus of the women's presentation, and where they placed the emphasis of their narrative—to the past, present, or future. Temporal focus concerns the women's ability to be agentive—to decide at what point in time they will figuratively place themselves and, in some cases, to literally and metaphorically move beyond being held hostage by painful memories.

73

THE LIFE STORY

Beginning the life story with an incident or event that occurred at a midpoint in life underscores the time period or event's significance to the narrative. We use Mrs. Grosso's life story as an example. She is a 73-year-old poor Caucasian divorcee who lives in a suburb of Philadelphia in the house that she once shared with her husband and now shares with her daughter, son-in-law, and three grandchildren. Mrs. Grosso, born and raised in "South Philly," drives to a South Philadelphia senior center each weekday to enjoy lunch and companionship with "old friends."

Mrs. Grosso began her life story by saying, "I got married at age 19 and every year after that there was a different sickness." She thus presented the two issues that consume her thoughts—her health and her marriage. Mrs. Grosso's next comment was that she was divorced; she went on to say that after 39 years of marriage "he [Mr. Grosso] just left."

Even though Mrs. Grosso's health had been poor since youth, her husband's abandonment augured further illness. Two months after he left, she suffered a stroke that paralyzed the left side of her face. She blames her husband. "I blame him because he just left without saying why. He ruined my life."

Mrs. Grosso admitted that several years prior to his leaving, Mr. Grosso brought his secretary (the woman he later married) to all the social functions that the Grossos attended. Still, she remains perplexed as to "why" her husband left her. She links her husband's abandonment to her mother's early prophesy of bad luck.

> I ask him what did I do that was so wrong? He won't say nothing. He says he was crazy. My mother told me I was born unlucky but she would never tell me why. I says I'll die with two things on my mind—why my mother said that and why he left me. I'll go to my grave not knowing why.

This interesting quote suggests at least three facts about Mrs. Grosso: (1) that she has retrospectively defined her expectations about life on her mother's prophesy of "bad luck," (2) that she sees her husband's desertion as the inevitable result of her mother's omen, and (3) that she links her mother's words and her husband's actions through her own bewildering response to them. She remains rooted in "not knowing why."

Mrs. Grosso's divorce occurred over 14 years ago. She relives the year before the event in painful detail.

> I guess I should have known something was going on. He took her [secretary] everywhere with us. But I blame her more because she knew she was

breaking up a family. He married her two months before the divorce was final. So he's not legally married.

Believing that the couple are "not legally married" gives Mrs. Grosso hope for a reconciliation. Mr. Grosso contributes to this "hope." He calls his ex-wife every morning and visits her several times a week.

I get upset after he leaves, but after 14 years, I'm getting used to it now. See, he was always good to me. You can see he regrets it. He calls me every morning. If she steps out he calls me. People tell me not to bother with him, but I say he helps me out. He left me the house. He plays ten dollars a day [on the numbers]. He gives me thirty, forty dollars when he comes down. Once, he gave me a winning [lottery] ticket for fifty dollars.

Mrs. Grosso accepts Mr. Grosso's role as a part-time husband to two women and continues to be defined by her marriage. When asked what she thinks about her life as a whole, Mrs. Grosso answered:

I feel like if I knew what would happen, I wouldn't have worked so hard in the house, you know, putting up curtains, making it look nice.

Mrs. Grosso's sense of achievement is based on Mr. Grosso's validation of her work. Because her marriage failed, so did the value of what she accomplished as a homemaker. Mrs. Grosso's home, once the arena for her source of self-esteem, is now the place she "can't wait to get out of every day." At the end of the interview, Mrs. Grosso was asked what she believed is the main purpose in life.

Main purpose in life? I guess God still wants me here and he left me here for a reason. I just wish he'd tell me what that reason is. I think about it all the time.

Mrs. Grosso's narrative demonstrates that she is "stuck" on the original question of "why." Unable to get clarification from her mother and husband, she feels powerless to answer her own question or define her own purpose in life. Instead, she continues to wonder why her mother portended misfortune for her life, remains trapped in a limbo between divorce and reconciliation, and now directs her questions about the mystery of life to God.

Like Mrs. Grosso, Mrs. Wexler began her life story with a "sad" fact about herself that occurred in childhood. This fact continues to inform her self-concept and worldview.

Mrs. Wexler is a poor African-American widow who lives in a large, well-maintained subsidized housing facility. She acts genteelly, stands rod-straight, and looks younger than her 84 years. When the interviewer asked her to tell the story of her life, Mrs. Wexler shook her head.

> That's the sad part. I only went to the second grade. My dad, he didn't have an education either. My mother, she had very little. We couldn't go to school. We had to work it [the plantation]. Some of us had to stay home and take care of the others.

Mrs. Wexler was one of seven children born in "a little place in Louisiana" to a family of sharecroppers who worked on a cotton plantation. Mrs. Wexler's painful childhood seems symbolized by her nightmarish memories of picking cotton and her visceral aversion to the worms that nestled in it.

> My nerves is bad now from worms because, on the cotton, the cotton is always beautiful. But the worms, you could see them when you work to get the cotton out. They looked like they was just looking at you. And that depressed me so, I couldn't make it but I had to do it. I don't know anything about slavery but that's the way it was under my own dad. One year, and I worked all year long and the man, you know, over the crops, he came and called my dad to the fence and said, this year you didn't do anything. You didn't make anything at all. You just cleared yourself at the grocery store. I was devastated.

Despite the fact that 70 years have passed, Mrs. Wexler graphically depicts the horror of sharecropping as an extension of slavery. Aware that her family was unable to escape their oppression, and falling herself under its emotional toll, she set out on her own.

> I don't know exactly what I was, maybe 14 or 15 years old, I had to run away from home because I couldn't stand it. I was going crazy. My dad had some change, I took half of that change and walked away with that on the railroad tracks all by myself. Sometimes I think about that now. I say, 'How did I do it. How did I survive?'

Mrs. Wexler paused pensively after this comment, as though trying to connect the young woman in her story to her present, remembering self. She realizes that part of her ability to link her two "selves" is her desire to reflect and make meaning of her past horror. "Now I have time to think about what happened to me."

After Mrs. Wexler set out on her own at age 14, she never returned to her family, nor did she tell them about the fears that forced her to flee the plantation. When Mrs. Wexler's "cotton job" ended, she found work as a domestic in another small town in Louisiana.

> That [domestic work] was very good only it was too heavy for a small person. But I did it and I liked it. Because at home we had to work. All we knew was work, work, all the time.

Mrs. Wexler recalls a childhood of little education, physical abuse by her mother, sexual abuse by an unnamed male relative, hunger, neglect, poverty, and fear of internal (nightmares) and external demons (worms). Her childhood provides the lens through which she viewed successive periods of her life. Although it included many painful incidents, any of which might have surfaced, haunting and unresolved, in the present, she names the "true" source of her shame and sorrow as her scant education. In the same way that cotton worms became the symbol of her abusive childhood, Mrs. Wexler symbolized her illiteracy as the cause of her adult loneliness and lack of self-esteem.

Mrs. Wexler admitted that she "looked forward" to the interview because of her chance to share her secret "with a stranger." The fact that Mrs. Wexler had little schooling informs feelings about herself, relationships with others, major regrets, and worries about the future. She zealously guards this humiliation from her closest acquaintances.

Mrs. Wexler: Even when I was young I didn't have too many friends because like I said when you don't have an education, you're afraid to talk to people, they'll find you out.

Interviewer: You must have been very lonely.

Mrs. Wexler: I had to have a lonely life because I was afraid.

Interviewer: What were you afraid of?

Mrs. Wexler: I was afraid because I had no education. Not everyone, but most people when they find out that you don't have no education at all, they just seem to not respect you, just feel like you're nobody. This friend I have now, she loves people that got good educations, but then she doesn't know nothing about mine. She calls them "big deals." I never made a lot of friends because I kept to myself. My friend, she doesn't know about my problems. When you don't have the education, you're frightened all the time. You can't hide it because times come—. Nowadays, when you go to the doctors, they give you one of these things [forms] to fill out.

Mrs. Wexler's lack of education follows her everywhere and threatens to expose her lack of worth. In this, she concretized her illiteracy into a "true" measure of personal value that she failed to meet. Perhaps in Mrs. Wexler's eyes, "enforced" loneliness is the appropriate punishment for her inability to reach her objectified, then internalized standard of worth.

Mrs. Wexler has been unable to make peace with her perceived failings. Although she is dissatisfied with herself, she doubts whether she has the wherewithal to change. When asked what she would do differently in her life, she answered:

> I would like to go into a nursing home. I would learn more and I would stop being so lonely and particular. I do want to do things in a nice way but I would, I really don't how to say it—. And not worry about my condition of my education. Because you see that's gone by now and I can't do anything about that because I'm too old I can't take the stress of learning, so . . .

Mrs. Wexler's narrative began and ended with her perception of personal incompetence, and the energy she extends in trying to hide it from others. Mrs. Wexler seemed weary of the inadequacy that locks her inside an invisible but impenetrable prison. Her desire to live in a nursing home suggests that she hopes to find rest from the memories that torment her, and from the life that has proved to be "too heavy for a small person."

Respondents' past expectations and current themes seemed reciprocally related throughout the life story. A respondent sometimes began her life story by relating a feeling or event that remained salient throughout the narrative and emerged as a life theme. An example of this intertwining of narrative is Mrs. Custer. She is a 70-year-old poor African-American divorcee who lives in a large airy row home in South Philadelphia, which she purchased in 1970. She began the interview by recalling:

> All of my memories are of my family trying to eke by, to eke out a living, just trying to eat. I mean not even trying to make a living, just eat. I can remember eating and not getting enough.

Mrs. Custer was the oldest of 9 children growing up in the muckland of the Florida Everglades. Her father worked as a sugar cane picker. The family lived in a shack that the owners of the land provided for their workers.

> You're talking about living in the raw. That's what we did. Whenever I hear that song, "I Owe my Soul to the Company Store," I think about the past. You never made enough to pay off your debt to the company store. The past blows my mind.

Since no schooling was provided for the children of the sugar cane pickers, Mrs. Custer's only schooling came from volunteers of a local Baptist Church. However, family obligations preempted education.

> I don't remember going to school for five consecutive days in my life because of the family situation. Still, I had that yearning and that love for learning.

Mrs. Custer compensated for her lack of education by reading voraciously. When discussing young people's opportunities and their need to "give something back to the community," she mused:

> You know, I was reading in the Analects of Confucius that without ritual there can be no harmony.

Mrs. Custer bore her only child when she was 15 years old. She later married her son's father, but separated from him after a year. When asked about her marriage, she replied:

> Well, I used to blame black people because they didn't have anything. I thought they didn't have sense enough to get anything. I didn't realize that the same thing carried over into my marriage. I thought by the time I was 40 I'd work hard, he'd work hard and we'd have this and accumulate that. And I blamed him for everything. But life taught me that the cards were stacked against him. Back then, you had a certain space you walked in, you had a crawl space and if you got out of that you was knocked down. So there was nothing he could do. But I thought he didn't have any ambition. So I just thought I could strike out on my own and do better.

Mrs. Custer and her son left Florida "for something better" when she was 21 years old. She traveled with a man whose family lived in Philadelphia. His undefined illness kept them from marrying, although they had intended to do so. Mrs. Custer recalls her early days in Philadelphia as a continuation of the hard work and financial deprivation she experienced in Florida.

> Ever since I was 8 years old I worked. I worked in the house, with the kids, and even with some of those white people. They would want children to come and do something and my mother would encourage me to go, to rake their yard or wash their dishes. I was accustomed to having it hard. I just thought, well join the crowd. Nobody expected anything and you didn't get anything.

Even though Mrs. Custer's work experience in Philadelphia might have squelched her hope for a better life, she remained optimistic. "I always thought tomorrow I'll make it." She recalled her various jobs as a domestic.

> Most of the people I knew, the easiest way to get a job was just to go and work for someone and clean someone's house. At that time you didn't just run a sweeper. You got down on your knees and scrubbed the floor from the front to the back for five dollars a day.

Mrs. Custer reviews her past with a kind of awe, realizing that the present is the "tomorrow" in which she believed she would "make it." She tries to connect the naïve girl she once was with the world-weary woman she became.

> I look back and I wonder, why didn't I ever think that I could do something different? But it had never occurred to me. I didn't know. I thought working hard was the only way to do it.

Mrs. Custer's encompassing remorse about her life is evident in the following exchange:

Interviewer: When you think about your life as a whole, what sorts of things do you think about?

Mrs. Custer: I just think about different times I could have done something and it would have been all different.

Interviewer: Can you give me an example?

Mrs. Custer: Well, if I had went to school. I started night school for older people back in the 60s. But I thought, well, I'm too old now. By the time I finished with school I'd be 40 years old. When I was coming along, at 40 or 50 years old, you didn't start anything. You was getting ready to die almost. And most black people was dead by 50. They was worked to death. My mother's mother was 11 years old when freedom was declared. I was raised by slave time people. So nobody in my family expected anything and I guess looking back, they didn't prepare me to expect anything.

Although Mrs. Custer states that her family's lack of expectations resulted in her own ignorance about a "better life," she had believed, in her youth, that she *could* achieve "something more." Her incisive ability to look behind and vividly see the path not taken results in her present anguish. Her scrupulous introspection prohibits her from painting the past in a rosier hue.

I didn't head in the right direction. I didn't know enough. Like education. I only looked at the negatives, because I had nothing to measure by. And I couldn't see the bigger picture. Education would have been my key.

Mrs. Custer highlighted the futility of her life of hard work.

I never ever not worked and I don't have anything to show for it. But I've always worked. You know, the human body can get accustomed to anything. You ever hear when people, they get out of jail, they say they want to go back? Here I look at my life and I say, 'Look at you! You're the same.' Because I never had any degree of success or anything and I just live day by day so I say I've grown accustomed to just having nothing.

Mrs. Custer realistically measured her ambition against the obstacles that society placed in front of her. Her life story became an anguished balancing between her drive to "make it" and her lack of opportunity. Her clear recollection of what she once expected from life equaled her awareness of what she was denied. However, Mrs. Custer's ability to change her arena of success—from the material world to that of the spiritual—allowed more "room" for "making it." We will return to Mrs. Custer in Chapter 7, Thoughts of the Future, and examine how she reoriented her goals to achieve her expectations.

Like Mrs. Custer, Mrs. Billson had examined her life, either for the purpose of the interview or because retirement allowed time for recollecting the earlier, most difficult periods. She expressed her feelings about life's hardship as eloquently as Mrs. Custer.

Mrs. Billson is an 85-year-old poor Caucasian widow who lives in a tiny subsidized apartment that overflows with plant cuttings and crafts. She moved there 17 years ago, shortly after her husband passed away. She describes her day-to-day life:

I'm comfortable and happy. I'm a collector. I buy day old fruit from the vendor and make juice. Last week I found a fan in the trash and cleaned it and fixed it up. I'll sell it at the flea market.

When asked to tell the story of her life, Mrs. Billson laughed incredulously.

From the beginning? My father died shortly before I was born. And I was born in Ukiah, in the hop fields of Ukiah, California. I don't even have a picture of my dad to fall back on. And my sisters are dead; my brothers are dead.

This skeletal outline provides the backbone of Mrs. Billson's life story. She was the youngest of six children born to a father she never knew and a mother weary from "being on the run."

From what I've heard my mother had to be on the run all the time because she was a widow with small children. And in those days it seemed they liked to take children away from widows and put them in homes.

The family eventually settled in a shack in New Jersey, where Mrs. Billson began school at age 8½.

We lived in a tent in Pennsauken. Through the years my brothers finally built a house. You want to know what they built it from? Packing boxes. [Pause] I can't explain my life. It was so hard, it was a matter of making a living. One of my granddaughters, on her sixteenth birthday I gave her a pendant I had. And I said, 'I never was 16.' I didn't feel I ever was.

Mrs. Billson's childhood ended when she stopped attending school, some 5 years after the family moved to New Jersey.

I had to go to work before I was 14. I had one job after another. I did restaurant work. I hated factory work. Finally I took children in. I boarded children day and night for parents who worked or mothers who abandoned them.

Mrs. Billson met her husband, a handyman who worked sporadically, "at one of the places I worked, I don't know where it was. He was divorced and he had three daughters." Mrs. Billson's marriage, though "good," did not ease her financial hardship. She describes her husband fondly.

He was handy, not easy to get along with, had an eye for the girls, very demonstrative, out in public even, possessive, a kidder and a curser. But we stayed married for nearly 50 years.

Mrs. Billson pointed to an enlarged portrait of a thin, smiling-faced man on the living room wall. "That's the old son of a gun! He had a mouth on him," she added with pride. "He was one of a kind."

Mrs. Billson eventually bore two sons of her own, and raised them along with her three stepdaughters in various rented rooms and houses throughout West Philadelphia. She painted a bleak financial picture of the family.

It was kind of tough. My first son slept in a bureau drawer for a while 'til he got too big for it. My husband wasn't a good man for making collections on the work he did. So I had to be a collector too. Just after the first boy, I had to hock my sewing machine and typewriter. I never did reclaim them but I had to do that to pay the rent.

The Billsons were married only 10 years when Mr. Billson became disabled due to heart failure. Although Mr. Billson lived another 30-some years, he never worked again. Since there was no disability compensation at this time (1930s) and Mr. Billson "wouldn't have been eligible anyhow—he didn't work enough," Mrs. Billson took on extra, "round-the-clock" jobs. She worked as a domestic, a waitress, a babysitter, boarded children, and occasionally nursed elderly people in the Billsons' rented homes. Like her mother, Mrs. Billson was often "on the run," forced to flee the unpaid bills of one apartment and start "clean" in another. Her one regret remains that she never owned a home.

Mrs. Billson often answered a question concerning her past with a look of wonder. Feeling forced to retrospect, she seemed to marvel not only at her hardship, but at the person who endured it. Mrs. Billson reviewed her life reluctantly for the purpose of the interview, admitting that she feels "more contented" if she does not think about the past. She prefers to live in the present, anticipating her next project or future trip. The present period of older age grants her small pleasures denied earlier in life: cooking for one, bus rides to the casinos, and time to putter with crafts and plants. At the end of the interview, Mrs. Billson summed up her life: "I had more sadness than anything."

THEMES

From the point in time at which and the way in which respondents begin their life story, we turn to the themes that respondents use to knit their narratives together. We use as our example Mrs. Bernini, whose motherlessness was the theme of her life story and became the frame for her past and current worldview.

Mrs. Bernini is an 81-year-old poor Caucasian widow who lives in her own home in South Philadelphia. She asked to be interviewed at a nearby senior center. Like Mrs. Wexler, Mrs. Bernini began her life story when asked how many grades of school she completed. "I don't know. I never really sat in a classroom." Mrs. Bernini grew up in a suburb of Philadelphia, the middle child of five siblings. Her parents perished during the flu epidemic of 1918. Although an uncle adopted all of the children, he was financially able to take only the oldest and youngest child into his home. Mrs. Bernini and two brothers lived in orphanages and foster homes until she was 11 years old, when her aunt and uncle, who were born in the "old country," retrieved her. Unable to speak Italian, Mrs. Bernini could not communicate with her aunt and uncle. However, she remained "deathly afraid of their coldness and their punishments" well into adulthood.

Mrs. Bernini's major responsibility at home was household chores. Her duties prohibited her from playing outside or having friends during childhood. She often lapsed into tears when recollecting this period of her life.

When Mrs. Bernini was 13 years old, a parish priest signed a false birth certificate testifying that she was 14 years old and able to work. Mrs. Bernini recalled her first day as a domestic.

I was given a bucket and told to scrub the floors and when they're dry they better be white. When I got home I still had to do all my chores.

The following quote exemplifies the spirit of Mrs. Bernini's adolescence. "I felt so all alone."

Losing her mother at age 4 lay the foundation for her reaction to life—a solitary quest for knowledge about her mother. Perhaps "knowing" about her mother would provide her with a key to self-understanding and the nurturance that was denied her in childhood, and for which she still felt the lack in older age. Mrs. Bernini remembers searching for people who might have known her parents.

I just wanted to know somebody who knew my father and mother. Just to tell me what did they like, what color did my mother like, what food did she like? What was she like? I couldn't find anybody to tell me.

Because she "hated" domestic work, Mrs. Bernini "luckily" found a job in a stocking factory during the Depression. While working at the factory she met her husband, Nick, through neighbors.

We met on the sly. Even though I was 21, they [the aunt and uncle with whom she lived] didn't approve [of marriage]. See, I never kept a cent for working. The money went into the house. And I was deathly afraid of them.

After 2 years of dating "on the sly," Mrs. Bernini finally received her family's blessing for marriage. Mr. and Mrs. Bernini made their first home in a small South Philadelphia apartment. She did not draw a clear picture of her marriage. When asked about her husband, she hesitated.

He was all right. He was a good man but he was very fussy, especially about his food. He wouldn't eat out of a plate that had flowers because there might be something in there he might not be able to see. He had his own knife and fork and water bottle.

Throughout his life Mr. Bernini did not hold a permanent job; he worked seasonally in a shoe factory and later for the Navy Yard. Mrs. Bernini was forced to work throughout their marriage, taking time off only to bear two daughters in quick succession. Her favorite job was as a salesperson for a large department store. Her pride in holding this job rested on the fact that she "never learned the times table," yet was a "whiz" with numbers. Unfortunately, Mr. Bernini did not share his wife's pride. He was neither encouraging nor complimentary of her achievements inside or outside the home, such as her "great" cooking and her sales work. Her one regret remains that she failed to open a pizza shop on the Atlantic City Boardwalk some 40 years ago, after her sister-in-law had encouraged the venture because "my pizza was so great. I would have been on easy street now." Mrs. Bernini lamented that her husband forbade such a risk.

Through Mrs. Bernini's "hard work and careful managing," the Berninis finally bought a small home in South Philadelphia where they raised their daughters. Both daughters married. Mrs. Bernini described the saddest day of her life as the day her husband of 29 years died. Her children and grandchildren as well as her work helped her cope with the loss. Although she had "offers," she decided against remarriage, but had difficulty articulating why. Her youngest daughter eventually divorced and returned to the family home where she currently lives with Mrs. Bernini. Mrs. Bernini identifies strongly with her two daughters and maintains an "extremely close" relationship with them. Her description of her daughters' reaction to their father is reminiscent of her own adolescence.

> They sort of feared him. But they respected him. They had to. [Pause] My oldest daughter doesn't talk about her father in a kind way.

When asked what comes to mind when she thinks about her life, Mrs. Bernini hearkened back to her original theme:

> I wonder where all these years went. All I wanted was to raise my girls, so they won't be an orphan like I was.

Mrs. Bernini's mix of the past and present tense reveals that the long ago loss of her mother keeps her in a liminal state. The specter of the past defines and determines her present. She carries the theme that was created in her grim childhood, continues to cry for the lost child that she remains, and views the world through the lens of motherlessness. Although Mrs. Bernini's theme gives her narrative an aura of "what might have been," it also provides the impetus for her strong bond with her children and grandchildren. When asked what she considers to be the main purpose in life, Mrs. Bernini answered:

> To serve God and to—I don't know, to keep up the family traditions, because it was so hard to lose my mother.

THE THEME OF INDEPENDENCE

As previously mentioned, most of the women in our study described themselves as independent and named "being independent" as "extremely important." What does independence mean for women in the poverty sample?

For poor women, independence was usually not equated with "having money." Making choices within the boundaries of poverty was the cornerstone of independence. If going without or getting into debt were the perceived alternatives, depriving oneself of a small or large pleasure seemed not only the sensible choice, but one that gave women an internal locus of control. In this, women viewed poverty as an obstacle to be confronted and manipulated under the rubric of choice. The decision of how to manage limited finances granted a sense of agency.

Life stories reveal the intersection between individual experience and historical circumstances (Josselson, 1993). It is important to note that the women in our study were raised during the Depression. The Depression was sandwiched between two world wars, marking this period of time as especially bleak in retrospect. Because the Depression occurred at an early stage in the women's personal development, it created a Depression mentality, in which "going without and making do" became not only a way of life, but a worldview that persisted throughout the women's lives. Although more nonpoor women said that they were affected by the Depression's economic collapse in the sense that their families' income appreciably diminished, poor women simply remained poor. Scarcity and want were aspects of life with which they were well acquainted before, during, and after the Depression.

It is interesting that in the nonpoor sample money *was* the vehicle to reach independence. Money held sway in granting choices and in allowing women to respond to those choices. In this, feeling independent, i.e., having a choice, even from a limited range of options, was the important variable, no matter how women accomplished that goal. For example, Mrs. Millson shows a strong sense of independence in what she chose to relinquish in her life.

Mrs. Millson, a 79-year-old poor Caucasan widow, lives in a handsomely decorated apartment in a subsidized housing facility. Mrs. Millson began the interview by saying, "I had the weirdest life of anybody you will ever interview." She then revealed that her artistic talent showed itself early in life.

> I received an award which was given to the most talented kid, to give them special ed in art, which was unheard of in those days.

Pride in her talent and in receiving the award were superseded by "love at first sight." For Mrs. Millson, there was no "having your cake and eating it." Marriage at 15 to an 18-year-old boy and pregnancy soon after thwarted her chance to attend a prestigious school of design. She describes the first time she saw her husband.

> I saw him walking down the street. He was gorgeous. It was physical attraction.

In recalling her decision to marry, Mrs. Millson remembers her parents' heartache. "I was damned determined to make this work." She accomplished her goal; their marriage lasted for 50 years despite the multiple obstacles of youth, financial hardship, illness, and family disapproval. The inequity of her marriage, however, did not hinder its success.

> He was bossy. His word was law. But he was also intelligent. I mean he might have had a closed mind, but it was a damned good mind. Life with him was difficult but good. He was jealous. He was possessive. He was intolerant. He was the one I wanted. I wouldn't have changed it a bit.

Mrs. Millson's expectations about a man–woman relationship matched her experience of marriage with Mr. Millson.

> In our day you kind of expected your husband to be bossy. You did not expect an equal break. At least I didn't. And you coped.

Mrs. Millson described her early married life as "not a dream life." In their small home in North Philadelphia, her father, who had lost money in the stock market crash, supported his wife, two unmarried children, his mother, mother-in-law, and the Millson family. There were "lots of conflicts" within this extended household. Mrs. Millson recalled this period with a shake of her head.

> I don't know how we got through it. There was just too many people. [Laughter] I didn't know what privacy was.

Although Mrs. Millson wanted to "go back to school for [her] high school diploma," Mr. Millson would not allow his wife to return to school at any point in their marriage. She supports her husband's decision.

> I guess it would have been impossible in our day for a girl to go back to school after having a child.

Mrs. Millson named her husband's "menial job" as a cab driver and his poor health as the major reasons for their financial hardship. When Mr.

Millson was drafted into the Second World War, Mrs. Millson held diverse positions, such as sales clerking, waitressing, and tending ovens for a large bakery. Mrs. Millson described this period as "very difficult, very rough. I was always exhausted."

Until his death in 1981, Mr. Millson suffered from various diseases such as ulcerative colitis, malaria, and heart disease, and worked irregularly. She admits to the financial struggle of life with her husband.

> Yes, he was ill for most of our life, but when you love a person, you don't care. You will sacrifice anything and everything you can.

Mrs. Millson named the years of her marriage as the hardest financially because she was often forced to decide between eating and getting health care for her husband. However, she saved "every penny to get out of apartments" and buy a home of their own. After 25 years of marriage, the Millsons bought a home in Levittown. Mrs. Millson laughed at the memory.

> To him Levittown was the end of the world. For me, it was a dream come true.

The Millsons spent 25 years in her "dream home." She names this period of home ownership as one of the happiest in her life, despite financial hardship and her husband's health problems. After her husband's death, Mrs. Millson was forced to give up her home. The labor and expense of its upkeep added to the burden of her own failing health from heart disease. She believes that one compensation for selling her home was finding a new sense of self-esteem.

> I had more self-confidence. I had to. I had to do everything. Because he had been ill for so long, it was like living on the edge. And you figure is he going to be living when I get home from the store or when I wake up? When my husband died, it was a relief.

Mrs. Millson describes the present as the best emotional and financial time in her life. After moving into her one-bedroom apartment, she is "just now" experiencing a freedom she "never knew." She found an outlet for her talent. At 70 years of age, and after a hiatus of over 60 years, she resumed her art studies at a local college. Her living room is decorated with her own still lifes and small sculptures.

> I never dreamed it would be so easy. I was able to go to college for art and I did better than most of the people in my class. I figure now I'm living a little.

Mrs. Millson described herself as "extremely independent." Her independence manifests itself in her ability to deprive herself.

I see things that I would dearly love to have, but I can put it out of my mind and settle for something less. I don't brood about it. I make choices. I think not accepting what happens to you in life is counterproductive.

Mrs. Millson links making choices and accepting life's circumstances with independence. For her, acceptance requires an active mindset to work hard, to strive for something better, but ultimately to be contented with the situation in which you find yourself. Mrs. Millson *chose* to marry a "bossy" husband, just as she chose to return to art school 60 years after she was awarded a scholarship. She views herself as the agent of her thoughts and memories as well as of her actions and decisions. When asked about the main purpose or task in life, Mrs. Millson answered:

Just to be contented with what God gives you. Be contented with your lot. You can't do much about it and if you can, do it. What can I say?

TEMPORAL FOCUS OF PRESENTATION

In this section we discuss respondents' temporal focus of presentation, or the time period in which women centered their current thoughts and feelings. We begin with Mrs. Meyer, a woman whose focus on the past was an anomaly in the sample of poor women. Her passivity and sense of being victimized by her memories contrasted with most poor women's strong sense of agency within the boundaries of personal and historical circumstances, and despite adversity. Her temporal focus on past hardship is an example of how her vantage negatively colored her daily life.

Mrs. Meyer is an 82-year-old poor Caucasian widow who lives in a small, neat, ground floor apartment in a subsidized housing facility. Her middle-aged son and daughter and their respective families live nearby. Mrs. Meyer began the interview by saying:

My family life was fine but my married life wasn't. My husband was an alcoholic.

So began Mrs. Meyer's theme—the course of her life, which should have followed the path of her fine family, went awry because of her alcoholic husband. Mrs. Meyer waxed talkative only when she discussed the misery of her marriage. She had difficulty articulating feelings about other personal matters, such as whether she enjoys attending senior events in her building, or opinions about current events. Requests for elaboration usually elicited the response: "I don't know."

Mrs. Meyer grew up on a farm in Bucks County, the next to the oldest of 10 children. She described her life as "happy then."

Coming from a good family I figured everybody was good. I didn't know
he [husband] came from a drinking family.

After high school, Mrs. Meyer and her sister came to Philadelphia to find
work.

Hosiery was the thing to get into because it paid good money. And that's
how I met him. Somebody I knew introduced us.

The Meyers went steady for 2 years before marriage. She described their
2-year dating period as "nice." In fact, Mrs. Meyer described the first 10 years
of married life this way:

We got along fine. It was his drinking that did it. Then you never saw him
sober. See, nobody ever drank in my family. And I had to walk into this.

Mrs. Meyer reiterated her lack of knowledge about "drinking men." Her
unfamiliarity with "drunks" did not allow her to foresee that tragedy was
inevitable. Mrs. Meyer's remorse about her marriage is an ever present and
all consuming regret. It allows no room for other memories.

Mrs. Meyer: You know, I think of it more now than I ever did, more
                 than I did when it was going on.
Interviewer: Why do you think that is?
Mrs. Meyer: I just think of how nice it could have been if he hadn't
                 been drinking. We never went no place. There was no
                 money to go nowhere. We could have taken trips.
Interviewer: What triggers those feelings?
Mrs. Meyer: Especially when I hear other people say, you know, they
                 went on trips. Oh, married 40 years and I never went
                 nowhere.

Mrs. Meyer dwells on both the past and present isolation that her unhappy marriage caused. Ashamed to admit her anguish to her parents and
siblings, she also tired of nagging her husband about his self-destructive
behavior. She believes that he "didn't know or didn't care" that his alcoholism was ruining their family life.

They don't think they're doing anything wrong. I heard this over and
over. I'm not hurting you or the kids. I'm only hurting myself.

Mrs. Meyer believes that her husband's death from lung cancer at age
59 related to his habit of "smoking when he drank." She also blames his
early death for her present financial hardship.

That's why it's so hard on me now. He wasn't old enough to get Social Security. And the way he was, he didn't have a job. I mean he did have a job for
21 years with the transit company. But the way he was, he got fired from there
because he would work nights and then he would drink, and they got rid of
him. Then he went from job to job.

The sum and substance of Mrs. Meyer's narrative centers on her unhappy marriage. It negatively affects her opinion of herself and results in
self-imposed alienation from neighbors or would-be friends. The interviewer asked Mrs. Meyer if she is currently able to share her sadness with
anyone.

I'm too ashamed to talk about it. They might think maybe I was stupid to
stay with him. Or, you must be in love or you wouldn't stay. But that was not
the reason. I just couldn't go nowhere. Nobody knows unless they go through
it. Nobody in here knows about my life.

Mrs. Meyer's use of the present tense to describe events that happened
20 years ago emphasizes her rootedness in the emotional poverty of the
past. Her belief that she possessed no control over her past or present situation cements her perceived status as a victim.

Mrs. Meyer: They [men of her generation] didn't want their wives to
              work. Therefore, they could do what they wanted to do
              and you're stuck. I guess if I had to do it over, I would
              have divorced my husband.
Interviewer: Why do you think you didn't?
Mrs. Meyer: I didn't want to go home to my family and I didn't want
              to stay with him. I was trapped. When you have children,
              and you're just working part time, where can you go?
              Now they have shelters.

When asked if she ever felt badly about herself, Mrs. Meyer answered:

Oh, sure. That's when I think of him. If he had been the right kind of guy,
it would all be different.

Mrs. Meyer is both driven and paralyzed by her memories. Her marital
unhappiness provides the fodder for her thoughts, the stimulus for her
feelings, and the substance of her narrative. Frozen within those memories,
she feels unable to push beyond her sad reminiscences. Instead, she chooses
to blame Mr. Meyer for both the past and present unhappiness of her life.
Although she has been widowed for 20 years, she allows her marriage to

enclose her in a prison. The area of her prison is quite small, permitting only painful memories, thoughts of what might have been, and shame for her role in the situation.

Although Mrs. Meyer admitted that she is "happy in [her] apartment," the comfort of her home and ease of financial worries cannot overcome her sadness. Likewise, although she described her children as "great," and sees both of them often, descriptions of them are subsumed under the rubric of her marriage. When asked to describe her son and daughter, she relayed their opinions of their deceased father.

> My son can't stand him. He had no time for his father at all. My daughter just won't talk about him.

Mrs. Meyer named the early days of her marriage and the birth of her first child as the happiest time of her life. Perhaps her early hope for happiness equals her disappointment when her expectations failed to materialize. Her emotional investment in the marriage reaped no benefits and drew instead on her own limited resources. When asked what she considered the main purpose in life to be, she answered:

Mrs. Meyer: I used to wish I wasn't here; I used to wish I was never born.
Interviewer: Do you still think that way?
Mrs. Meyer: Once in a while.
Interviewer: When you're feeling better, why do you think you're here?
Mrs. Meyer: I'm here because I'm here. I don't know.

Perhaps this last comment sums up Mrs. Meyer's self-concept and worldview. The circumstances of her life seem mysterious and random. She feels overwhelmed by her bad fortune *and* her inability to make sense, interpret, or impute meaning to her life. Her lack of understanding as to why she is here speaks to her powerlessness to create purpose for her existence.

Contrasting Mrs. Meyer's past focus of presentation is Mrs. Bowser, whose strong sense of self-reliance and future orientation negate her past and present hardship.

Mrs. Bowser is a 71-year-old poor African-American divorcee who lives in a dark and dank subsidized apartment in a poorly maintained building in West Philadelphia. She blames the dampness of the building and its poorly constructed windows for her arthritic knees. Despite her disability, Mrs. Bowser "gets up early, gets dressed, and gets out" every day, even if it is just to play bingo in the building's drafty community room.

Mrs. Bowser was born in Virginia to a woman who gave her away shortly after her birth. She never knew if her mother bore other children and does not know if she has "birth brothers and sisters."

> She kidnapped me from my adopted mother when I was 7 years old. She thought she could get some work out of me. She [adopted mother] went to court and my real mother sold out my birthright for $80. She never bothered me anymore.

Because Mrs. Bowser's adopted mother worked as a live-in domestic, Mrs. Bowser's early years were divided between living with her adopted mother at one home and "this boss lady who had taken me as her own and raised me, too." Mrs. Bowser and her adoptive parents eventually moved to New Jersey to live in the home of other employers.

Mrs. Bowser was introduced to Mr. Bowser while visiting an aunt in Philadelphia when she was 15 years old. The Bowsers married the next year and had their first child 13 years later. Although Mrs. Bowser said, "I always wanted 2 children," she described her 10 pregnancies as something that "just happened. You have to let Mother Nature take its course."

Mrs. Bowser named the period of her marriage and pregnancies as the worst financial time in her life.

> He wouldn't give me the money. One Friday I went to the highway where he was working while it was snowing to collect his paycheck. He handed me $14 for two weeks for me and the kids and left.

Her husband's co-workers, realizing that Mr. Bowser had rebuffed his wife, invited her to have lunch with them at a nearby bar. When they entered, Mrs. Bowser saw her husband with another woman.

> I never opened my mouth. One of the fellows said, come on over here mama, sit over here. I sat there and laughed and talked with the fellows. We clowned and cut the food.

Neither of the couple spoke of the incident when they returned home. However, Mrs. Bowser delivered this ultimatum:

> 'Tomorrow morning, you get your ass out of here and bring me some money for these here kids. Wherever you carried that money, you go back and get it or else don't come back in here.' When he came back, he had the money.

Mrs. Bowser, tired of replaying this scene throughout the 10 years of their marriage, left Mr. Bowser and several of their younger children to live in an apartment a few blocks away. However, she refused to "feel bad" about her husband's infidelities or her eventual separation from him and their children.

> I laughed it off just like it was a joke to me.

However, Mrs. Bowser did not hesitate to provide care for Mr. Bowser when he fell ill several years ago, months before his death from cancer. "When he was on his deathbed, he needed me, " she admitted proudly, adding that she knew there would come a time "he would come begging because what goes around comes around."

Presently, Mrs. Bowser has contact with only 2 of her 10 children. Of the other 8, one has died, one is in prison, and two are "on the street." She has not heard from or about the others in "years." Although she raised two of her grandchildren, they also are estranged from her. However, she learns about the comings and goings of her children and grandchildren from her grandson who "uses [drugs] but will not go to rehab." Mrs. Bowser denies worrying about her current family situation.

> I don't let it worry me. It did for a while. Then I got to thinking. You are number one. You got to think about yourself now. You thought about them when they was small. And look how hard that you worked, rain or shine, gray or blue, you was out there, pulling all through the snow to protect them. If they don't come to see you, let it be like they are strangers, somebody you never seen.

Mrs. Bowser delivered the above remark in a theatrical manner with strong inflection and a dramatic pianissimo at the end of each sentence. This way of speaking occurred throughout the interview and marked revelations that might have been emotionally charged for her.

Mrs. Bowser prefers to think of the activities that she currently enjoys, such as playing bingo and going to the casinos. When she thinks about the past, she "remembers the good." She is especially proud of her job as a school aide which she held for 16 years in a local elementary school.

> I never let nobody come between me and my work. I had them kids almost eating out of my hand. They needed somebody to be firm. When them kids found out I was leaving, they cried.

Although Mrs. Bowser sees her life in terms of a "fight," she is proud of her tenacity in dealing with her financial and familial struggles. She also takes pride in finding imaginative ways to stretch her limited finances, such as buying shoes and clothes from thrift stores and "old" vegetables for soup.

> I have been through the thick and the thin. I don't think there's a woman at my age that has been through the ups and downs, the knots and bruises as cruel as I've been through And I have lived to tell it.

In fact, Mrs. Bowser names the present as the happiest time of her life because

> I have no worration, no aggravation, no wondering where I'm going to get my next meal from.

Mrs. Bowser's major strength seems to be her self-reliance. This characteristic ran as a theme throughout her narrative. Witness her playful quote on first meeting her husband. Mr. Bowser, wondering if she was dating or going steady, asked, 'Do you have anybody?" Mrs. Bowser, fully comprehending his meaning, answered, "Yeah, I got somebody. I got me." Mrs. Bowser proudly named her accomplishments.

> I have accomplished a whole lot. I know how to handle money. With five dollars I fed 12 people for a whole week. They never went to bed hungry. Now, I have a place to live and I can buy a pair of shoes for myself. I have accomplished that.

Mrs. Bowser refuses to live in the past and believes it is foolish for anyone else, such as her neighbors, to do so.

> I can't live in the past. In the first place, there's nothing back there to go back there for. You can't take Old Man Used To and bring him up here. Because Old Man Used To wouldn't know how to live today. He knows nothing about up here. I got to live in the present and the future time.

Some might construe Mrs. Bowser's cavalier attitude about her difficult circumstances as denial. However, she fully admits her hardship, and chooses how to counter it. She decides what people or situations she will allow to "hurt" her, how she will react to the past, and on what memories she will focus. She also *chooses* to live a somewhat isolated existence— in the midst of a busy apartment complex filled with seniors, she discourages friendship. When asked the purpose of life, she answered definitively.

> Minding your own business. You can't have close friends in a place like this. They be knocking on your door, looking in your refrigerator. If you don't have, how do you expect me to have? See, it takes 6 months to mind your business, to get it together, and the other 6 months for you to live by it. So you ain't got time to mind nobody else's.

SUMMARY

Telling the life story describes your journey through life. You are both observer of and participant in what happened along the way. Pitting the "person you were" against the present self highlights moral agency. With knowledge accrued in the intervening years, you are both the same and different from the past self. In looking back, you either chose to keep on the perceived "right" course despite negative circumstances or you "lost" your way. In this, the life story grants a moral value as well as the value of retrospection.

Mrs. Custer's theme of "not making it" knits her story together with a clear sense of futility. Believing that "tomorrow I'll make it" collides with the fact that tomorrow is now. We return to Mrs. Custer in Chapter 7, Thoughts of the Future, to show that despite Mrs. Custer's regrets about life, she did not despair, but channeled her ambition toward another goal, and that her expectations for "making it tomorrow" remain.

Mrs. Wexler, although ashamed of her "secret" illiteracy, stated her shame clearly and in detail to the interviewer. In this, perhaps she is ready to "try out" the reactions of others concerning her perceived inadequacy. Still, Mrs. Wexler remains the agent of her thoughts and actions, deciding what and to whom she will reveal herself.

Mrs. Meyer also experienced a complex shame that causes her to focus on her past unhappiness and constantly relive its pain. Although she blames her husband for life's disappointments, she also questions her part in the perceived tragedy of her life. Her shame is a complex of regret, rue, an inability to impose meaning onto her sorrow, and a sad wondering if it could have turned out differently.

Mrs. Bowser presents herself as an adaptive loner who enjoys her own company. Her focus on herself and daily entertainment allows little or no regret about past or present hardship.

Women's self-presentation may be seen as a point of departure for the subject of Chapter 5—Strategies and Techniques of Coping with Poverty. In Chapter 5 we continue to look at our respondents through their own eyes—and through the way they met and managed their lifelong adversity.

5

&

Strategies and Techniques
of Coping with Poverty

In this chapter we will look at the methods women use to cope with poverty. Because of our focus, we will use case studies primarily from the two poverty groups. We acknowledge that because the women interviewed did not necessarily equate poverty with lack of money, we will also probe for issues of perceived emotional, relational, and spiritual impoverishment in all of the groups, and how women cope with this non-material type of poverty.

Poor women handled their hardship in various ways; we will examine their coping methods in terms of three general strategies used to counter the deleterious effects of poverty: (1) through their generativity of raising, nurturing, and having hope for future generations, (2) through the comfort received by their spirituality and religion, and (3) through the pride of personal accomplishment perceived as a contrast to financial poverty.

GENERATIVITY USED AS A COPING STRATEGY

We will begin this section by presenting the story of Mrs. Warren. We devote more attention to Mrs. Warren because her narrative displays a complex intertwining of the topics discussed in this chapter as well as in preceding and forthcoming chapters. This case demonstrates the aforementioned weaving of themes into the life story. It also depicts the problem, for some women in our study, of using their generativity as a coping method. Because Mrs. Warren thinks of motherhood as her greatest accomplishment, and making a home for her family the achievement in which she found and fostered her self-identity, she would like to rely on her children and grandchildren to help her manage the difficulties she faces in the latter stages of life. However, due to the problems her own children face, she must search elsewhere for support.

Mrs. Warren is a 90-year-old poor Caucasian widow who describes herself as a "shut in." She walks with difficulty because of a hip broken in a fall several years ago. Although she maintains her own home (where she has lived for 58 years) in the Northeast section of Philadelphia, she maneuvers through the three stories slowly. A myriad of pictures covering every surface in the living room testifies to the significance of family in Mrs. Warren's life. When the interviewer commented on the coziness of her home, Mrs. Warren beamed, "There's a lot of love in here."

Mrs. Warren was born and raised in Fishtown; the family moved to Kensington when she was 14 years old. Because of her father's unnamed illness and inability to work, Mrs. Warren was forced to quit school and obtain working papers shortly after her fourteenth birthday. She cleaned a three-story house for a local doctor in exchange for medical services provided to her family. Mrs. Warren is pleased to share her long-term perspective.

> When you get older you think a lot about your younger years. You know you're taking a long, long range when you say 90 years old.

Mrs. Warren is extremely proud of her heritage—one of her ancestors fought in the Civil War and a Philadelphia street is named for another family worthy. She is gratified that her own children and grandchildren observe holiday traditions in their homes that *her* mother initiated. A strong sense of family and tradition permeated Mrs. Warren's narrative. However, Mrs. Warren spoke little about her family of origin. She said only that she was the sole child of parents who separated after she was grown.

Mrs. Warren "married a boy [I] knew all my life" when she was 20 years old. She succinctly described the practice and practicality of choosing a mate when she was a girl. Although she does not depict the arranged marriages of some cultures, her portrait is also not the romantic ideal that became the stuff of American myth.

> It's one of those things. A boy and girl goes to school. You know him and you just gradually get to a point, well he likes me, you like him and you start seeing each other even if it's only sitting on the steps together. Then the first thing you know you start going out, and then you get engaged and you get married. And it's one of those things you don't give too much thought about.

Mrs. Warrens' parents and the newly married couple pooled their savings to buy a large home in Tacony. Mrs. Warren was the financial manager in the Warren home.

> I don't think my husband ever wrote a check in his life. But I kept a good strict budget. When money was slow I made my children's clothes.

The careful, but progressive way in which Mrs. Warren managed her home was integral to her self-concept. When asked to describe herself, Mrs. Warren answered, "I had the first automatic washer. I had a modern viewpoint."

The Warrens' loss of their home during the Depression remains a major sorrow for Mrs. Warren. She considers the 10 years of the Depression as the worst financial period in her life and blames it for negatively affecting the course of her economic future.

> We lived from hand to mouth. You save your money and you say well, maybe in six months I can do such and such a thing.

Throughout the interview Mrs. Warren talked about items that she purchased through "scrimping and saving" such as a player piano, dining and bedroom sets, and storm windows. Again, Mrs. Warren's self-image is intertwined with the home that she created for her family.

> I used to look at others' homes that weren't so nice and be so proud of what I had. So, when in 6 or 7 years we had the Depression, that was an awful thing. I always had the expectation that things were going to be better. I foreseen me doing things better but these here obstacles come in your path.

The above statements underscore the integration of Mrs. Warren's financial and social expectations with her self-concept—personal pride hinged on improving the lot of her family. The comments also highlight important themes in her narrative: (1) she described the method whereby she and others of her generation fulfilled their desires—they sacrificed immediate gratification for the sake of achieving material goals and were proud of their willingness and skill in doing so, and (2) although she believes that the Depression changed her economic future, it did not change her goals—a nice home with new furnishings and pride in constructing that home. Despite the financial setback of the Depression, she continued to be optimistic, forward thinking, to improve her family's life and her own self-concept within the framework of that era's struggle.

Considering Mrs. Warren's ability to modify her plans and succeed within her immediate environment, it is not surprising that she saw some benefit to enduring the hardship of the Depression. Her ability to learn from "hard times" is crucial to her self-esteem.

> I learned more. I learned how to count a penny. I learned how to use half an onion. I learned how to take a stalk of celery and cut it up and freeze it.

Mr. and Mrs. Warren raised three daughters in the home they purchased in the late 1930s. She stated that child rearing was "[her] job" because her husband worked at night. Mrs. Warren described her husband as a man who performed his duty as provider, but little else. In some ways, Mr. Warren existed on the periphery of family life.

> I never told my husband anything the girls did. I just didn't feel as if he could handle it. He was honest and quiet and he demanded his meals were on the table when he came home. He was a fisherman, and a fisherman is usually a loner, so he was a loner.

Mrs. Warren's syllogism about her husband demands acceptance of his taciturnity and precludes questions as to why he was the way he was. She did not disclose whether she was unhappy with her marriage or merely had few expectations concerning her husband's role in the family.

> I always initiated everything. I don't know if it's a good thing or not. We didn't go anyplace unless I planned it.

Mrs. Warren presented herself as a consummate mother whose greatest delight was raising her children. Although Mrs. Warren's full time job was childcare, she "helped out" financially by taking part time jobs in factories or stores when the children were small. Also integral to her self-concept is her record as a "good" employee. Although she failed a test to become a telephone operator, she proudly confided:

> I had the gift of gab I guess, because I talked myself in and I was only in the telephone company a short time when I could do everything.

The ethic of hard work as a moral victory resonates in all areas of her life. Mrs. Warren's present dismay over family problems equals the amount of effort that she extended in working hard, especially in nurturing her children. Mrs. Warren's eldest daughter, Edna, is 67 years old, lives nearby, and is partially estranged from her mother and siblings. Mrs. Warren explained the estrangement this way:

> There's a little bit of bad feelings there when Dad died because of Dad's car. There's been about 10 or 12 years that I haven't seen them much and I've heard about 10 different reasons why, but none of them is what I see.

Mrs. Warren does not see Edna on holidays, nor does she speak with her on the phone. "I do get cards and gifts from them" Mrs. Warren clarified, pointing to a tape deck, a VCR, and the television cable box for which Edna pays.

Mrs. Warren's middle daughter, Marian, aged 66, is suffering from a long-standing depression triggered by three losses that she endured 13 years ago. Marian's father, husband, and 32-year-old daughter died within a 4-month period. Although Mrs. Warren understands that it is Marian's pain that causes her to lash out at her, she has difficulty comprehending why these hurtful things "need" to be said.

> Several weeks ago she said, 'Mother, I know you're not anxious to go into a nursing home, but I just want to let you know that don't depend on me because I could not be able to take care of you.' She didn't have to say that. Marian would be the last person I knew that was capable of it.

In reflecting upon Marian's grief, Mrs. Warren revealed her own method of experiencing and handling loss.

> You can't let losses weigh you down. Life just hands you so much, you can't cry anymore.

Mrs. Warren admits to a "moderately close" relationship with her youngest daughter, Joan, aged 59. Joan lives nearby and grocery shops for her mother.

Mrs. Warren's consuming worry at this period of her life is her problematic relationships with her daughters in light of her own future. She cannot live with her daughters; she does not want to go into a nursing home, and her income does not allow her to enter area life care communities. What is not entirely clear is Mrs. Warren's part in the family drama. Although the interviewer probed to understand how events unfolded to result in family animosity, Mrs. Warren explained cryptically:

> This is one of the bad heartbreaks of a mother. When you think almost, like you think, well, gee, I've been almost like a perfect mother. But see, when you're older you're all adults. My daughters are on Social Security. So then you become just another woman in the senior citizen groups.

Bemoaning her sense of being "equal" to her daughters may represent a perceived loss of status for Mrs. Warren as "special" or as hub of the family. Perhaps her relational sorrows also highlight each generation's measure of success in the Warren brood. For Mrs. Warren, family, relationships, and community involvement defined her notion of accomplishment. For Mrs. Warren's daughters, marriage and motherhood held neither the status nor the rewards that it did for their mother. Mrs. Warren mentioned that two of her daughters, Marian and Joan, berate her for not sending them to college. Marian stresses to her mother that a career might have assuaged the tremendous grief she suffers. Mrs. Warren's grandchildren, who are accountants, business executives, and physicians, wear badges of success that are quite different from their grandmother's. However, Mrs. Warren complains that she never sees her grandchildren. Family closeness, which held the apogee of meaning for Mrs. Warren, is less important for her grandchildren. When asked how she spends her days, she sighed and answered with questions of her own. "Why am I living? Why don't he [God] take me home?" When asked where home is, Mrs. Warren offered, after a long pause, a concrete and idiosyncratic picture of the afterlife.

> No more pain. What's wonderful is that I sit here and think back of all my aunts and uncles, even the Civil War veterans and every one all the way back. I remember them so vividly and know that they all loved me. That to me is the greatest thing. Because I can think of all the relatives in my family and knowing that they all really love me and that I can feel the love. If they see me again I know they will love me again. If I meet them, I know they will be happy.

Because she no longer feels loved by her children and grandchildren, it is to her dead ancestors that she turns for the acceptance and family pride that are crucial to her self-concept.

Mrs. Warren, a Catholic, also finds solace from her faith. When asked what her religion means to her, she answered:

> Oh, God. God. I'll say he walks with me and he talks with me and he tells me that I'm his own.

Mrs. Warren's family crisis informs her belief about God's involvement in her daily life and shapes her personal spirituality.

> I guess God came along and made it so that I can't walk. I can't go to my daughter's house and straighten this thing out. I can't do that. I pray, that's all I can do.

Mrs. Warren believes that her inability to "straighten this thing out" is ultimately determined by God. This perceived link between God's disallowance of her "walking to her daughter's" and her disappointment in her children results in a sorrowful acceptance of how things turned out for her as a mother. She also views her faith in light of her daughters' estrangement from the religion that she taught them as children. However, she wonders how her daughters, especially Marian, judge *her* faith.

> The day my granddaughter was buried, I could stand and sing at the church. My daughter was in the row in front of me and she must have heard me sing and thought, 'How in the world could you sing, Mother?' And I

don't know how I could sing. I still just thought, you know, that God should be praised.

The intricacy of doubts, hopes, suspicions, and wonderings about her daughters' feelings toward her provide the major theme of her narrative. Her impotence to understand or change their emotional and physical distance from her colors every aspect of Mrs. Warren's life, When asked what she considers to be the main purpose or task in life, she answered wistfully:

> What I would love is to feel that my children love me very much.

It is unfortunate that after being a mother for close to 70 years, Mrs. Warren does not feel she achieved her "main purpose" in life. However, she continues to rely on family to provide self-esteem, and turns to those who cannot disappoint her—her ancestors. She imagines their "happiness to see her" in response to her own strong needs, which remain unmet by her "living" family. She has therefore created a future home with her ancestors similar to the one in which she raised her children—one that holds "a lot of love."

We now present the story of Ms. Simmons, a 74-year-old poor African-American woman whose method of coping with poverty is to rely on, and take pride in herself. Although she continues to "have it hard" emotionally and financially, she also persists in "making it through."

Ms. Simmons looks quite young when seated, but seems to age when she stands because of swollen legs and arthritic knees. She endured several unsuccessful operations on her knees. Ms. Simmons blames her physical pain on "doing days' work, scrubbing floors and everything, that's what started the arthritis on my knees."

Ms. Simmons has lived on the first floor of a large, porch front row home in North Philadelphia for over 20 years. She rents the apartment from her "baby sister Edith," who lives on the second floor and owns the building. Ms. Simmons began her life story by relating that she grew up as a sharecropper's child on a farm in South Carolina.

> I always had a hard life. My mother died when I was about 11 years old. My mother had 12 children and I was the seventh child. When my mother passed away me and another one of my sisters, we had to take turns and go to school because me and this sister of mine, we had to do all the housework. We had a big farm. We grew cotton, corn, potatoes and we had to work this farm. It was so hard. Yeah, it was rough.

Ms. Simmons left the farm when her first opportunity arose. She found a job as a babysitter and housekeeper for a minister's family in West Virginia.

Although Ms. Simmons worked for this family for only 5 months, much of her narrative dealt with her lonesomeness in this "mostly white" community.

> I think I must have been about 18 or 19 years old and I had a chance to leave home and look for a job. But I didn't like it too good. I didn't have no friends there.

Ms. Simmons secretly planned to visit her sister in Philadelphia and not return to the minister's home.

> I had to ask her [the minister's wife] can I come to Philadelphia to visit my sister because she was sick. She wasn't sick but I just tell them that so I would get away [Laughter]. She said no, my father wouldn't like it and they wasn't going to let me go. I said okay. So, with that little bit of money what I was making, I was saving it, you know. One Sunday, after they ate, I cleaned up and I had my suitcase packed because I had done find out what time the bus was going to leave for Philadelphia. So that afternoon he went somewhere to preach and she went upstairs to feed the baby. I took my suitcase and slipped out the back door. I got on that bus and I came to Philadelphia. I wasn't scared. I wanted to get away from that place.

Although she was employed by the minister and his wife, Ms. Simmons' role was that of a bonded servant. The need to break loose, at any cost, pervades the story. Since she was not permitted to leave, she finds the wherewithal to escape. She overcomes her sense of servitude by taking the risk to "get away from that place," and to live with her sister. She clarified that the minister's wife lied to her; her father *had* given his blessing for her journey to Philadelphia. Ms. Simmons arrived in Philadelphia and never looked back; she lived with her sister and brother-in-law in their North Philadelphia home and eventually found domestic work.

> My aunt got me a part time job doing domestic work. It was all right for the time being but I didn't stay there long. I got work in a laundry. I liked that much better.

Ms. Simmons has four children. The first, second, and fourth sons were fathered by someone whom Ms. Simmons had hopes of marrying.

> When I first came up here I met this guy. I wanted to marry him but he didn't want to marry me. He seemed to be nice, making like he wanted children but I don't know, he didn't like me. He just didn't like me. I guess he figure he could do me like he wanted to. I had to get me an apartment for me and my kids. He left me with my kids and went and married another woman.

This man, whom Ms. Simmons never named, neither supported nor kept in touch with his children. Although Ms. Simmons admitted that it took her a long time to "get over him," she shrugged with nonchalance at her past heartache. "I don't even think about it no more. He's dead now," she added, as though to prove that he was completely dismissed from her life. Ms. Simmons said that she, but not their sons, attended his funeral because "his sister sent a car up for me." When asked how she felt during his funeral service, she shrugged again.

> I didn't care. She [the present wife] was much heavier than I am. She had three children for him. But my children was older.

Ms. Simmons's older children and lesser weight elevated her perceived status in relation to the "wife." An important aspect of Ms. Simmons' narrative is how she chooses to look at certain events in her life. She actively lessens the pain of past injuries and proves her self-worth by noticing some aspect of a hurtful situation in which she emerges either feeling or looking "better" in relation to the person who has hurt her.

Ms. Simmon's third son was fathered by someone she met coming home from work one day.

> That guy wasn't no good either. He liked a lot of women. He know I was having it [the baby], because I had put him in court and all. I think I got two checks from that guy. I ain't seen him in a long, long time.

Ms. Simmons broke off relations with this man because of a comment he made to her. One evening, when he came to her home uninvited, Ms. Simmons complained.

> You don't care nothing for nobody so why do you keep coming to my house? So he said to me, 'Well you say you don't want me to come to your house but each time I come here you always let me in.' So I said, 'Thanks for telling me; you'll never get in my house no more.' He came out there a whole lot of times and I could peep out the door. [Pause, in a whisper] And that guy didn't never got back in my house no more.

This man revealed to Ms. Simmons that she was complicit in allowing him to "use" her. Once she was let in on this secret, she could no longer claim ignorance and still demand respect. For Ms. Simmons, this unhappy liaison and the self-awareness it engendered precluded a relationship with another man.

> I had a rough time during my life. I don't want to get in touch with nobody else, that's for sure.

Ms. Simmons said that although she has "never been too financial set," the present is the best time in her life financially because it drastically contrasts the period when she was raising her sons. "Yeah, I feel better now because I didn't have all them children to feed."

Despite the difficulty of raising her sons alone, Ms. Simmons is proud of the men they have become. She is especially pleased that each of her sons has a good job of long standing. When asked to describe her sons, she answered:

> Well, they all work. I told them ever since they was young children going to school, I tell them I'm doing the best I can until they got old enough to work. Because you're boys and when you get old enough to work you have to get a job and keep a job because I won't be able to work for you. And that's what they did. They work hard.

Ms. Simmons' son are dutiful. They assist her by carrying heavy items from the store, shoveling snow, or taking her to church when her legs are "especially bad." Still, she prefers not to ask her children "for anything."

> With food stamps and that little check I get, I have to manage. My sister don't charge me much rent.

Although Ms. Simmons is grateful for her sons' occasional errands and for living in her sister's home, she relies mainly on herself for social and relational support. When asked how she feels about her life as a whole, she answered:

> I really don't know. I been through so much, so I just forget about everything. Now that I'm old I don't worry about nobody or nothing.

Ms. Simmons admitted that she had "worries enough to last a lifetime." Now, she blends bemusement and pride when she views her past hardship. She looks at her life and at herself, from the past to the present, as from a great distance, with surprise at how far she came. Because her sons "work hard," she has succeeded in terms of motherhood. Because she is happy where she lives and has "enough to live on," she has also succeeded in resisting homelessness. In achieving her most important accomplishments—raising "good" sons and having a "nice place to live"—she has also overcome her greatest fears. Ms. Simmons described herself as

> Quiet, very quiet. And a whole lot of time I just like to be alone. So I can think better about anything, nothing special, about a whole lot of things I had forgot all about. It come back to me, so I don't know why, things that happen

a long time ago. All I can say and all I can remember—I always had a hard time. It was really hard. Somehow or other I made it through.

Because the worries of the past are over, Ms. Simmons seems to marvel about the difficulty and eventual victory of her life story. She enjoys linking the struggling young woman with the elder who "doesn't have to be on my knees no more," who has time to attend church services regularly, and "thinks about nothing special."

SPIRITUALITY USED AS A COPING STRATEGY

We now present the story of Mrs. Jonas, a 72-year-old poor African-American divorcee. We devote this section to Mrs. Jonas because she is representative of many poor African-American women who used their spirituality as a coping strategy and a way to live life. We are using the term spirituality to include two aspects of the women's sense of the sacred. First, their internal, private sense of the sacred, which includes belief in a personal God, talking to God, and imagining God to be both immanent and transcendent. Second, their external sense of the sacred prompts them to adhere to the tenets of a religious denomination, which comprises public worship as well as the social aspects of belonging to a church group. In this sense, women's spirituality is not unidimensional, but is a complex of private beliefs and communication with God as well as communal worship and rituals. This belief system culminates in a conviction that it is not only God who is intimately involved in their daily affairs, both public and private, both sacred and secular, but that they approach God on both public and private levels and in both sacred and secular domains. The sense of a relationship with God is a reciprocal one; Mrs. Jonas reciprocated God's perceived gifts by external worship, as well as talking about God or witnessing. It is important to note that Mrs. Jonas, like the poor women she represents, did not passively expect God to better her lot in life. Instead, she actively strove to improve her situation through a "partnership" with God.

Mrs. Jonas lives in her own home on a small street in South Philadelphia. Although the facade is in disrepair, the inside is well-maintained and decorated with feminine touches, such as ruffled placemats and holiday crafts that she creates at a nearby senior center. Mrs. Jonas suffers from bad eyesight and a heart problem. She admits that ill health keeps her from working because "working would be better than staring at these four walls."

Mrs. Jonas was one of five children born to a family of sharecroppers in North Carolina. She began her life story this way:

I was the yelling baby. The other three was older than me and the real baby was a boy. I was the yelling baby. My mother said it was hard. To me I guess it was and it wasn't because we never went hungry. But I always said I ate so much cornbread that when I get grown I wasn't going to eat no more cornbread [Laughter].

Mrs. Jonas remembers her childhood as "hard, but we didn't expect no different. We [the family] all cared about each other, though." She left school in the sixth grade to help her family with home and farm chores. She married her husband, a neighbor, before she was 18.

I thought I was in love with my husband; I thought he was in love with me. Anyway my mother and father both had to sign for me to get married. [Pause] He didn't beat me or nothing like that but he was too much of a baby-getter for me. Besides, he run around too much.

Mrs. Jonas left her husband and returned to him three times; each time she returned she became pregnant.

I married him in '41. I had three babies [middle baby was stillborn]. I left him in '45, three months before my last baby was born. I went back home to my mother and I didn't go back no more. I just hated him. I tried to get his Social Security but you got to be married ten years. So I couldn't get nothing.

Mrs. Jonas was only 21 years old when she left her husband for the last time. Although her marriage was brief, it remains one of the "worst" periods of her life both emotionally and financially. Mrs. Jonas was happy to "return home" to her parents. She "had nothing to do" with her husband after their separation. He neither supported nor kept in contact with their children. When asked if she ever thought of marrying again, she answered decisively:

No. Because I ain't seen nothing to marry. And still, there ain't nothing out there. Not for me there ain't.

Mrs. Jonas came to Philadelphia in 1956, temporarily leaving her two sons in North Carolina in the care of her mother.

I left home for the better. There wasn't enough work there other than working for white peoples in the kitchen or domestic work and I didn't want that. They didn't have no factories for us to work in; those were for white people. I found a room with a lady and her husband [in South Philadelphia] and I got a job in a rug place [factory] up here.

When the interviewer commented on the mix of feelings that leaving her children must have caused, Mrs. Jonas shook her head, as though reliving the pain of leaving her beloved family for an unknown city and uncertain future.

> The way I feel about it today and I felt about it for a long time now, I says nothing but the Lord helped me because I wanted to make it. I didn't want to go back to North Carolina and so I asked God to let me stay away from there.

For 2 years Mrs. Jonas roomed with the couple, saved money, and finally sent for her children to join her in South Philadelphia in an "apartment of [her] own." Although this period of Mrs. Jonas life was fraught with financial hardship and physical ills, she was proud of her determination to "make it alone."

> I was working in a candy factory. I was working, then I would get sick; I was on the DPA off and on. I had a partial hysterectomy.

Mrs. Jonas worked as a domestic only once more in her life. Finding this job through an employment service, Mrs. Jonas paid 25 dollars a week (for an unremembered number of weeks) for securing the job.

> She [the employer] thought I was a fool, but I let her know I wasn't. She told me that the girl before me did all the work, even the windows, but she got sick and died. I said, 'You worked the hell out of her [Laughter]. You won't do that to me.' I worked there one week. But anyway God was with me. I left there on Friday and then I got a job that same day. On Monday morning I went to work in a candy factory. All I did was line the boxes up to put the candy in. But I kept getting laid off. When she laid me off the last time I said to the Lord, 'Let me get me a job someplace else because I'm tired of getting laid off.' When she sent for me to come back to the candy factory, sure enough I had me another job. I was working in an egg plant place.

Mrs. Jonas does not focus on the societal framework that allowed blatant exploitation of her by the employment service, the callousness of the employer, and the stressful uncertainty of factory work. Instead, she focuses on her faith in God, which she sees as a route to her own empowerment. Her faith effected a confidence that she would find a new job through prayer. Her faith also engendered a self-esteem that did not permit her to accept maltreatment from her employer despite her desperate need for a job. Her faith grants beneficial results that are practical as well as psychological and spiritual.

Despite financial hardship throughout her life, Mrs. Jonas never considered herself poor. She remembers the period of raising her children as "fair" financially, but "very hard" physically.

> In '66 I went blind. I was working in this factory and there was dust. I call
> it the rag factory. They was new clothes and used clothes. I had to quit that
> because they told me at the hospital not to go to work in that dust no more.

Mrs. Jonas' illnesses were directly related to the work and housing that were available to her. In the 1970s she suffered a heart attack due to the physical stress of living in a housing project. Unable to use the elevators in the building because they had been "taken over by the drug dealers," Mrs. Jonas was forced to walk up and down 16 flights of stairs several times a day.

While Mrs. Jonas lived in the project, she prayed to be able to save enough money to purchase a home of her own. She realized her dream in 1981, buying the house in South Philadelphia where she currently lives.

> I prayed hard to get out of there. And nobody but the Lord helped me get
> out of there. I lived in the project for nine years. Still the Lord brought me
> through. With the little money, I never made much, I saw this house on sale.

Mrs. Jonas smiled as she looked around her living room, darkened by drawn blinds. Her home is an enclave of safety and respectability, representative of the fruit of her hard work, independence, and faith in God.

When asked to describe the hardest financial time in her life, she answered:

> My younger son, Alfie, he went to jail when he was sixteen. He got in with
> the boys robbing these meters. When his trial come off, he admit he did it
> with his gang. He got six months. And that kind of went hard with me. He
> did it, and I was mad with him.

It is interesting that Mrs. Jonas does not mention money when she names the hardest financial period of her life. Rather, she describes a time when she was angry about her son's crime and its repercussions for his future. Mrs. Jonas described her present relationship with Alfie, who has two children of his own, as "fine." When asked what kind of man Alfie is, Mrs. Jonas answered, "He don't give me no problem, that's all I can say."

Alfie's estrangement from his two children *does* worry Mrs. Jonas. Her own emotional distance from her grandchildren seems to cause her little concern.

> His [Alfie's] son is in and out of jail. He would call his Daddy. Then he'd
> borrow money. Now they don't communicate. But Alfie don't care. I don't
> see either of them [Alfrie's children]. I let my granddaughter come live with

me, but something was going on. She wasn't working. They told me she was selling dope; I don't know what she was doing. I called the cops. I had my locks changed on my door. That was over four years ago. And I ain't seen her since.

Mrs. Jonas denies feeling hurt by her granddaughter's actions and subsequent estrangement. She is no stranger to family loss. Mrs. Jonas lost her older son Jon in 1981 at the age of 38. Although his death was attributed to natural causes, Mrs. Jonas heard through neighborhood gossip that he was poisoned, but refused to pursue the rumor.

> He wasn't living with me then; he was living with some girl. When I got to the hospital he was dead. I didn't want to go through it all. If he was poisoned, I couldn't bring him back and I would rather not know. I just let it go as it was. Also, I thought maybe my other son would go and get in trouble if somebody done poison his brother. So I just let bygones be bygones.

This statement addresses many complex issues: (1) that Mrs. Jonas could not or would not trust the "authorities" to find out if her son had been murdered, (2) that she feared "losing" her other son if he tried to avenge his brother's death, and (3) that she is able to put the uncertainty of how her son died out of her mind—knowing that he was poisoned would cause greater heartache than uncertainty about his death. When the interviewer commented on the tremendous heartache her son's untimely death caused her, Mrs. Jonas responded:

> Yes and no. They said it was a natural death so I just went along with that. I accept that. Besides, he wasn't living with me so it didn't take me long to get over it. My son was dead before I moved into this house. [Pause] See, God knows and I didn't know. And I still don't know. I don't really think about it.

The above narrative indicates how Mrs. Jonas uses her faith as a coping strategy. The fact that God knows the details of her son's death satisfies her need to believe that "someone" knows the "truth" about what happened to Jon. This knowledge, although hidden within God, may be revealed to her at a later time, perhaps when she is better able to handle it, especially if her son *had* been poisoned. Mrs. Jonas employs her faith in God's omniscience to protect her against the uncertain cause as well as the pain of her child's death.

When asked about Jon's three children Mrs. Jonas responded:

> I see them once in a while, but that's all. The only thing they come to me for is a loan that they never pay back. So I got to the place I didn't have no loan, I had nothing to loan. They don't bother me period and I don't bother them.

The sustenance she receives from her faith assuages the painful shards of her relationships with her son and grandchildren. Her partnership with God gives purpose to her life. It allows her to imbue a painful past with meaning, to draw acceptance for family losses, and to provide comfort for present loneliness. She also finds within her faith the strength and self-esteem that permit her to forgo closeness with family members rather than be ill-used by them.

Mrs. Jonas: I talk to God. Talking is a prayer. I know they say how can you love something that you ain't never seen. But God is the one to look to. Because God will never turn you down. He talks to me.

Interviewer: How does he do that?

Mrs. Jonas: By letting me know how to manage my money and like that. Within me.

The above dialogue shows that God is a "concrete" friend who dispenses practical advice. Throughout the interview, Mrs. Jonas spoke of God with more familiarity than family members or neighbors. When asked to name her accomplishments, Mrs. Jonas answered:

Mrs. Jonas: Getting closer to the Lord, that's my accomplishment.

Interviewer: How did you accomplish that?

Mrs. Jonas: I prayed and asked God to get me out of the project, so he did. And one Saturday night I dreamed this as plain as anything: God said, 'Didn't you say that if I would get you out of that project that you would give me more of your time?' Sunday morning I wake up. I walk to the corner, Seventh Avenue and Sugar Street. I look up the street; I look down the street. I said, 'Well, Joy Baptist is the closest.' And I've been going to Joy Baptist ever since.

The above dialogue shows that Mrs. Jonas has a reciprocal relationship with God. God fulfilled his part of the bargain in getting her out of the project; she must repay God with her time. It also shows that she is an important member in the relationship. God expects her to keep her part of the personal convenant they made.

When asked where God fits in concerning the heartaches of her life, such as the death of her oldest son, the imprisonment of her younger son, and the estrangement of her grandchildren, Mrs. Jonas answered:

God didn't let it all happen to me. I mean everybody's days is numbered. That includes my son that passed away. When Alfie got those six months [in jail], well he was of age. I accept it. See, there's nothing but the Lord. The Lord saw, the Lord knows it all. He knows what you're going to do before you do it. So I feel this way about it; that's why I'm living today. Because of the little bad things I did, God knows there was good in me and I was going to change from all those things. Because I used to drink but I don't drink now. The only thing I do—I smoke my cigarettes.

Mrs. Jonas places God inside and outside the minor and major details of her life. By acknowledging both the hardship of her life *and* God's loving concern for her, she admits to her sorrows, but keeps the goodness of God intact. In this way, God becomes a two-fold partner in her life—an active participant and silent observer. In sharing her experiences, God is immanent to her pain. However, as transcendent, God watches the trajectory of her life from a distance, standing back, observing the manner and length of time she chooses to "change her ways."

Mrs. Jonas seems to live in two worlds: She acknowledges the larger world, which includes overt oppression, especially for poor African-American women, in a peripheral way. That is, she recognizes and is forced to work within the boundaries of racism and sexism, but refuses to be bowed by their destructiveness. Her smaller world is her intentional world. This is the world she creates according to her own design, and which she experiences as a haven from the larger world. Because God is her partner in this smaller world, she is empowered not only to find new jobs, but to remove herself from situations that lessen her self-esteem. It is also within the parameters of the smaller world that she does most of her "living" and "remembering."

Mrs. Jonas named the present as a "happy and contented" period in her life. She feels secure in her home environment and comforted by her spiritual life. She accepts that her relationships with her grandchildren are unsatisfactory but refuses to blame herself. She sighed when she told the interviewer that no one in her family attends church. When asked if that was a problem for her, she answered:

Well, if it is a problem it's their problem, not mine. When I go [to church] I look all right to myself. I put my teeth in. I put a little powder on my face. I look good.

ACCOMPLISHMENTS USED AS A COPING STRATEGY

To illustrate how a sense of accomplishment may be directly used as a coping strategy we present Mrs. Cummings, who perceives her achievements as a woman, wife, and mother as a means to combat her feelings of impoverishment in older age. Mrs. Cummings is a petite 82-year-old poor Caucasian woman who lives in a tastefully decorated apartment in a subsidized housing facility in Center City. She began the interview by describing her childhood as "very happy," and that currently "everything is fine." Her present contentment because of a "supportive" family is the theme of her interview and the major accomplishment of her life. Mrs. Cummings was one of eight children (four sisters remain) who were born and raised in the "back of a grocery store in North Philadelphia."

> We all got along. I had such a wonderful family and we still are. I mean I'm not alone. Besides, who has four sisters at my age?

Mrs. Cummings, whose husband died 20 years ago from heart disease, admits that she thinks about him every day because he had been an "outstanding" husband and father to their three children.

> We met at H. [a restaurant and bakery]. He was the fountain manager. He'd give me free sodas. All my girlfriends were jealous. I guess I was a little surprised when he asked me to marry him. I placed him on a pedestal. You know when he left this world he didn't have an enemy.

Mr. Cummings' character engendered no enemies but provoked girlfriends to be jealous. Mrs. Cummings became special when her husband chose her; she reflected his specialness. After the couple married, Mr. Cummings was made manager by Mrs. Cummings' father in the family grocery store. Her parents had "some hurt feelings" when Mr. Cummings left the family grocery after 2 years to manage an "American Store," the first crop of supermarkets that sprang up in the 1950s. According to Mrs. Cummings, the best time of her life, emotionally and financially, was when her husband was alive. She related the ease of her life under the care and protection of her kindly husband.

> We got along nicely. We never had an abundance of money but we always had enough to get by on with three children. We managed, and he took care of everything. I was never much for handling money.

The unfolding of Mrs. Cummings' life matched her expectations. Although the couple hadn't "planned" the number of children they would have, Mrs. Cummings "knew" that her husband would be a wonderful father to their two sons and one daughter. When asked if she thought that she would be better off financially in older age, she answered definitively.

> No, I knew I wouldn't be better off. In my family there was no money so I didn't expect it. My husband had steady work, but not a lot of money. But we weren't extravagant. We couldn't take vacations, Well, sometimes we

went to Ocean City with my mother-in-law. We didn't go to shows. We went to movies. I wasn't greedy. I was contented with my married life.

Mrs. Cummings' emotional contentment was not linked to having "a lot of money," but to the fact that her husband took care of her, their children, and their modest finances. Although financial security was not integral to Mrs. Cummings expectations about life, her husband's presence *was* crucial; she "never imagined" life without him. However, the continuing concern of family members tempers the sad surprise of spending the latter part of her life without him.

Well, I always thought my husband would be here. And I never thought I'd have a hard life because I have children and they look after me. We're close. They would do anything for me. I'm contented.

The day following Mrs. Cummings' interview was Thanksgiving. When asked where she would spend the day, she answered cryptically. "Well, all the children will be away. I'm going to stay in my building."

Mrs. Cummings named the present as the worst financial period of her life due to the fact that she recently gave up her job of 30 years. She is also experiencing a trying time emotionally and physically. She worries about her failing memory.

I'm just hanging on financially. I'm a little pressed. I sold cosmetics for 30 years. I just stopped 6 months ago. I couldn't remember things. I mean I had to pay my own money if I made a mistake with the customers.

Although Mrs. Cummings feels pressed financially, she reiterated that she is grateful to live in subsidized housing where her utilities are paid. Also, she is proud of her strength and independence in the way that she handles her limited finances.

I am independent. If somebody wants to go out to the shows, I deprive myself from doing it because I can't afford it. So I don't go out to movies or shows. Maybe people who have husbands go out, but I can't. Shows are expensive. The last one I saw was Mame. It was marvelous. I see people there. But I'm a happy and contented person.

Mrs. Cummings' choice to deprive herself of social pleasures influences the type and amount of camaraderie that she enjoys with her neighbors.

I have many acquaintances but no friends. See, I can't get in a conversation if others talk about shows. Shows are too expensive. But I'm a happy and contented person.

The words "happy" and "contented" are Mrs. Cummings' code words, which telegraphically relate how she thinks of herself and how she prefers others think of her. Like Mrs. Corner, introduced in Chapter 3, who consistently used the words "deep" and "level' to describe herself and her family, Mrs. Cummings both protects and presents herself by her self-description.

Mrs. Cummings' independence also asserts itself by her self-imposed isolation. Mrs. Cummings' alienation from neighbors keeps her from being judged by them. In this, she protects her reputation from real or imagined criticism. However, she remains aware of her standing in relation to her acquaintances. She listed her co-tenants by who had gone to college, "saw shows," or were skilled at bridge. When asked what she would "do over" or "do differently in life," she answered:

> Nothing. I'd marry the man I married. [Pause] Of course, I'm very sorry about not having an education. There are things that I read that I don't get. But, I'm happy. My family keeps in touch with me.

The above response—an affidavit of satisfaction after an admission of lack highlighted Mrs. Cummings narrative. No matter what adversity she faced in the past or might confront in the future, the love of her family provides a cognitive haven and a psychological refuge that engenders positive feelings. However, Mrs. Cummings balances her emotional closeness with physical distance from her family. Although she likes hearing from her family, she prefers their limited contact.

> Sometimes I think I would like to travel. I could go to Florida bcause my sister lives there. But I feel contented being home. She [sister] calls me a couple times a week, but she's very critical. She says, 'why don't you do this or that,' or she criticizes the way I speak. I went to visit her and I couldn't stand the pressure.

Mrs. Cummings laughingly admits that although she is gratified by her childrens' daily phone calls, she feels relieved if they don't stop by.

> The children—I love them dearly, but there's always something they find fault with. They are sometimes too critical. My son likes "real" coffee, but I don't like to make a whole pot just for one. He complains. The younger one is always finding fault. But I don't say much because they're very handy. They do things around here [the apartment] that I can't.

Mrs. Cummings admits that even with her children she does not "expose" her "true" feelings. She fears their censure as well as their refusal to help her with household chores.

Despite her careful interactions with family and neighbors, Mrs. Cummings remains active. She takes dancing lessons, volunteers 2 days a week at a geriatric facility, and sits on an art museum committee. She explained, "I like to be in with the crowd." Her desire to be "involved" contrasts her passivity when she speaks of the future. When asked to whom she would turn for care if the need arose, she replied:

> No one at this point. I'm sure the children would [help], but you don't know what's going to happen. Maybe they would put me in a home. Maybe I wouldn't care if I don't know what's going on. [Pause] I think about it once in a while.

Contradictions surface in Mrs. Cummings narrative: she describes her family as "close-knit," yet will spend Thanksgiving alone, she makes definitive choices about the present but feels confused about the future, and her financial struggle counters her emotional contentment. Perhaps these contrasts speak to the complexity of Mrs. Cummings as well as to the issues that women in this cohort confront, such as saving face with their acquaintances, a disinclination to become a burden to their children, and a need to "show a good front" to a stranger. Another personal incongruity emerged when Mrs. Cummings was asked if she believed she had gained wisdom with age. She laughed heartily.

> No, I got stupider. I don't know. It's the way my mind generates. I don't think you think the way you used to when you're older. But I'm very happy with my family. I mean the younger generation is having babies and I enjoy being with them. Things go on and they go on for me.

Mrs. Cummings places her personal denouement into the "big" picture. She accepts her place at the end of a long line of productive women and is gratified that the cycle continues. Her family provides an overarching canopy to provide meaning in *her* life as well as to ensure that "things go on."

Mrs. Cummings did not define herself through her lack of financial resources. Instead, she characterized herself by the fact that she was well-liked and, like her husband, "has no enemies." Also, she is delighted that she is considered "good-looking" and is adept at fixing her hair and applying make-up. When the interview was over, Mrs. Cummings pointed to a picture of a newly married, 20-something-year-old Mr. and Mrs. Cummings. The interviewer commented on the couple's good looks. Mrs. Cummings replied with pleasure, "You know, I look in the mirror and I really don't see too much difference."

Although Mrs. Cummings never envisioned the financial hardship that she now experiences, she continues to believe that "things happened for the best." Her pragmatic optimism precludes her from being a victim. Despite financial hardship and concern about her failing memory she literally "sees" herself as happy and youthful and believes that the future holds "good tidings for me."

SUMMARY

Most women in our study, like Mrs. Jonas, related having hard times financially with an event or incident that spoke to an *emotionally* difficult period. It is interesting that although financial poverty certainly engenders complex and negative feelings, the poor women in our study equated poverty with an emotional, familial, or relational deprivation. This speaks to the paradox of poverty—women in this study experienced deprivation as not *primarily* financial. However, it is important to note that a serious social problem such as poverty never stands alone, affecting one aspect of an individual life. Rather, it becomes one difficulty in a composite of problems that influence the emotional, physical, and spiritual lives of those affected and their network of family and friends. Our study highlights the women's stories and the complexity with which they meld their subjective feelings with the objective facts of poverty.

With this in mind, we conclude that for women in our study, asking for or receiving financial or emotional support from family did not usually emerge as a primary coping mechanism. Women did not look to their children and grandchildren for support. Physical distance, dissimilar values, and the need to be considered independent and not be a burden to the family were named as reasons why our respondents did not ask for emotional or physical assistance from their children.

Women did rely on their religion and spirituality to cope with hardship. Both Mrs. Warren and Mrs. Jonas considered their religion and spirituality as their major resource in dealing with the stresses of life. Although the organized church community was often a source for moral direction and social support, women employed a more personal spirituality, idiosyncratically defined by their particular racial, ethnic, and personal history, to sustain them during trying emotional and financial times. We further examine the role of religion and spirituality in the women's lives in Chapter 7, Thoughts of the Future.

Another means to actively cope with poverty is to focus on personal accomplishments. Reminiscing about past successes, such as "being a good wife or mother," or "being a dedicated employee," or "never asking anybody for help," remained, for women in our study, a well-traveled route toward maintaining independence and self-esteem in the present. Also, like Mrs. Cummings, respondents often tempered a story of past regret or financial hardship with a story of personal achievement or gain. Besides viewing life's sorrows and joys as balanced, this equalizing method of narrating your life speaks to the importance of telling your story, especially at the latter stages of life. Summing up life events and having more on the debit side grants integrity not only to the life story but to life as lived.

We turn now to Chapter 6 and to women's sense of being privileged or impoverished in relation to finances, social class status, as well as personal characteristics.

6

୫

Class and Self-Concept

This chapter examines how women's perceived class status informs their self-concept. As mentioned earlier, the construct of class has at least two aspects—financial and social. Although the two aspects might be thought of as interwoven, the women in our study saw the weaving of social and financial class less clearly. Some women determined to be objectively poor according to federal income standards described themselves as "rich" because they "want for nothing," or "upper" class because their friends were "refined" or "very intelligent." Some nonpoor women talked abut the poverty of their past in relation to the financial ease of the present. As mentioned in Chapter 5, women in our study grew up during the Depression. Its particular historical circumstances intersected with the early development of all women interviewed to create a mindset in which financial security, because elusive, became a primary goal. For many poor women, the present, with regular Social Security or SSI payments, and assistance from utilities programs or subsidized housing, was a relatively secure time. However, the meaning of financial security could be different for each group, as well as for each individual within each group. As discussed in previous chapters, emotional and relational contentment were primary factors in achieving a sense of security, especially for poor women.

For our research the objective measure of government income tables for 1992 was used to determine poor and nonpoor women in relation to finances. A subjective measure of class was used as part of our screening process for inclusion in the study. We asked the question: "In terms of social class would you say that you are (1) upper class, (2) upper middle class, (3) middle class, (4) lower middle class, (5) working class, (6) poor."

In this chapter, we will explore women's subjective notions of class—their perception of privilege and poverty, and the extended meanings of these rubrics. We acknowledge that situating yourself in a particular class implies self-awareness in relation to others' class status. We will also attempt to answer one of the major questions posed in our study of women living in chronic poverty: Do poor women see themselves as poor? We will examine women's awareness of the social forces that contribute to poverty and to the oppression that poverty leaves in its wake.

Finally, we will discuss the interview itself. The depth and breadth of the qualitative interview, although pleasing for most women, were confusing to some. A few women questioned what interest or importance their life story held as well as the motives behind and value of qualitative research. Some women sidestepped interview questions with monologues of their personal agendas. Other women felt that the interview tapped into uncharted portions of their psyche and dredged up long-forgotten feelings and memories. To some women a question such as "How would you describe yourself as a person," was difficult or even impossible to answer. This question sometimes elicited laughter, shyness, or an admission that they had "never even thought about it."

In all cases the interview was a dialogue in which interviewer and interviewee had expectations about each other and the interview, and "made each other up" within the unique process of telling and listening to a life story.

PERCEPTION OF PRIVILEGE

In discussing how women perceive that they are privileged to be in their current emotional and financial situation, two intertwining themes emerge: that of financial security and personal agency. Although poor women strongly expressed their personal agency without enjoying lifetime or even recent financial security, nonpoor women often linked the two themes. Mrs. Greene, a 73-year-old nonpoor African-American woman, connected the constructs of financial security and personal agency in her narrative. Widowed for just over a year, she lives alone in a large, semidetached home on a quiet street in a racially integrated neighborhood.

Mrs. Greene led the interviewer past a dining table covered with books and papers into a bright breakfast nook. She pushed aside a thick folder, and offered coffee from a silver service. When the interviewer commented on the graciousness of the silver service, Mrs. Greene clarified her intent. "Oh, no. I do this for me." After pouring coffee, Mrs. Greene pointed to the file folder she pushed aside and began her life story.

> Eighteen years ago I went into stocks and bonds. My husband said, 'What do you know about the stock market?' I said, 'I don't know much but I'm going to find out.' I read everything I could. I read that there is a better way to make money than a passbook saving. That's one reason I'm comfortable now.

Mrs. Greene's initial comments frame the focus of her narrative and expose three salient personal themes—the significance of financial security, especially at this time in her life, her courage in seeking it, and her solitary agency in acquiring it. She explained that her family of origin galvanized her determination for success. Mrs. Greene described her childhood in West Philadelphia as "wonderful," and named her father as a model of economic achievement and provider for his wife and three children.

> My dad had a job for 44 years when things were really tough—the Depression. He bought his first house in 1921. He subsequently bought three more homes which he passed down to my mother, and my sister got two houses and I got two. Oh, I had a good childhood. Since my dad worked I never really knew about the Depression. Because we took vacations and my mother made all of our clothes and we always looked nice. We seemed to have everything.

Mrs. Greene saw herself as privileged because of a normative lifestyle, even during the Depression, filled with "vacations and nice clothes." Since her entry into the "good life" came early, she admits, "I never knew any different." Her sense of past privilege matches her present gratitude for a network of supportive relatives and a religious upbringing that she now realizes were critical to her development.

> I'm grateful for the parents that I had. I'm grateful for the family—my grandmother, aunts and uncles. I didn't realize how wonderful they were until I started looking at television and I see the problems. I had so much going for me that I just took for granted. I'm very grateful that my parents brought me up in church.

After "enjoyable years in grammar school, junior high and high school," Mrs. Greene met a man 15 years her senior at a high school basketball game, grew increasingly attracted to him, and quit school in her senior year to marry him. Mrs. Greene's parents were disappointed; her mother envisioned her daughter as a nurse. Plans for nursing school went awry when Mrs. Greene fell in love with the man who was "like my dad." Her father's stalwart trait as a hard worker became the symbol for what she envisioned in a husband.

> I knew I wanted a husband who wanted children, wanted to own his own home and wanted to work. I knew what I wanted in a man because I saw my dad. I wanted the same thing from my husband—stability. And I knew that he [Mr. Greene] liked the same things that I liked, and that was the *good life* [authors' emphasis]. [Pause, with a smile] I handled money and I dressed nice and I looked good.

Mrs. Greene connected the "good life" to choosing the "right" man, managing the money that it took to acquire "things," and "look[ing] good." Her worldly goals and personal ambition were parallel; both emerged as significant in her perception of privilege.

Mrs. Greene named her marriage as her greatest accomplishment. She spoke wistfully of early married life and her husband's romantic attentiveness. She summed up its idyllic nature with a wave of her hand.

> I met and married. He loved me; I know he loved me and I loved him. We just wanted to have a good marriage and have children which is what we did. I had a good marriage and today that's almost a miracle.

Mrs. Greene admitted that the couple struggled financially in the early years. Mr. Greene often worked "at two or three jobs so that we could be comfortable." Although Mrs. Greene longed for six children, and her husband began to "make good money" as a policeman, they decided that six children would strain their budget and blur their dreams.

Mrs. Greene gave birth to four boys in quick succession and named "having them" as one of the happiest times in her life. She credited her husband's "specialness" and his role as a "strict disciplinarian" with "raising four kids who never gave us any trouble."

Motherhood further motivated Mrs. Greene's desire for social and economic advancement. Her prescription for the boys' success included not only a standard by which her sons should measure themselves, such as advanced education and personal dignity, but a warning against the world in which they would compete.

> *Mrs. Greene:* When the children were small, we would stress: Don't get in trouble; don't go to court because you will never get a fair trial. And don't let anybody tell you who you are. Define who you are. Education. I always stressed to them that they had to go to school and be the best they could. I said, 'It's not enough for you to be Edward S. Greene, you want some letters behind your name.' I always said that.
>
> *Interviewer:* What do you mean?
>
> *Mrs. Greene:* Like a Ph.D, DDS, whatever. Get all the education you can get and make liars out of what these people say about you.

Mrs. Greene knew well the competitiveness and racism of the business world; she had used the assertiveness, pride, and motivation that she instilled in her sons for her own professional advancement. Starting out as a cosmetics representative selling door to door, she quickly became a district manager with "two hundred people under me." Traveling from one city district to another gave her an opportunity to contrast her own "changing" neighborhood with "nicer" ones.

> West Philadelphia was beginning to change and I wanted a different place to live, to finish raising my children, and for us, too. When we moved here, the realtor went to some neighbors and explained who we were. We were nice. And he was a policeman and I was a manager and I had boys that were nice. All this crap that we go through because we're black and have more class than some of the white ones that lived here.

Mrs. Greene remains embittered by her need to "prove" herself to her Caucasian neighbors. Although her family moved into their home over 30 years ago, she is also disappointed, but not surprised, by the neighborhood's lack of community. "We don't socialize [with neighbors], never did." She would prefer to live in a "nice all black area," but explained the reason why such neighborhoods are difficult to construct and maintain.

> The realtors put all kinds of black people together in neighborhoods. You got the nice, the hardworking people, you got people who are being subsidized and they're the ones who throw trash out, who do graffiti, who don't sweep. You got all different kinds in a neighborhood and that's what starts bringing it down. You got poor blacks living with middle class. It's like a jigsaw puzzle. Background, background. My church is my backbone. My faith gives me strength. But I don't believe, as opposed to poor women, that God is going to come here and give me a nice home or a nice husband or nice clothes. He gave me a brain to go out and get the things that I want. Had I married a no-good man, he couldn't have kept me down too long. If I had to work harder, or if I had to work and get more education, that's what I would have done.

Mrs. Greene's empathy for "poor" women's status as victims coexisted with a refusal to imagine herself (for too long) in such circumstances. Although she is acutely aware of the circular and perpetuating nature of social problems, such as racism, poverty, and destructive behavior, she places the onus for the undesirable results of those problems, such as "doing graffiti" and "not sweeping," on sources (realtors) external to the actual agents. Yet, she emphasizes her own agency and responsibility to wrest herself out of similar circumstances.

Although Mrs. Greene acknowledges racial injustice in the "larger" world and has warned her sons about its tragic effects, a perception of her own privileged status distances her from this larger world and from the "poorer women" who endure the effects of this injustice. Her sense of agency allows her to claim her place as the center of her "smaller" world.

> I've had a good life. I didn't say easy. The getting has been fun. I think I've been a leader in my family. My idea has always been I cannot control the world, but I have a little family here, this is my circle and it's up to me to do the best that I can with my family. I'm not out there. I'm not a leader; I'm not this, that and the other thing. But in my family circle I am. And if everybody did that we wouldn't have the problems we have today, that's for sure.

Implicit in the perception of privilege or poverty is the ability to see yourself in relation to others. In the four sample groups, nonpoor African-American women, like Mrs. Greene, mentioned their "status" within a social sphere more often than other groups. Perhaps the obstacles they overcame in their struggle to achieve the "middle class" made this lifestyle more desirable and more a subject for discussion.

In the case of *poor* African-American women, awareness of others who had "more problems" or "even less than I do" led them to definitively name themselves as *not poor*. For the African-American poor sample, the term poverty was often used to describe negative character traits, such as "I think of a person as poor if they are always depressed or in trouble," or even a lack of faith, such as "poor is when you don't believe in God." We present the case of Miss Mary (the title she preferred) as an example of a poor African-American woman who described herself as "rich" and defined her own "good life" in regard to her expectations, achievements, positive feelings about herself, and reciprocal relationships with others.

Miss Mary is a 78-year-old woman who has been widowed for over 30 years. She lives in a three-story row home on a small street in South Philadelphia. Several homes on her block are handsomely ornamented and display tiny landscaped lawns. They sit beside vacant houses that are boarded and covered with graffiti.

As the interviewer approached Miss Mary's home, an attractive white-haired woman, bent from the waist from osteoporosis and severely bow-legged, watched a small dog from the corner of her eye as she leaned against the railing of her stoop and chatted with a neighbor. Turning to the interviewer, she identified herself as Miss Mary and climbed her steps with difficulty. The dog and interviewer followed Miss Mary into a tiny vestibule, a large living room, and an old-fashioned, cozy kitchen. After being introduced to her "babies," Cubby the dog and Boo the cat, Miss Mary offered the interviewer coffee. She began the interview by saying:

My mother told me I had beautiful skin. Most people, everywhere I go I get that compliment.

Miss Mary was born in South Carolina, the youngest of two daughters. The family moved to Philadelphia when she was a baby so that her parents could escape the servitude of sharecropping and "improve themselves."

My mother and father worked for the land that they lived on. It was a white man's land. I don't know anything about the South except that I was born there.

Her home in South Philadelphia is the first home her parents owned and the only home in which Miss Mary ever lived. She speaks of the neighborhood with affection, attachment, and a sense of ownership.

It was always a mixed neighborhood. Portuguese, Italians, Jews. There's several of us that were here in the '30s.

Although Miss Mary witnessed her neighborhood's decline, she believes that the strength of her personality transcends any danger that might lurk in a deteriorating area.

Everybody knows Miss Mary. If I'm coming up and the young boys are using some profanity, one says, 'Hey, man, don't you see Grandmom or don't you see Miss Mary?' Sometimes four or five of them are on the corner, and I walk into the middle of them shooting craps. And I say, 'Oh, no, boys, not here on Miss Mary's corner.' I can walk in my neighborhood any time of night. Every section I go in I'm well known. If I'm out on that street, anybody that comes by, I don't care who, I say, 'Good morning, how are you? Yeah, I'm talking to you.' I'm not a stranger nowheres from Kansas Avenue to Maple Street. To everybody I say, 'Hey, how are you?'

Although Miss Mary continues to enjoy a close relationship with most of her neighbors, she decries some of the new residents' lack of concern for "how things look." Indeed, she places a priority on respectability—on the right way to conduct yourself and live your life. Her measure of respectability, gleaned from her parents and from the cherished memory of her past, sometimes causes the present to fall short.

Sometimes I just sit and reminisce. We used to all have flower boxes. Our poles we painted white. The curbs, every other pole had a trash can. And we would paint the addresses on the curbs. Others came here, migrating from wherever and you could see the neighborhood beginning to deteriorate.

Miss Mary admits that she is currently "just making ends meet" and that throughout her life she "just got by" financially. Although she cannot afford badly needed repairs to her beloved home, she refuses to describe herself as poor.

> I have always lived good since I've been in this world. I've never wanted. I had a home. I had a piano. We had a victrola.

A home, piano, and victrola were accoutrements of the "good life" into which Miss Mary places herself. Perhaps she feels that to call herself "poor" would dishonor the memory of her parents' hard work. Miss Mary met her husband, "a neighborhood boy," at a South Philadelphia high school.

> One day I was out in the school yard. He [future husband] came over from the boy's side. My neighbor introduced me to him. Things was so different then. My mom used to go out and say that little boy is out there on the corner [Laughter]. We were *young*. I was 14, 15. He was two years older. One day my mom said to him, 'You like my Mary? You don't have to stand on the corner; you can come down, you know. But when you come to visit, I want you to come in a necktie and jacket. When you get here if she gives you permission you take off the jacket 'cause it's hot.' This is how my mom was raised. This is how she had us raised. This was raising children years ago. Nowadays these children are raising themselves.

Although Miss Mary did not graduate from high school, she has no regrets about the path she chose.

> During that time, the Depression, the teachers in all the schools had cards. One had cards for clothes, one had cards for shoes or food or what have you. This was before they started giving out stamps. School was so crowded because all of those boys and girls that had dropped out to get jobs to help their parents, they came back to finish. At the age of 16 I got so disgusted I just politely got up and walked out. I said it was no use. The teacher, when she would be explaining something, here come somebody with a card for shoes or food. So I stayed home and kept house. My mom and dad worked. They worked for Jewish people. My mother kept their house; my dad drove their truck.

Miss Mary married her husband 2 years after she quit school. She spoke warmly of their 20 years together.

> I was 18 when I got married, it was during the Depression. My husband would go out and look for work. He would stand out on the corner and some guys would say, you want to make a day's pay? He was very, very good. He

was a good provider; he loved and cared about his children. After the Depression he worked with the city, driving one of those big trash trucks.

Miss Mary and her new husband set up housekeeping with her parents, her grandmother, and an unmarried aunt in the house on Iris Street. The strong bond of the extended family unit made a safe haven of their home. She smiled at the memory and repeated a theme that pervaded the interview.

> We lived with my mom and dad period. I never left. Sometimes I just sit here and reminisce in my mind, how nice it was. I never wanted. I always lived good. I always knew what it was to have a nice home.

The family home was the site of Miss Mary's happiest memories—raising their four daughters, three "natural" born children and an adopted daughter, Susie. It is also the site of Miss Mary's deepest losses.

> My sister and her husband, they lived up in the next block. So it was my dad, my mom, and my kids and my husband. My dad was 75 when he died. Right here at home. Susie was holding his hand. My mom, my dad, and my grandmom, they all died right here, and my husband died right here.

Miss Mary worked throughout her married life first as a domestic, then as a school aide. She realized her dream of attending nursing school when she was 35 years old.

> My oldest was 7. I graduated at the L.H. on Main Street. I was so elated. I'll never forget it. My husband was working, so my brother-in-law came. He bought me a black and gold Chinee lounging set. Right out of nursing school I went to the very first hospital which was T.H. at Tenth and Watson. I worked there 21 years until I had the two heart attacks, one in '74 and '79. I went back and I wasn't there two hours I was passing out. My supervisor said, 'Don't come back.' I said, 'Honey, the Man Upstairs just told me what to do.' That was it. But I always figured that the time I was there served a purpose.

Miss Mary soon intends to move into her eldest daughter's home due to her difficulty in climbing stairs and doing housework. She did not mention her grief at leaving the home in which she was born and raised, raised her own children, and believes the spirits of her relatives still dwell. Instead, she sees her life as planned and the situations in which she finds herself as serving a purpose not immediately apparent to her. Indeed, even though she is physically debilitated, she describes herself as independent and assesses her situation realistically and humorously.

I have a degenerating hip and knee. I fight it. I go on. I have Mister Cane
here. Most people are amazed that I am as old as I am. I wear high heels. Some
of the women say to me, 'Mary, why don't you wear the lower shoes?' I pull
my dress up. I says, 'You know why? Because I got damn pretty legs.' You
know I still do the rug cuttin' too. I put the stick up side the wall and honey,
I'm out there.

Miss Mary related that she worked hard for the "extras" in life—such as
an ocean cruise. Gaining concrete rewards through hard work seemed the
key to her perception of privilege. Inherent in her sense of privilege is how
she sees herself and presents herself to others.

There was a little Jewish pharmacist on the corner. My mom used to work
for his wife and at times I used to do a little cleaning for her, too. That's why
I went back to school, to get money. The cruises that I've had, about 4 or 5 is
because of that. Like I say, I have lived; I won't complain. The world owes
Mary nothing.

Like Mrs. Jonas, discussed in chapter 5, and Mrs. Greene mentioned earlier in this chapter, the world that Miss Mary inhabits is "small." It is an intentional world constructed of her expectations, achievements, memories,
and, perhaps especially, feelings about herself and her impact on the
"larger" world. Miss Mary seems able to stand outside of herself, and to
take stock of her personal assets and physical liabilities. For Miss Mary, the
scales balance; she and the world have done right by each other. When
asked what she accomplished in life, she answered:

I accomplished everything that I ever wanted to do. I have lived good since
I can remember being born into this world and I won't complain. The Lord
has really been good to me. I got married, had a good husband. He treated
me nice. And I've always lived here with my parents.

Miss Mary's optimistic worldview includes her belief that the world,
especially her family, church, and neighborhood community, needs her.
This need convinces Miss Mary that she continues to achieve her purpose
in life:

To do for yourself and do for others. I love doing for people. I wish I could
do the world. Others say to me, 'Mary, are you ever unhappy?' I say, 'What
for?' I'm alive. I have lived a good life, happy and it still is. All my friends
say, 'Boy, Miss Mary, you something. Ain't nothing like Mary.' I'm a great
teenager, you know.

Miss Mary relates the past, sums it up, and foresees the future according to a particular image of herself as a person with a lot of living ahead of her—"a great teenager."

PERCEPTION OF POVERTY

Most women living in poverty did not use the word poor to describe their social or financial circumstances. Indeed, as mentioned throughout this book, most poor women did not think of themselves as poor. One reason may be that in American culture, the word poor carries a moral and social as well as financial stigma. Interestingly, some nonpoor women did define themselves as poor in the past, when the circumstances of the Depression contrasted with their normative economic situation. Perhaps the temporal and emotional distance of past poverty reduced the moral sting of the word "poor."

Although all of the women in the poverty groups and some women in the nonpoor groups admitted to "having it hard" at times during their lives, most poor women experienced poverty as *not* akin to financial lack. As mentioned in Chapter 5, the paradox of poverty was salient in most poor women's narratives. That is, emotional or relational security often precluded a self-perception of poverty. Contrasting most poor women's notion of contentment and highlighting the moral connotation of poverty, we present Mrs. Pierson, whose unresolved shame over past behavior results in a perception of extreme impoverishment.

Mrs. Pierson is a 78-year-old poor Caucasian woman who looks older than her years. Her skin is weathered, her voice is raspy from years of cigarette smoking, and she walks with a labored gait. Mrs. Pierson lives in an efficiency apartment in a subsidized apartment building. The small window in her single room looks out onto the deserted main street in a small depressed suburb of Philadelphia. The room is neat and modestly furnished. A vase of silk flowers graces her small wood dining table, tiny crocheted hats hang on the wall, and a worn red rose bedspread covers her single bed.

Mrs. Pierson was born in the Blue Ridge mountains of Virginia, the second of four daughters. She quit school in the fifth grade when her younger sister was born to help with child care and housekeeping chores. Mrs. Pierson waxes nostalgic when speaking about her early childhood.

> We didn't have the very best but my father always seen that we had something to eat. And my mother could take nothing and make the best meal out of it.

Mrs. Pierson named the period when her father was alive as the happiest time in her life. However, after his death, when she was 6 years old, her mother remarried.

> He [stepfather] hated me. My mother married him to keep all of us together so we wouldn't be put in homes. He treated me so bad because I was so much like my father.

Mrs. Pierson recalled an incident that occurred shortly after her stepfather had beaten her with a strap. It typified his brutal temper, the family's fear of him, and Mrs. Pierson's violent reaction to him.

> Once, I aimed a fork at him and it stuck in his forehead. He came around to me; I think he was going to kill me. My mother got in between us and said to him, 'Oh, no, you asked for that.' [Pause] I didn't have no bed of roses.

Although Mrs. Pierson was only 14 years old, she left home shortly after this incident, worked as a laundress, and roomed with "other young girls from no-good families [laughter]." Mrs. Pierson never returned home but communicated regularly with her mother and sisters. After her stepfather died, Mrs. Pierson's mother moved in with another daughter and "had peace for the first time since him [stepfather]." During the war Mrs. Pierson became a welder in a shipyard in Virginia, where she met "the best looking man I ever saw." After a brief courtship, they married, but the marriage lasted less than a year. Mrs. Pierson blames her husband's jealousy over her higher salary, his alcoholism, and his abuse as the reasons for their divorce.

> He hit me hard one time. And I said, 'So long, brother.' I'll remember that 'til the day I die.

Mrs. Pierson sneaked out of their apartment one night and traveled north to Pennsylvania. She never saw her husband again, nor does she know to this day if he is living or dead. "I had kin people, cousins and uncles by the dozens up here."

Mrs. Pierson worked as a waitress in a local diner. She was quickly dubbed "Little Cricket, on account I could wait the tables so fast." She remained a waitress in and around the surrounding area for the rest of her working life. Although she never remarried, she had "lots of boyfriends" and "good times." Mrs. Pierson does not think of those times as "good" anymore. In fact, she feels ashamed of her heavy drinking and the numerous love affairs she had during this period.

Mrs. Pierson cried often during the interview, especially when talking about her mother, who died over 30 years ago, or her only remaining sibling, a younger sister who is dying from cancer. Although this sister lives a few blocks from her apartment, Mrs. Pierson is unable to visit her because of her difficulty in walking.

> The only thing I do is pray. Sometimes I say, Lord, please, my sister can't eat. Take this suffering off my sister and put it onto me.

Mrs. Pierson identifies strongly with her mother's and sister's past and present pain. Throughout the interview Mrs. Pierson answered questions by recalling her mother's hard life or her sister's suffering. The memory of her mother's hardship, her sister's illness, and the "bad things" she did in the past are the loci of Mrs. Pierson's present thoughts. When asked what she would do differently in her life if she could, Mrs. Pierson hesitated.

> If I could go back—[Pause] I want my mother. But I don't want her the way she suffered. She died when she was 69 years old from cancer. She had the eating cancer. Like my sister.

The memory of her mother is both bitter and sweet. It is the repository for Mrs. Pierson's longing for emotional support, fears about her sister's imminent death, and regrets about her behavior as a younger woman. When asked to describe her accomplishments, Mrs. Pierson recalled her mother's achievements, such as the wonderful meals she made "out of nothing." She idealizes her mother to assure herself that she came from something "good." When pressed to name her own accomplishments, Mrs. Pierson could not think of one; she believes she has yet to achieve her goal.

> I want to be a better woman, don't say nothing dirty. I talk awful nasty and dirty. [Chuckle] Somebody on the bus said, 'Lavinia's got the dirtiest mouth for a woman.'

Mrs. Pierson's deep shame for past behavior settles in the forefront of her consciousness, shaping her self-concept, memories of younger adulthood, and thoughts about the future. Only her memories from earliest childhood remain untainted by regret.

> There's a lot of things that I have done in life that I'm going to pay for. You shouldn't do a lot of things but you do them anyway, and then after—it's too late. There was a time when I thought I was something. I had no flies on me. I just don't like to talk about it. It brings back old memories and I just want to forget them.

This interesting comment offers a window into Mrs. Pierson's mindset. Her belief that she must "pay for" her actions causes her despair in the present and makes her fearful of the future. Her inability to let go of the past and forgive her own "badness" renders her painful memories as ever-present. When asked to describe herself, she used the past as her mirror.

> I was a good looking woman, you better believe me. I had long blonde hair and I wore a size 11 dress.

Mrs. Pierson wages an internal battle between her past self—who was pretty and had a good time—with her need to become the morally upright person she must become in order to "pay" for past "sins." Perhaps this inner skirmish forces Mrs. Pierson to describe herself as "dirt poor" since her notion of poverty does not include her past or present economic situation. Although she has no savings, she "wants for nothing."

> I thank God for what I do get [from SSI]. It means I can have two pennies of my own. I got enough so that I can eat a piece of bread and be satisfied with it. Look at the rich, they can't use that money in heaven and if they go to hell that money will burn. Some think they can do this and that and cheat the world but he [God] knows. They pay for their own and I'm paying for mine.

Throughout her narrative, Mrs. Pierson connects the idea of money and payment with sin. This complex intertwining of material and spiritual constructs indicates her deep shame, her rootedness in the materialism of American culture, and her belief that she must "pay" to be relieved of that shame. Mrs. Pierson feels poor because the price of her sins is indeed more than she can afford. It is exacted through her guilt about the past, her fears about death, and her inability to help her dying sister. Perhaps she would prefer to endure her sister's "eating cancer" because it would exact its payment more quickly in physical pain. When asked how she thinks about her life as a whole, Mrs. Pierson laughed ruefully.

> I think about the crazy things I did. You know, being with men and all the drinking. I wasn't no angel and I'm still no angel. I wouldn't want to go back. [Pause]. And I'm trying to change.

Mrs. Pierson laughed again when she was asked what she believed the future held for her—"Just to die." However, she worries about what she will face in the next life.

> The Lord made me in his own image. It's up to me. He didn't tell me to do this and do that. He didn't make you go with this one and go with that one because he didn't pick nobody out for you. You did that yourself. [Whispered] Oh, Lord, forgive me.

This quiet aside shows that a glimmer of hope resides within her shame. She explained that she continues to struggle against a powerful enemy who shares some of the responsibility for her past behavior.

> *Mrs. Pierson:*   That old man with the horns, he is still trying to get me.
> *Interviewer:*   Who is trying to get you?
> *Mrs. Pierson.*   The devil. I want to go up there [heaven] but I don't know. [crying] My cousin says, don't you worry, you're going there. God is a forgiving God. But I want my people to go, too.

This complex dialogue highlights the black and white nature of Mrs. Pierson's worldview, as well as the depth of her present loneliness. It also permits her an accomplice in her wrongdoing. Some of the responsibility for her "sins" must be placed on an external agent (devil).

Mrs. Pierson's "immoral" behavior informs her self-concept. Day-to-day pleasures, such as bingo playing, craft making, and casino trips, are thwarted by the painful, all-encompassing memories of her family's sufferings and this "bad" behavior; hope about an afterlife is shadowed by her fear of heavenly retribution. When asked about the main purpose in life, she whispered:

> The things I could have done. Too late.

This quote encapsulates Mrs. Pierson's life story. Her belief that it is "too late" for change causes her to replay scenes of anguish—her mother's death, her dying sister, and her own shame—from which there is no escape. Perhaps the replayed scenes are her self-inflicted punishment for a "badly" lived life. Perhaps she fears that her own death will be similar to her mother's and sister's tragic end. Her inability to make sense or take meaning from her "mistakes" and her guilt concerning them result in despair.

When the interviewer was ready to leave, Mrs. Pierson began to cry, explaining that she's been "crying for nothing lately." Her depression certainly speaks to the hardship of her life. This difficult interview highlights Mrs. Pierson's tremendous needs and her internal poverty in meeting them.

CLASS AWARENESS

Situating yourself in a certain social or financial class implies an awareness of yourself in relation to other classes. We present Mrs. Dickson, a 75-year-old nonpoor African-American woman who, similar to Mrs. Corner mentioned in Chapter 3, knew that her family's legacy of talent and her own good choices and hard work augured success. However, Mrs. Dickson, like Mrs. Greene discussed earlier in this chapter, was also cognizant that poverty was woven into the fabric of society through its institutions and mores. This cognition of the ethos of the "larger" world caused Mrs. Dickson to construct a "smaller" world. Within this smaller world Mrs. Dickson tried to shield her family from the assault of racial discrimination by nurturing, within her sons, a strong sense of self-esteem and a desire to achieve a social and financial status that would be "accepted" by the larger world.

Mrs. Dickson has been widowed for over 20 years. She remains in the large row home that she and her husband bought over 40 years ago and in which they raised their two sons. Although she had asked to participate in the study, she asked why *she* was being interviewed for research on chronic poverty. When the interviewer answered that she was a member of a group that served as a contrast to the group that included women in poverty, Mrs. Dickson offered one of several themes in her narrative—that the polarity between herself and the poverty sample was well-drawn.

> Early in daddy's life he was a butler in a very wealthy family. And all right, mother was a maid in a very wealthy family. [Pause] An Irish woman that I worked with when I went back into government work said, 'Faye, I have to ask you and say this of you. First of all,' she said, 'you are a lady, such a nice lady. Did your parents work in private families for wealthy people? Because you instinctively know what to say and what to do and it's evident that you were raised this way.' I said, 'Yes, that's true.' And then I thought about it and I said, 'Yes, they learned a lot from this exposure and experience.' And so mother set certain standards for us in our home. We would always sit down as a family and eat. But for these women that marry sorry men—they are sorry. Society has a lot to do with it. And I've thought about it. I really have. Not so much in contact with women like that but in reading and even through the church seeing various women from broken homes. I have thought about so many of these things. Because it's like a generational thing.

Mrs. Dickson's opening remarks show her awareness that societal structures contribute to the perpetuation of poverty. However, family legacy bequeaths models of values and lifestyle. Mrs. Dickson sought the middle-class values that her parents witnessed through the back door of domestic service and upheld in their home. Her comments distanced her from those women whose parents had not set "certain standards" for their children.

Mrs. Dickson is the youngest of two children born to a family that grew up in West Philadelphia. She described her family home as "filled with love and laughter." Although she admitted that their family "had it hard" during the Depression, she quickly added that the social status and goals of their family were high.

My mother was born in Delaware. See we've had two priests and three nuns from my mother's family. The others were all prosperous farmers. My father is from Darby. The boys all played an instrument. Daddy played the viola.

Her mother's disappointment in her own limited education fanned a hope that her only daughter would attend college.

She [mother] was very resentful because her uncle educated all of his children. Her father, he ran the post office. But he didn't think that education was important for women. And she was responsible for raising the two youngest children. And she was always bitter that she wasn't educated like her cousins.

However, Mrs. Dickson's swift promotions and "good pay" earned from office work made the penury of "college girls" seem unappealing. Although her brother graduated from college and "did very well," Mrs. Dickson chose a different, but equally successful path.

I was fortunate enough to get a job in the government because when I started working and with my overtime I made more money than my father. I was the talk of the family. Oh, they were all so proud of me. So I never really had a desire to go to college. I didn't want to scrimp and save and I didn't want to work and have to go to school.

Mrs. Dickson met her husband through her brother; they were fellow students at an out of state college. Mrs. Dickson liked her husband "the first time [she] saw him." She was 19 when they married; he was 2 years older. Although Mr. Dickson did not graduate from college he found "high level jobs" in the city government. Mrs. Dickson described her husband as a "peaceful" man whose "goals were similar." When asked if her expectations in life included marriage and motherhood, she smiled.

No, but see the example was set for me. And also by my husband's parents. Oh, I wanted to be married. I wanted to be a mother. But I don't know, those things were there, just there. But to say that it was a plan that I had in mind, no. There again, I was conceited enough to think these things would just happen [Laughter].

Mrs. Dickson sees her weighty role as an African-American woman, wife, and mother as eminently crucial for the well-being of her race. Her need to protect her family springs from her personal experience in a world divided into "us" and "them." Her philosophical yet realistic worldview reacts to the unfairness of this world by creating another world—the haven of home for her family.

Man has a need to look down on someone. And we black people are at the bottom of the heap. People come from all over the world to this country and they in turn begin to look down on the black men themselves. Other races of people, other cultures. And so it's just a way of life and you do learn to live with it. As I said, I hurt more for my boys than anything that I've experienced. I hurt for my husband because he was refused promotions and other men with far less education and experience would get the job. And this was very, very hard. So there again the black woman—and our's is a matriarch society—and the black woman has always had to be strong for her family and her mate. So home had to be a refuge and a place of peace at least.

Mrs. Dickson carefully constructed her home as a safe haven for her husband and children. She described her married life of 34 years as "enjoyable" and named raising her children as the happiest time in her life. Her primary job, until her youngest child was 11, was to guard her children from the cruelty of discrimination. Despite her hard work, she could not keep bigotry from her doorstep.

Vincent [older son] experienced unpleasantness from the priests at school. And see they kept these things from me. They never told me until they came out of high school because I think then I would insist they not go there any longer. These things are—. There are people that have these prejudices within them. They've been raised that way and it's been a part of them. And just because they go into the religious life it doesn't change. And you may keep them hidden for a while but they will surface somehow.

Mrs. Dickson's gentle manner glosses the ugly truths of racial prejudice. However, she feels she excelled in her job as protector of her family; she is proud of the successful men her boys have become. Both are professionals who live nearby; her oldest son has children of his own. Stories about her grandson's college awards and her granddaughter's writing talent dotted the interview. She takes pride that she and her husband showed, by example, the importance of education.

I loved history and I know my husband had said when we both retired we were going to take courses in things that we were interested in, you know, on a college level.

Although Mrs. Dickson admits to "still" missing her husband after 21 years of widowhood, she feels "extremely contented" with her present lifestyle. The memories of a "whirlwind romance" at age 50 something, her work as a Eucharistic Minister at her church, and social activities with numerous friends allow no time for boredom or "unhappy thoughts."

When asked if she would change anything in her life if she could, she answered definitively.

> Oh, no, I would go on as I am. I have everything I need to make me comfortable. And I have the wherewithal for the extras. So I'm fortunate. I guess I've always thought that I was just so fortunate to be born into the family that I was and to be raised the way I was raised. Some of the values that I saw with my friends were not the same as the values in my family. Because you tend to associate with people you're comfortable with. Even in the past, I dated a few men that I knew would not be accepted by my family. That this man does not want out of life what I want. Whether I even thought it through I knew, so I moved on.

Mrs. Dickson, like Mrs. Quill in Chapter 3, is grateful that her parents set her on the "right course" early in life. She recognizes her "good luck" as she contrasts her family's values against a lesser standard.

> I know when mother came to live with me, my husband said, you know, you do need someone to come in and help with the responsibilities of cleaning, etc. So that's when I started having someone to help me in the house. And now I'm on the third lady. And she's aware of my grandson's career, his going through college and everything. And her child is on dope. She has several sons, and another one's in jail. She's such a fine woman, but she's had to raise four grandchildren.

Mrs. Dickson ended her narrative in the way she began—by drawing a contrast between herself and women living in poverty. Although never accusing the poor of moral turpitude, she nevertheless grounds their poverty in a legacy of poor family values and personal bad fortune that she, through the foresight and hard work of her parents, never experienced. Like Mrs. Greene, she was well aware of the social forces that leave poverty in its wake, but chose to name her own "good" family and "luck" as reasons for her present emotional and financial contentment.

Mrs. Dickson offered the interviewer brewed coffee and home baked cookies on the blustery day in January when the interview took place. Her graciousness made her home exactly what she planned it to be—a warm refuge in a cold world.

SOCIAL FORCES

The feminist axiom that the political is personal resonates to the poor women we interviewed. They lived, endured, and usually thrived within the framework of opportunities permitted by society at large. The idea introduced earlier in the book of two worlds—the smaller and the larger—has a special place in this section. Most poor women saw the trajectory of their life history, family poverty, lack of education, and limited job opportunity, as the boundaries of the "larger" world. These boundaries showed what life paths were open or closed to them, what goals were reachable or untenable, and what choices were permitted or denied. Behind the invisible but "real" stanchions of the larger world, women created their smaller worlds, which became the focus of their life story. It was within the "smaller" world of family, work, and daily joys and sorrows that everyday life was lived. Still, poverty, scant education, poor health, and limited job opportunity bonded poor women to the particular ethnic, gender, and racial norms of the larger world. These norms cause us to focus, in this section, on the concept of oppression.

We acknowledge that a macrolevel of oppression is institutionalized and woven into the fabric of a society that represses certain groups. We suggest, through analysis of our data, that a microlevel of oppression also exists. It is within this microlevel of culturally specific oppression that the women we interviewed situated their experience of hardship. Personal experiences of oppression were perceived as such through relationships with absentee fathers, cruel mothers or stepmothers, abusive or unfaithful husbands, unwanted pregnancies, and drug-dependent children or grandchildren.

The voices of our respondents speak to the experience of oppression as a culturally unique result of society's construction, sanction, and tolerance of poverty. We suggest that although poor women conceived of their life as being related to the social conditions of their larger world, the demands of "getting through" the hardship of their smaller worlds required all their mental and physical energy. In other words, oppression at the microlevel left little time to ponder the cause and effect of oppression at the macrolevel. We present the story of Mrs. Rose, who speaks eloquently to the "trickle down" effect of powerlessness and despair, and the legacy of tragedy and oppression that poverty bequeaths to subsequent generations.

Mrs. Rose is a 75-year-old poor African-American divorcee who gave birth to seven children, five of whom are living. She lives in a subsidized apartment on a busy street in North Philadelphia. Her apartment is large and airy; her kitchen sports an old-fashioned red metal table, sheer green curtains, and several likenesses of Jesus Christ in the forms of pictures and magnets.

Mrs. Rose's experience with loss came early. She recalled her first memory—the moment she realized that her mother abandoned her, her five older sisters, and their father.

I remember she [her mother] took my baby sister to the clinic. She told us—
she said, 'Stand to the window, and watch when I come back. You all be to
the window watching for me.' And we were still to the window when my father came home. He said, 'What you looking for?' We said, 'We're looking for
mamma.' Ain't that something?

Mrs. Rose never saw her mother or youngest sister again. Her mother
died less than a month after she left Philadelphia to begin a new life in New
York. Mrs. Rose believes that her mother's boyfriend poisoned her through
"rootwork."

My father went up [to New York], buried her [mother], and that was it.
We never talked about her after that.

Mrs. Rose described her early family life as "harsh." When she became
pregnant at age 17, her older sister "forced" her to marry the baby's father.
After 5 years of physical abuse, financial hardship, and emotional heartache,
she demanded that her husband leave.

He used to beat me up terrible. Besides, he was not a worker. He did a
day's work every now and then but he didn't have no steady job. Yeah, I had
a terrible time. I worked as a domestic and I cooked. I sold dinners on weekends. When he [husband] came back [from the service] I was hip. I told him
to go when I found out he was going with this girl. My baby was three months
old. I said I'm just tired. So he left.

Although Mrs. Rose bore five children by the time she was 22, she graphically relates her attempts to "get rid" of them.

Every one [child] I had I tried to get rid of. They all came anyway. I took
everything they told me to take. My girlfriends said take turpentine and sugar.
I took everything. Everything I tried to get rid of my kids. Bluein', what you
put in clothes, get in a tub of water and let it all over your head, all the way
down. But they all came anyway. A boy was going around giving abortions
out. He said, 'I'll get rid of the baby.' So I paid him the fifty dollars. And the
next month, I'm still pregnant. Never wanted no children. Every time I look
around I was pregnant. I couldn't get rid of them.

Mrs. Rose's recollection of her pregnancies as unwanted may be shaped
by her suffering as a mother. Her deepest sorrow, the murder of her son
Jules in 1979, capped years of emotional turmoil for both Mrs. Rose and Jules.

My Jules, he used to come to my house every morning before he went to
work. Once he came and stole my pocketbook. He pull up his sleeves and

showed me the needle marks. He said, 'Look, Ma, I been on drugs for six years.' That took everything out of me. He got killed over crack in '79. You never get over nothing like that. You never get over murder. It was a debt over drugs. He was supposed to pay them when he got paid and he didn't pay and they went and killed him. Oh, that thing killed *me.*

Mrs. Rose's oldest daughter died of a heart attack 2 years ago. Her youngest daughter suffers from schizophrenia, and because she has assaulted Mrs. Rose, is not permitted inside her home. Her other children, burdened with financial and familial problems, seldom visit her. When asked what she thinks about her life as a whole, she answered with a sigh, "Everything. The children, the children, the children."

Mrs. Rose was adamant that *she* is not to blame for her children's lifestyles. She contrasted her own behavior as a young mother to what she "could have been."

> When my husband walked off and left me with 5 kids, I could have been the worst bum in the world, but I raised them all, all decent. My kids have never, never seen me in bed. Whenever they got up, my bed was made up and I was up.

Although Mrs. Rose once found her self-esteem in her role as a mother, she has, because of concern for her own safety, estranged herself from her family.

> All my grandkids is on crack. I got 30 grandkids and about 20 of them is on crack. Yep. I don't want them to come around. They don't bother me because they know I don't want them here. Their mother [Mrs. Rose's daughter-in-law], that's the one that got killed [murdered by a drug dealer], she had nine kids. And out of nine, six of them is on it and three of them's in jail. It's too much.

Mrs. Rose suffers no guilt over her family's dissolution. She weaned herself from any emotional closeness to her grandchildren because of their destructive lifestyles. She blames her own children for not transmitting *her* values to their children.

> My children did not send their children to church. My kids had to get out there every Sunday and they know that. I don't know why they didn't do that. And all of them turned out to be nothing.

Mrs. Rose does not succumb to self-reproach despite her anguish, nor does she dwell in the mire of "what could have been." Instead, she turns away from her family circle to find companionship and joy. Several years ago, she set her eye on a dapper widower at a senior center they both attend. At age 72, she searched for and found a new route to self-esteem and meaning in life.

> I said to him, 'I been looking at you a long time.' He said, 'I didn't know nobody was watching me.' I said 'I was.' [Laughter]

Mrs. Rose filled her relational void by adopting a new family. Every Sunday she invites her gentleman friend and his two middle-aged daughters to dinner. She also creates a new self-image by incorporating some former tasks as a mother (homemaker, cook) with the optimism of a woman being courted. When the interviewer asked her about the happiest time in her life, she fingered a dainty gold necklace, a present from her gentleman friend's daughter.

> Right now, since I met this man. I never had a man that was so good to me. He has never said anything out of the way, no kind of way. He's the wonderfulest person I ever met in my whole life, at 72. Best thing that happened to me in my whole life. Honest to God I never knew you could meet nobody like that at 72. God saved him for me.

Mrs. Rose adamantly urged the interviewer to learn from her hard-earned motherwit.

> And no sex period. It's companionship. I never had anything like it. I thought, like in middle age and all, I thought you had to have sex. It's not the answer no more. No, sex is not the answer, baby. Respect is what you want.

Mrs. Rose delights in her platonic relationship. She has sharply severed her notion of happiness from sexual union—an activity that produced seven children who assaulted her identity as a "good" mother." In an act of psychic survival, Mrs. Rose rebuilt her self-esteem by interpreting her relationship with her gentleman friend in at least two ways: (1) he acts as a mirror in which she continues to see herself as familial and relational, and (2) he is a gift from God. Mrs. Rose believes that she was given practical help from an anthropomorphic God who occupies a central position in her life as a friend who is empathetically aware of the details of her life. It is God who knows what she has endured because of her mother's abandonment, her son's murder, and her grandchildren's addictions. It is God who rewarded her trials with a gentleman friend who "respects" her and helps refashion her identity as a worthwhile person.

Mrs. Rose's personal identity is set squarely within the parameters of her historical identity—and is defined by limitations imposed by her class, gender, and race. The microoppression that she suffers due to her family reflects the macrooppression that society inflicts on its most vulnerable members. However, despite the pain of her small world and the encroaching boundaries of the large world, Mrs. Rose takes the choices that are open to her to actively find meaning in life. She decided to climb out of her family's well of tragedy and fashion a new self by giving her love to those she believes reciprocate—her gentleman friend, his daughters, and God. Perhaps this ascent is too steep for Mrs. Rose's children and grandchildren to follow.

THE INTERVIEW

The qualitative interview is an interaction between two people. Within our study, the first question asked of respondents is to tell us their life story. A request to hear the life story is significant to how the interview is framed. Since the framework is broad, narrators often begin with a chronological unfolding of their lives. Sometimes they begin by relating a significant feeling, event, or incident that becomes a salient theme throughout the interview. The interview's open-ended structure is dependent on probes for elucidation, requests for elaboration, and follow-up prompts. Despite a format of questions and answers, the interview remains an interaction that depends on the ability and desire of two people to be open to each other. It is within this interactional, social context of the interview that the narrator creates her story. Its setting is both formal, because of the professional intent of the interview, and personal, because of the private information in its content.

Although respondents initiated the interview, in some cases they seemed confused by the interview's (uncertain) demands. We present the case of Mrs. Curston, who, by wondering why her life story would be of interest to anyone, seemed hesitant to let the interviewer inside her home, gave monosyllabic answers to many questions, hastened the end of the interview, and highlighted the often mysterious process of interviewing.

Mrs. Curston, a 78-year-old poor African-American widow lives in a row home on a small street in North Philadelphia. She and her husband bought this home in 1956. The dilapidation of her front porch typifies the facades of the entire block. However, the lush interior of Mrs. Curston's home contrasts with its outer shabbiness. Plush green carpeting covers the living and dining rooms; wall mirrors add an illusion of size to the small first floor.

Mrs. Curston initiated the interview process by calling the interviewer, requesting to be interviewed. She mentioned that she had learned about the study from a friend and "was interested." A time convenient for Mrs. Curston was settled on. However, when the interviewer rang Mrs. Curston's bell, Mrs. Curston took 10 minutes to answer. She seemed suspicious during the interviewer's introduction. She said that she had tried, without success, to call the friend from whom she learned about the study to ask what the interviewer would be like and about why her life story would be "interesting or important."

Mrs. Curston shares her home with her two teenage greatgrandchildren, ages 14 and 18. Mrs. Curston has been caring for the boys for 7 years. The children's mother is incapable of raising the boys because of drug use. The boy's grandmother, Mrs. Curston's 58-year-old daughter, is too busy with work to keep them in her care. Mrs. Curston receives a modicum of emotional support (talking to the boys man-to-man) from her grandson—an uncle to the boys. She receives financial support for the boys from welfare. Mrs. Curston explained at the outset of the interview: "I don't like handouts. I'm getting welfare because of the boys."

Mrs. Curston's relationship with the boys seems conflictual. She worries about their future because of the drug use that is rampant in the neighborhood.

> I try to keep some change in their hands because they see other guys pulling out money—money from selling drugs.

Mrs. Curston urges them to "get a good education." She disapprovingly related that the eldest child did not take advantage of a scholarship he received. She explained her disappointment.

> I achieved the little I have achieved without higher education. But now you need to go farther than the 12th grade. So, there's a future for them but there's no future for me.

The boys seem to be a source of both hope and vexation for Mrs. Curston. Although she encourages their success, she is reminded, through what the oldest boy was offered and rejected, of the chances that never came her way. She also resents the financial and emotional burden of caring for two youngsters.

> I'd like to see what it would be like to be by myself. I'm too old—there's a time to raise children and a time to cut it. They get on my nerves but they don't want to leave me.

Mrs. Curston's conflict about the boys arose often during the interview, adding ambivalence to many of her answers. Although she conveyed her sure love for the boys by telling stories about their "good natures" and "politeness," she made it clear that she was tired of being their sole caretaker.

She also seemed uncertain about the interview process itself. As the interviewer reached a halfway point in the questions, Mrs. Curston asked, "You should be about finished with me now? You asked me a thousand questions." At times, Mrs. Curston warmed to the interview process, such as when she proudly showed pictures of her family, named each member, and located them in the family tree. She then shared a poignant memory— her mother once asked her to list her dreams.

> I wanted to be a nurse, drive a car and play the piano. I bought me a car.
> I'm a nurse, not a graduated nurse, but a nurse. I accomplished that. But I
> never learned to play the piano. That's a dream that will never come true.

At other times during the interview, Mrs. Curston answered in monosyllables or refused to give details to unusual stories. For example, she was one of 16 (7 of whom survived) children raised by sharecroppers. Although she said that "the family moved around like gypsies" to find work, she offered no details of her childhood other than "it was very hard." Another example of her reticence occurred when she said that "my father got killed in Florida" when she and her siblings were youngsters. When asked about the circumstances of his death, she shrugged. "Some guys killed him."

Mrs. Curston's family came to Philadelphia in 1941 where Mrs. Curston found work as a domestic. She often lived with the family for whom she worked, or arrived early in the morning at her employer's home and left late in the day. Mrs. Curston blames this work schedule for her lack of closeness with her only daughter.

> I did domestic work for the white people. A lot of times it kept me away
> from home because I went to their summer homes. I had to go with them and
> I was away from my daughter. I think about that quite a bit. I think that's
> why my daughter and I aren't too close This bothers me but what could I do?
> I made out somehow. I never went to welfare. I never wanted a handout.

When Mrs. Curston "got tired" of domestic work she entered a training program to become a licensed practical nurse. She "liked working with the sick" and found work as a private duty nurse for several years. To receive "some kind of pension," she sought hospital nursing. Eight years ago she retired from a local hospital after working there for 23 years.

There is a history of shared caregiving throughout Mrs. Curston's family. Mrs. Curston's mother helped her raise her only daughter. Mrs. Curston cared for her first grandchild because her daughter was "wild and young and didn't understand how to raise children." The fact that no one is able to help her raise her greatgrandchildren may add to her ambivalence about their dependence on her.

Mrs. Curston married Mr. Curston when her daughter was 11. Although Mr. Curston is not her daughter's father, Mrs. Curston offered no details concerning either the girl's father or the earliest part of her daughter's life. Although the Curstons were married for 32 years, Mrs. Curston's description of their married life was sparse. She described her late husband as a drinker.

> I met him here [in Philadelphia], but I don't know too much about his life. He was all right. It could have been better.

The happiest and saddest times of Mrs. Curston's life involve only herself. Perhaps her experience with connection has either disappointed her or has involved so much conflict that she prefers solitary pleasures.

> The happiest time was when I was single until I got married. I was happy because I didn't have the responsibility I have today. The saddest time was when I wanted to go to school and I couldn't. I worry about that quite a bit because I always wanted a better education.

Mrs. Curston's worry about her lack of education parallels her concern about her greatgrandchildren's lack of desire for higher education. In this, Mrs. Curston's love for them, worry about them, and annoyance with them conflate. Although she may have found satisfaction through her greatgrandchildren pursuing the route that was denied her, their lack of interest in learning annoys and stymies her. Mrs. Curston is neither emotionally nor financially content. She believes that her financial situation continues to negatively affect the choices that she makes in her life.

> [With more money] I would have a fine home, cars. I'd move. Better neighborhood.

Failed aspirations is another theme in Mrs. Curston's interview. However, she admits that she would like her life to continue "the way it has been" because she is "too old to change." Perhaps an unwillingness or lack of motivation to change convinces her she has "no future."

> There's no future for me no more. I'm on my way out. You're just living from day to day. Is that a future?

She believes that it is better to "keep things as they are" rather than risk making the situation worse; better not to hope than to call up further disappointment. Perhaps a refusal to change and a refusal to anticipate a better future are Mrs. Curston's defenses against past dreams that had not come true, yet continue to haunt her with what "might have been."

Pictures of Mrs. Curston as a girl were displayed on her fireplace mantel. She pointed them out to the interviewer and described her looks as well as her personality in negatives.

> I'm not attractive but I used to be when I was young. When you get older you don't look the same as when you're young. I'm not a very interesting person. I feel a little lonesome. If I could have more friends, but some people— you never get too close.

The above statements, telegraphically relayed, seem to encapsulate Mrs. Curston's thoughts about herself and her life. She is disconnected from the young, pretty, single woman who held dreams about life. She is a different person from the girl in the photographs—unattractive and uninteresting. Perhaps the interview highlighted the events she prefers to forget as well as the attributes she believes she lost or lacks. She shields herself from letting others know that she is "not very interesting," yet is painfully aware that the price for self-protection is lonesomeness.

Mrs. Curston's responses highlighted the interactive nature of the interview. A complex of many feelings, such as annoyance with her greatgrandchildren, guilt for her annoyance, and resentment and shame over failed dreams made her feel vulnerable to the probing eye of the interviewer. Mrs. Curston did not tell her life story in isolation. Whatever she saw within the interviewer and believed about herself caused this particular interaction to take place.

SUMMARY

For most women in our study, the absence or presence of money alone did not determine a self-perception of privilege or poverty. These perceptions were tied, along with "having enough" money (which was idiosyncratically formulated by each respondent), to emotional and relational contentment. Money, in itself, had little bearing on women's sense of past meaning, present achievement, thoughts about the future, and a sense of personal integrity throughout the life course.

For example, Mrs. Pierson perceived herself to be "dirt poor" although she was satisfied with her financial income. Perhaps the term "dirt poor" better describes Mrs. Pierson's shame for past behavior, her inability to connect with her sister during her suffering, and her remorse concerning her mother's painful death. Mrs. Rose, who "gets along" on her present income, reacted to her relational poverty by seeking and finding new familial-type relationships. Mrs. Dickson, like Mrs. Greene, considered herself "privileged" in terms of her current financial *and* emotional circumstances.

Both women attributed their success in life to adopting the values of their parents, to bequeathing those same values to their children, and to their strong sense of cultural and racial dignity and personal agency in maintaining their privileged status for themselves and their children. Mrs. Curston was neither emotionally nor financially content. Greatgrandchildren who "refused" educational advancement caused Mrs. Curston to reflect on her own lack of chances, throughout her life, to "better" herself. Raising teenagers at age 78 caused her to question life's meaning because of her conflictual feelings toward them, her own "tiredness" in caring for them, and her worry about what will happen to them when she is no longer able to keep them.

The above case studies show that women's story lines seldom stand alone, but are multiple and intertwined. Various themes intersect at different loci and times of the life course. Likewise, significant others' story lines intersect and inform respondents' life stories. In this, poverty, for women in our study, is not a single concept. It has cultural, emotional, financial, historical, relational, and spiritual components that do not stand alone, but intermingle complexly. Women use the term poverty to describe aspects of the self through time rather than a financial state.

A "self through time" speaks to a woman's present self-concept in relation to her past. It also addresses women's thoughts about their personal future and those of their children and grandchildren. It is to this subject, and others, that we turn in Chapter 7, Thoughts of the Future.

7

&

Thoughts of the Future

One of the questions asked in the interview schedule was: What do you think the future holds for you? The specificity of the question encourages an equally specific response, with the answer opening a window into the women's worldview. It reveals whether respondents possess a sense of hope, are thinking mainly of "finishing up," or believe that life will continue according to a plan developed earlier. A personal future is built on life circumstances and self-concepts held in the past and present. In this, the future is integrated throughout the life story.

In this chapter we explore women's responses to questions about issues they confront in relation to their future—issues of finitude, death and dying, spirituality and the afterlife, and thoughts about subsequent generations. Because reactions to the above issues are based on women's personal histories, we present, as we have done throughout the book, case studies that show how life events, pervasive themes, and self-concepts inform thoughts of the future.

We present the case of Mrs. Emil, whose grim childhood wove feelings of fear throughout her life and her narrative, and resulted in a reluctance to anticipate future joys. Mrs. Emil, a 77-year-old poor Caucasian widow, lives in a suburban subsidized housing facility. She met the interviewer in the lobby of the building, where residents take turns as volunteer receptionists. Mrs. Emil, who is slim, straight, and husky-voiced, led the way to her cozy basement apartment. When the interviewer asked Mrs. Emil if she also answers the phones and greets visitors, she answered, "Not anymore. I don't like to be in the center of anything."

Mrs. Emil was widowed 15 years ago, 2 years after the Emils moved to the senior facility. Her son and daughter and their respective families live in nearby suburbs. Mrs. Emil sees her children occasionally and reiterated throughout the interview that they "would do anything for me."

Mrs. Emil's description of her early life was grim. After her mother's death at age 25, when Mrs. Emil was 5 years old, she was placed, along with

151

her 2-year-old sister, first in an orphanage and then in various foster homes. When her father remarried, Mrs. Emil and her sister were brought home to a "wicked stepmother." Mrs. Emil lived in "constant fear" during her childhood, afraid of her stepmother's beatings and her father's absences. Mrs. Emil remembers crying when her father left for work, hanging onto his arm and begging him not to leave.

> My father knew what was going on, but he was in love with her I guess. A childhood I never had. I had one doll and when the doll broke, that was it. I didn't have much of a childhood. When I was 17, it was the last time she [stepmother] ever hit me because then I spoke up. But I had a fear of her even after I was married.

Mrs. Emil's stepmother, a beautician, eventually bought a beauty shop in North Philadelphia, where Mrs. Emil "was forced to work for no pay." She "hated" this work and described this period of life as a time "I lived in fear." To earn money for herself, she also worked part time in a factory and baby sat for neighbors.

Mrs. Emil met her husband, who worked in his family's grocery store (which was near the beauty shop), when she was 19. They married 2 years later. Mr. and Mrs. Emil lived in an extended family household behind his parents' grocery store. The family included their two children, Mr. Emil's mother and father, an unmarried uncle, and an unmarried sister.

The Emils sold the grocery store after her father-in-law's death and the Emils lived "privately" in a small apartment for the first time in their married lives. This period was difficult financially. Since Mr. Emil could not find work, Mrs. Emil took "whatever she could find." However, without the buffer of Mrs. Emil's mother-in-law, her marriage faltered.

> My husband drank but he was a good man. I often wanted to leave him, but for the children I stayed and because he was not a mean person. See, he was never, I can't say he wasn't a father, but everything was up to me. I often felt like there was no togetherness. I was there, his mother was there and we waited on him. He never wheeled the baby in the coach. My daughter for years didn't accept him as a father because of the early years. I mean she wasn't hateful. We weren't a family to curse or holler or anything like that. I did the hollering. He wouldn't fight back.

In the mid-1950s the Emils bought a grocery store and lived in its rear apartment for 17 years. She remembers the heyday of the store as the best financial time in her life despite the overwhelming work and responsibility. Mr. Emil's increasing debility due to phlebitis forced her to "do everything in the store." Finally, repeated burglaries and her "tiredness" caused the

Emils to sell the store, at a loss, in 1964, and buy a "tiny" home nearby. Mrs. Emil worked as a clerk in a check-cashing business until the couple came to live, in 1980, in her present apartment. Mr. Emil "hated leaving the neighborhood" and died 2 years after the move.

Financially, "things were okay" for the first 10 years after her husband's death. However, Mrs. Emil's monthly social security check of $550 does not rise in pace with her rent and utility bills. Although she stated that she was "satisfied with the little I have" she regards the present as the worst financial time in her life.

> It's hard for me to pay my medical insurance. I'm just making it. At times I would like to have different things, but I know I have to have my money for bills. I say, 'Please God, don't let my dentures break.'

Mrs. Emil described herself as "very independent." Like most poor women interviewed, she exercised her emotional and financial independence by active choice. With limited funds, she chose which pleasures she would accept or forego.

> If we [acquaintances] go out for a drive and they want to go for dinner I have to know if I've got the money to go for dinner with them or am I just going to have a piece of cake and coffee. They don't know that. I just say, 'I had dinner. All I want is cake.' But I'm satisfied with the little I have. I'm comfortable. I'd like to have fancier things, but I'm happy with what I have.

Due to a family disagreement, Mrs. Emil is estranged from her only sister. Despite "feeling close" with her children, their busy schedules preclude seeing them often. Although her neighbors are women similar to her in age, income, and religious background, she has, by choice, few friends.

> I don't want to be alone all the time. But I don't get overly friendly anymore. It's not worth it. You get friendly and then they die [Chuckle].

Mrs. Emil explained that the passing of several good friends deeply grieved her. Therefore, rather than open herself to this kind of sorrow, she protects herself against loss by remaining alone. Although she often feels lonely, imposed isolation is preferable to anticipated grief. Perhaps Mrs. Emil's reluctance to make friends is also intertwined with negative thoughts about herself.

> I don't feel that I'm the brightest of people. To hold a conversation, it's hard for me to speak out. I hesitate because I don't know if I know the right answers. I'm not a worldly person, but I like to dress nice.

Throughout the interview, Mrs. Emil weighed the negatives of her personality and lack of financial resources against the positives of having "a
nice place to live" and her children's affection. In summing up her life, Mrs.
Emil said philosophically:

> I got my food; I got my bed. It could have been better. But I feel I survived.
> But I have wonderful kids. A lot of people around here have families that
> don't come near them. I guess I believe if a person has love, it's more impor-
> tant than money.

Mrs. Emil, like many respondents, distinguished between "types" of
poverty. When asked what sorts of things she thinks about in quiet moments,
she answered, "I enjoy being with my children." Mrs. Emil seems to live
in a small, balanced world where the love of her children acts as reimbursement for financial poverty and a perceived lack of positive personal
traits. When asked if she ever held a dream or vision about how her life
would unfold, she laughed.

> Yeah, to meet a tall handsome fellow with a lot of money. But this is it. I
> guess years ago if you would meet someone and have children, that was the
> goal. And my husband was tall and handsome. We didn't have a mansion
> but we lived comfortably. I guess I didn't think too much about it. I was con-
> tent just having peace. I didn't want a mansion, I just didn't want the fear
> of—Is someone going to beat me?

When asked what she thought the future might hold, Mrs. Emil laughed
again.

> *Mrs. Emil:*   How much more do I have? I don't know. What could it
>   be? I just hope that if I live longer that I don't become a
>   burden. My burial arrangements are made.
> *Interviewer:* Do you believe in an afterlife?
> *Mrs. Emil:*   No I don't. But if I come back I want to be a bear so I can
>   hibernate. I have good children. That was my life.

The above answer echoes Mrs. Cummings' (mentioned in Chapter 4)
affirmation of contentment after a confession of deprivation. Mrs. Emil's
loving children compensate for an afterlife. Also, because she has based a
projection of the future on her past, the afterlife might contain something
that would hurt her. Indeed, Mrs. Emil's lack of hope about her fate mirrors
her distant past. The abuse she endured in childhood continues to haunt
her and shapes her perception of days to come. Therefore, hibernation is
preferable to what she might find in an afterlife. Perhaps her paraphrased

question—Is someone going to hurt me—makes a future of sleep more appealing than consciousness.

ISSUES OF SPIRITUALITY

As mentioned in Chapter 4, Strategies and Techniques of Coping with Poverty, many respondents, especially poor women, used their religion and spirituality as a primary means to cope with hardship. This method of coping discloses differences between religion and spirituality and how each of these constructs help women cope with their hardship. For our purposes, we are defining religion as adherence to the tenets of an organized religion. In this sense, religion has an *external* focus, with the emphasis on "keeping" the guidelines and rules of the doctrines of the denomination, i.e., publicly adhering to the religion's system of beliefs and worshipping through the religion's liturgy. We are using Pargament's (1997) definition of spirituality as a sense of the sacred. Spirituality has an *internal* focus, with the emphasis on spoken words or prayers addressed privately to an individualized concept of a Supreme Being and beliefs held quietly that *may* be contrary to a religious doctrine. For women interviewed, their spirituality often combined the beliefs of an organized religion with a belief system idiosyncratically built from their particular life circumstances.

To show the intricacies of a personally constructed spirituality, we present the case of Mrs. Eldredge, a 75-year-old poor Caucasian widow who lives in a subsidized apartment facility. Mrs. Eldredge's small apartment was striking; fine art reproductions cover the living room walls. Its sophistication contrasts with the apron-covered, anklet-clad dress of Mrs. Eldredge.

Mrs. Eldredge lost two of her three children. One son was killed in an auto accident in 1964 when he was 21 years old; Mrs. Eldredge's only daughter recently died from breast cancer at age 55. Her surviving son is a 54-year-old artist who lives with his family in Maine. The weekend before the interview Mrs. Eldredge attended her granddaughter's wedding. It was held in the same church at which her daughter's funeral Mass took place 6 months earlier. Mrs. Eldredge commented that returning to the church for a happy event evoked "mixed" feelings.

Mrs. Eldredge comes from a "family with money" that was lost during the Depression. When she became pregnant at age 18, she married the father of her child.

> I liked him from the moment I saw him. But I now realize that sex played the largest role in our marriage. He was a man who couldn't handle responsibility.

Mr. Eldredge enlisted in the Navy during the Second World War. Their second child was just 6 weeks old. After the war, he lived with his family until 1948, when he left again and eventually filed for divorce. Mrs. Eldredge stated that although their marriage lasted 10 years, she actually lived with her husband "very briefly. Only long enough to have three children."

Mrs. Eldredge named her married life as the worst time in her life financially and recalled "going hungry many a day." Although her husband worked as a roofer's helper, he "never held a steady job." Mrs. Eldredge does not blame her husband's lack of ambition for the hardship of her life. When asked who or what controls how her life unfolded, she answered:

> You are ruling your own destiny, but most people are not aware of it. Things happen to you and you have a decision to make and you can go one way or the other. Sure my life would have been different if I had behaved myself and not let him touch me. It was my fault that I was out of control.

Mrs. Eldredge connected her misbehavior with her impoverishment. She believed that being *sexually* "out of control" as an unmarried teen ultimately determined the *financial* course of her life. She is convinced that worse punishment awaits today's youth. Later in the interview, when asked whether future generations will be better off financially than she is, she answered definitively:

> I think we don't have too many future generations. I feel terribly sorry for people because of the television, the filth. There is no innocence. They're honoring the devil. I think the end [of the world] will be in not too long. God can be forgiving, but only to an extent. He's not forgiving and forgiving and forgiving.

It is notable that for Mrs. Eldredge, one attribute of God is limited forgiveness. It is also noteworthy that her concept of innocence or its lack is linked to sexual behavior. Mrs. Eldredge has created a God whose attributes are shaped by *her* perceived strengths and weaknesses. She believes herself to be closest to God when she is "good," i.e., when she sacrifices worldly happiness for what she believes God expects of her.

For example, in 1955 Mrs. Eldredge suffered a nervous breakdown. When asked what precipitated it, she answered, "I fell in love." Mrs. Eldredge described a "confused" period in her life in which she had an affair with a divorced man, confessed her perceived sin to a priest, and was instructed never to see the man again. Owing to her decision to obey the priest and break off the affair, she endured a breakdown. Interestingly, Mrs. Eldredge names this same period as the happiest time in her life.

> December 2, 1955 [was the happiest day of my life]. December 1 was the day I went to confession [to confess the affair]. And I came home and I was terribly upset. I went to bed and I'm not much of a crier, but I was broken-hearted. And that night, about two o'clock in the morning was the happiest time of my life and I won't go into any more details. I was consoled by God, let's put it like that.

God, through her priest, demanded that Mrs. Eldredge give up this relationship. After she did so, God rewarded her with a greater happiness—intimate consolation. However, she no longer practices the Catholic faith that forced her to end her love affair. In light of her "falling away" from the Church, the interviewer asked Mrs. Eldredge if she would make the same decision if she could go back in time. She answered:

> More so. I had a choice. And I chose God. See, we make a choice for him or for something else. I chose God. We do have choices, and I made the harder choice.

Mrs. Eldredge's choice for God in 1955 determined the course of her earthly life as well as her beliefs about the afterlife. When Mrs. Eldredge asked what the future holds for her, she answered:

> I can't wait until it's time to go to heaven and I feel I'll get there. I think the big thing was when I did give up Ted [the divorced man] and put God first.

Mrs. Eldredge could not find God in human love and amid worldly happiness. To her, God stood alone: unforgiving of her weakness and comforting her secretly in the night after she paid for her moral lapse with a mental breakdown.

Mrs. Eldredge also named her marriage as the worst emotional period of her life. Like many respondents, she weaves her sense of financial hardship with her emotional dissatisfaction.

> I've often thought about the fact that I had to get married. It was such an ugly period in my life. Those few years were very ugly. I still regret that I wasn't better behaved.

It is noteworthy that Mrs. Eldredge's only regret in older age is her misbehavior of 60 years ago. Mrs. Eldredge is convinced that "there was nothing really good about it [marriage], except the children." Despite her remorse about her marriage, she did make peace with her husband just before his death.

He was dying, but I didn't know that. His sister told me later that he said
that myself and the three children appeared to him at the foot of the bed and
he asked us to forgive him for what he had done. The same night he appeared
to me. I thought he was dead; I didn't know he was still living. He looked
like the wrath of God. He said, 'Can I go home now? I'm sorry.' I said yes. It
wasn't a dream. I was wide awake.

Mrs. Eldredge felt no sympathy for her husband's sufferings before his
death. She believed that his pain was the payment required for his wrongdoing, especially in regard to "not supporting" his children. This indicates
that Mrs. Eldredge believes God shows more justice than mercy; God exacts
stiff punishments for transgressions.

After a lifetime of "just getting by," Mrs. Eldredge named the present as
the best financial time in her life.

For the first time in my life I have not had a financial worry. I have enough
to bury me. I don't have much but I don't want much. I haven't any huge
amount of interest in money.

She named the present as an emotionally satisfying time as well. She loves
living alone after a life spent caring and being responsible for others. She
has reached a stage in life

where I can't worry too much about others. Up until now my life has been
devoted to my family. I don't want the responsibility of family any more. I
don't intend to get involved anymore. A lot of people, even around here,
confide in me. And a lot of people come to me for guidance. I think I've done
my share. I would be just as happy not to be bothered with that for the rest
of my life. I've had enough. See, I'm completely independent, and not a
dreamer. I'm a very practical, responsible person. I have no need to confide
or talk to anyone. I do my talking quietly.

Mrs. Eldredge happily admits that she has no personal goals. "Nothing
affects me personally any more. That part of my life is finished. I'll be happy
to go [die]." Indeed, she holds even that great unknown, her own death,
firmly in hand.

Mrs. Eldredge: I have no fear of death whatsoever. You'll die, you'll be
judged and you'll go to heaven, purgatory or hell.
Interviewer: How about for you? What do you believe will come
after this life for you?
Mrs. Eldredge: In my house are many mansions. St. Theresa said that
all the flowers in God's garden are content with what

they are. In other words, you will be content with what you have. You won't have what everybody else has. There's no question about that. Some people are going to do much better than many people. I look forward to it. I think of it quite a bit. I feel pretty certain that I know more than I should. You know the old expression, to go through the eye of the needle? Well, I think I've been through the eye of the needle.

Interviewer: Can you tell me what you mean?

Mrs. Eldredge: Simply that I look forward to the time when I'll be called home, literally. I'm very fond of Almighty God. He's a pretty good kid.

Mrs. Eldredge's belief in a personal God and in the afterlife God planned for her causes her to face her own death not only with equanimity, but with anticipation. Her steadfast faith also allowed her to trust in God's wisdom while facing her daughter's painful death from cancer.

Mrs. Eldredge: I am completely at peace regarding the death of my daughter. We had 7 months where my granddaughter and I really nursed her. So we had a real good time. I'm very peaceful where she's concerned She died a good death. In fact, I can see a lot worse things happening to my daughter than that.

Interviewer: Like what?

Mrs. Eldredge: I can think of a lot worse things. We won't go into that. God knows. It was her time. I definitely feel that way. And I don't ever question it.

Mrs. Eldredge believes that her sense of humor also eased her grief. Just before she visited her dying daughter in the hospital for the last time, she leased a Cadillac from a car dealer.

It took me on a different plane. It took me out of it. She knew she was dying. And then I went in with my usual joking self and told her about the Cadillac. Well, she got a kick out of that. She knew I knew and I knew she knew.

Mrs. Eldredge distinguishes her spiritual acts, which include "quiet talking," from the prayers and rituals of organized religion. She no longer attends Mass and has "no time" for the group of Catholic women living in her building who get together for a daily rosary prayer. She describes herself as spiritual—which includes an "intimate" relationship with God. The interviewer asked her how and when this relationship with God began.

I think my very first personal relationship with God—and I didn't realize it at the time, but years later I could pinpoint where it happened. It was June 4, 1944, D-Day. And I was making a novena to the Sacred Heart. And I was in church that night and my husband was over in England. And I was kneeling in church and I thought, you know, if Howard were to die now, I'd get the 10,000 dollar life insurance. I knew it was a horrible marriage. It was never going to last. It just would make my life—everything would be fine. And in fact it was so clear and it looked so good. And then a thought occurred to me, well you know, he's only young. He's only 27 and he hasn't even had a chance to live. He grew up in the Depression. And I prayed that he would live. And that I think basically pinpointed everything. I had a choice. And we do have choices in our lives and I took the harder choice because I was the one who suffered, not him. The other looked so good, for him to die, and it would have. I would have been free.

It is interesting that Mrs. Eldredge believed her prayer to be so potent that it would decide her husband's fate. Her prayer also reflects her either/ or mindset. Because she made the "harder choice," she was rewarded with a blossoming spirituality. If she had prayed for her husband to die, *she* would have changed the course of both their lives. In this, she seems to be the more effectual partner in her relationship with God. The plan of her life is not random or mysterious for Mrs. Eldredge, but follows a pattern of cause and effect that *she* initiates.

I think most everything that happens in this world is the result of things that we have done. But still, out of a bad decision, good can come. See, all people are born with a conscience. Some people have a delicate conscience. I have a strong conscience.

Making a choice between opposing forces, such as good or evil, God or the married man, praying for the life or the death of her husband, seems a primary lens through which Mrs. Eldredge views her world. In this tidy landscape, Mrs. Eldredge is like one of St. Theresa's flowers, content with her lot, but convinced that her "lot" is determined by *her* choices. Mrs. Eldredge definitively named the purpose of life:

Mrs. Eldredge: To know, love and serve God in this life and be happy with him in the next, and maybe to bring a few along with me along the way

Interviewer: How would you do that?

Mrs. Eldredge: By being a good example; to let others see God in you.

Interviewer: Do you see God in others?

Mrs. Eldredge: [Pause] I can't say that I do.

THE AFTERLIFE

Women's thoughts about the afterlife were often shaped not by the tenets of their religious denominations, but by their personal experiences throughout life. Crucial events, found or missed opportunities, and the deaths of significant others, especially their mothers and children, led women to construct ideas of the afterlife that were unique interpretations of reward, punishment, or simply a time of rest. In this, life events informed personal spirituality and reshaped religious belief and practice. We present the case of Mrs. Davies, who displays an idiosyncratic version of the afterlife that combines her past experiences with her present concerns. Mrs. Davies is a 78-year-old poor African-American widow who lives in a narrow, dilapidated, two story home in North Philadelphia. Her house is one of three that remain on a street that resembles a bombing site.

Mrs. Davies is small in stature but not frail. She answered the door amid barks of an off-white, sweater-clad poodle named Gus. The inside of Mrs. Davies' home reflects her poverty and her disablement—torn shades cover the front windows; discolored linoleum barely hides wood-planked floors. Years of structural and cosmetic neglect render the house bleak and splintery.

Mrs. Davies sat at a cluttered kitchen table placed between the two front windows in the living room. An elderly cat, Gert, sat on the table between Mrs. Davies and the interviewer. Gus kept watch at Mrs. Davies' feet. Her table and chair comprise Mrs. Davies' primary living space. She does her paperwork here, and from this vantage point she can see the comings and goings of her neighbors as well as strangers. Also, her friends are able to keep watch on her. At 11 a.m. on the day of the interview, a woman peered in the window, waved, and nodded. Mrs. Davies explained that this daily ritual allows her neighbor to know that she is all right. A half hour later, carpenters from the factory a half block away knocked on her door, ready to refurbish her vestibule as part payment for Mrs. Davies' cleaning the factory's offices. Contrary to what the interviewer initially thought, Mrs. Davies is part of an active community in which its members share mutual assistance and concern. Mrs. Davies said proudly, "I'm the oldest one on the street."

Mrs. Davies was born and raised in Philadelphia, the oldest of three children. Mrs. Davies' two younger brothers are deceased. She remembers when she lived in a thriving community that included varied ethnic groups.

I spent the majority of my life in these three blocks. And now they have all them black schools, all them white schools. We were all buddies, the Polish and the Irish girls. Not only did we go to school together, we went to each other's houses after school. On Saturday we went to the movies. The only thing about that was the movies was segregated. We'd sit together regardless. They'd [ushers] come down and they'd say you're not supposed to be there; you're supposed to be over there. When they'd come down again I'd be in the same place [Laughter] because the Polack said to me, 'Don't you move a damn bit. We came together and we'll sit together.'

Although Mrs. Davies' childhood friends eventually married and moved away to "all white areas," she recalled this period as happy and the neighborhood as "beautiful." She liked school, loved learning, and planned to continue her education beyond high school.

I went to Eastern High. After graduation I went to work because that's when my mother got sick. I worked in the YWCA. I worked on several lots in North Philadelphia as a phys ed teacher and I worked at the Youth Center. Then I decided I would take my chances to go to college. I wanted to be an obstetrician because our doctor, a woman from Guyana, told me that I had the hands for an obstetrician. When I started at college my mother began to have [health] trouble.

Mrs. Davies suspended her dreams of medical school to care for her mother full time. She minimized her disappointment at being unable to complete her education and realize her dream.

I seem to be a person that if I can't do it, sooner or later I make myself satisfied. I worry for a while, whatever it is. Then after a while I say, 'Well, if I can I can; if I can't I can't.'

Mrs. Davies lived with her mother in a house two blocks away from her present home. She enjoyed single life and admits that she "never really wanted to get married in the first place." Mrs. Davies met her husband

at a neighborhood birthday party. I liked him but just as a friend. Evidently he liked me differently. I had to tell him that I was older [10 years] than him and I didn't want him. But he kept right on after me. [Laughter] We got married in 1950. I told him I wasn't raising children. I was 34. I got pregnant with three and lost all three of them. Once I said something about adoption. 'No sir,' he said. 'If I didn't make it, I don't want it.' And that was the end of it.

When asked to describe her husband, Mrs. Davies said:

He was good. He brought the money home. But he had one weakness, he gambled. And on the weekends he drank. He wasn't mean to me or anything. The only thing we fought a lot about was he gambled up his end of the money and then he'd come looking for my end. Loan me, loan me, loan me. [Pause] Still, it was nice. I have lots of things to laugh about.

In 1954 the Davies bought the home where Mrs. Davies currently lives. Mrs. Davies' mother, who helped the couple financially throughout their married lives, lived with them. Mrs. Davies recalls this period with ambivalence. Although she was glad she had the time and strength to physically care for her ailing mother, she resented not being able to "go out" to work. Her mother and husband colluded in making decisions for her.

Bernie didn't want me to work and I had to go along with it because my mother was on his side. He was the man of the house. And my mother loved him. He could do no wrong.

Mr. Davies, a long-distance truck driver, died at age 38 from a stroke. He suffered two previous heart attacks that rendered him unable to work for several months. She poignantly remembers the night her husband died.

I think he knew when he was going to die because he began to talk silliness to me. See, we had to put the bed down on the first floor because he couldn't walk the steps. He said, 'But we have to keep the shades down because everybody outside will see what we're doing.' I said, 'Just worry about getting well, don't you be worrying about that junk!' Then he started shaking and I said, 'Are you going to stay with me, baby?' Then he died.

Mrs. Davies names the period of her marriage as the best financial time of her life and widowhood the worst. Although her neighborhood was deteriorating rapidly, she was unable to move. She also had difficulty reinstating herself in the work world. This complex of factors triggered a major depression.

I was stuck. I couldn't move. And time had passed and things were different in the work world. It was a terrible time. I lost my mother first, then my husband. Then I was in this house by myself. I used to stay awake at night and go to sleep in the morning when it was light. I'd put a pillow in the window and that's how I got to know those fellows [carpenters] that work over there. When they came to work in the morning I'd be on my knees, laying on the pillow in the window. The foreman from the factory over there said, 'How would you like to come over here and work? We have five offices in the front. They need dusting.'

Mrs. Davies began cleaning the factory offices and rest rooms 22 years ago and continues to work a few hours each week. Although she has difficulty bending and stretching due to arthritis, she believes that the benefits of working, such as "seeing friendly faces and talking" outweigh resting painful joints.

> It was a God send. I said, well, thank God I got a roof and I got heat and I can pay my bills. God is good to me. I retired once about 10 years ago. I'm not going to stay in this house with these four walls. I went right back over. I just don't go as often.

Mrs. Davies diligently oversees her limited finances in order to pay bills and keep up her old home. Her income barely exceeds her outlay. When the interviewer asked her how she manages financially, she answered, "Determination, that's all I know." However, a book club's monthly invoice in the pile of bills to be paid shows that although Mrs. Davies is impoverished, she refuses to be victimized by her circumstances and continues her "love of learning" by buying a book each month. "That's my book club. I do that for me!"

Mrs. Davies attends services at the nearby Baptist Church two times a month. Her reasons for joining a church are eschatological as well as practical. She does not apologize for the pragmatic motives behind her actions.

> I join a church to have a church home. Somewhere when I leave here they could lay my body out. That's important to me. I told God the reason why I'm going to church. I told him that every Sunday that church opens I'm not walking in the front door.

Mrs. Davies relationship with God is egalitarian and reciprocal. She believes that God is a friend of long-standing who holds a powerful position both in this world and the next. This friendship with a powerful "Other" empowers her to have hope that she will "never hit rock bottom." She trusts that God not only knows about her hardship, but provides substantive help during times she is most needful.

> The things that I went through, with my mother, my husband, I think God traveled along with me because I think that I wouldn't be here and able to walk around and whatnot without him. I think that some of the things I have done he's blessing me now for. I think he knows what I'm going through and he's not going to let me go down but so far because he knows I'm not that bad.

Mrs. Davies believes that God is purposefully instantiated within her everyday world as an incidence of good luck, or disguised as a happy coincidence.

Sometimes things look pretty dreary. And maybe later on, in a couple days things perk up, my little quarter number will come out and I'll say, 'Thank you, God.'

Mrs. Davies' thoughts about dying, death, and an afterlife combine fear of dying, worry about her "children," and a longing for love and affection. She believes that she will be repaid for her selflessness with an untroubled afterlife. Her hopes about an afterlife integrate those creatures who give her so much pleasure in this life—her pets—and show her strong identification with them. When asked about an afterlife, Mrs. Davies paused, then shrugged.

Dying doesn't scare me, but it worries me. I don't want to leave the animals here. Nobody is going to treat them like me. I don't want nobody being nasty to them. I mean my children are something. That's what I call them. My children. [Laughter] But I sort of believe in coming back in some form or other. If I come back I want to be little and cute like my dog for somebody to take care of me. I don't want to be a stray dog. I want to be little and cute for somebody to love me. I think I deserve that.

Despite Mrs. Davies' adherence to the Baptist religion, which does not hold reincarnation as a tenet of belief, she believes she will "come back." The manner in which she will "return" speaks to her sense of deservedness and her belief in God's ultimate justice. For Mrs. Davies, religion is the place she visits—her church home—both literally and metaphorically. Her spirituality—her private beliefs about God and the afterlife—is the place she lives.

We return now to the narrative of Mrs. Custer, first presented in Chapter 3, who channeled her strong desire for success into another arena—the afterlife. Mrs. Custer admitted that two incidents that occurred in mid-life constructed her present spirituality. One was the realization that she was not going to reap material rewards for her continuous labor.

I began to read the Bible when I was in my late 50s. Then having things began not to even matter. Because whatever I had it wasn't going to prepare me for the hereafter. When I was young I wanted to have the this, the that, but I don't long for them now. They're not worth losing your soul over. Some people would sell their soul to the devil for the things of this world. And I'm not sure if I had the opportunity if I wouldn't have did it when I was younger.

Mrs. Custer said that her mother's accidental death also led her to question her materialistic goals. After her mother's death, Mrs. Custer worked fewer hours at her factory job and decided to store up spiritual rather than material treasures.

My mother was killed in a car crash. This man [who was driving the car] was wrong and God will deal with him. Actually though, I couldn't sleep, so I turned to the Bible and started to go to church.

These two events—mid-life awareness that she was "never going to be rich" and the recognition of her own mortality due to her mother's sudden death—led Mrs. Custer to review her life, revise her goals, and rechannel her strong drive to succeed. Recharting her life course convinced her that despite thwarted efforts, unnoticed talents, and impoverishment, her life had meaning. Toward the end of the interview, Mrs. Custer admitted that she "just now" realizes that God "walked" with her during the worst times in her life. "He never left me nor forsaked me."

Currently, Mrs. Custer's life revolves around church duties and study of the Bible. Mrs. Custer seems not so much to enjoy the camaraderie of church sisters as much as she revels in the "hard work" of study. She rerouted her high level of energy, intelligence, and ambition into "learning" the Bible. Although Mrs. Custer revised her goals, she did not change her method of achieving success. She claims the spiritual promises of scripture with the same single-mindedness that she once pursued material goods. Mrs. Custer was surprised when asked if she believed in an afterlife.

In heaven? Oh, yes. If I didn't believe that I'd go charging into the Delaware River. I have to believe in that. If I didn't believe that what would the purpose be? We're only here for a few days! What's here? Then in a few days you're hushed up and you're gone.

Despite material disappointment and poverty, Mrs. Custer conceived of a way to succeed. She reconstructed her goals to accommodate her lack of material achievement without losing her dream of "making it." She used her spirituality as a blueprint to resketch her original aims and a means to broaden their parameters. For Mrs. Custer, if you work hard you *will* succeed—in the afterlife.

PARANORMAL EXPERIENCES

Many respondents, both Caucasian and African-American, shared their experiences of the paranormal, such as seeing visions of dead loved ones while awake, dreams in which the deceased communicated about an important matter, or prescience concerning the death of a family member. Although paranormal experiences occurred inconsistently and usually in relation to a traumatic event, such as the death of a child, respondents' systems of belief and sensitivity to extrasensory perception permitted an openness to this type of experience. We introduce Mrs. McFadden, whose appreciation for intuitive knowledge typifies many women's responses to paranormal events.

Mrs. McFadden is a poor 79-year-old Caucasian divorcee who lives in a modestly furnished apartment in a subsidized housing facility. She has fair coloring and speaks with an Irish brogue.

Mrs. McFadden's salient personality trait is her ability to connect quickly with others, and therefore to evoke a positive response from them. She appears to understand the feelings of others, and is able to articulate her own.

Mrs. McFadden is proud of her Irish heritage; she believes it bequeathed both positive and negative characteristics to her. She explained that Irish people are warm and sensitive, and are therefore prone to the political and religious suffering that has been inflicted on them by England.

Mrs. McFadden keeps many "souvenirs" of Ireland in her cozy apartment. A green and white afghan made by her beloved grandmother, colorful Irish pottery, and scores of photographs of relatives in Ireland remind Mrs. McFadden of "home." Even her talkative parrot evokes memories of Ireland. "Just like an Irishman," she commented when the parrot whistled as the interviewer walked into the living room. A painting above Mrs. McFadden's sofa—that of a lone cliff battling an angry sea—symbolizes her brief childhood in Ireland. Seeing the interviewer look at the picture, she commented, "I reminisce about the sea. I think it haunts one." Although she has lived in America for over 60 years, Ireland is home to Mrs. McFadden. She hopes to return one day and eventually be buried there. Her apartment is her personal museum—she displays items that show where her treasure and her heart remain.

Mrs. McFadden lived "only briefly" with her mother, father, and older sister in Scotland where her father hoped to find work. Learning that the family was in "dire straits," Mrs. McFadden's maternal grandfather brought his daughter and the two girls home to Ireland. They were permitted to live "free in a furnished thatched cottage" provided his daughter and grandchildren "never go back to him" (Mrs. McFadden's father). Mrs. McFadden never saw her father again, nor did she learn where he "ended up" or "even when he died." Not knowing him has "always bothered" her. Her mother told her very little about the man she "probably still loved."

> Once, when we were walking, she pointed to a man and said, 'He looks like your father.' [Pause, then laughter] Oh, well, all Irish people have sad stories to tell.

Mrs. McFadden's mother was one of 13 children and a talented seamstress. Desperately unhappy after she left her husband, she eventually emigrated to America to find work. Mrs. McFadden and her sister remained with their grandparents in the cottage by the sea.

The two daughters were called to America when Mrs. McFadden was 15. They settled in Philadelphia with relatives and made the area their home for the rest of their lives. She remembers this time of her life as painful because she could not measure up to the standard of feminine beauty in America. Her anguish over her physical "inadequacies" is strongly felt after 60 years.

> I was heartbroken at leaving my grandmother, but I never mentioned it to my mother. And when I got here! I saw myself as so horrible looking. And I wanted so much to look like an American. American girls were so slender and pretty and they had nice slender legs and I had heavy legs. A lot of Irish people have heavy legs. See, I'm a country woman. When you're a country woman you have to have sturdy legs.

As Mrs. McFadden reminisces about her adolescence, she reveals the integral nature of her body image to her identity. As a youngster, she was embarrassed by her brogue as well as her "sturdy" appearance. Mrs. Mc-Fadden did not like school or learning; her shyness alienated classmates. She finally left school at age 16 to become a mother's helper. She does not regret the path she chose; she named her lifelong career of child care as one of her major accomplishments.

> I always loved children and I envied the girls who took care of children in Ireland. When I was little no one told me they loved me, so I always told them [the children for whom she cared] I loved them. Many of them called me Mama. One little boy, an angel, he told me, I love you. What more can you get out of life than that?

Mrs. McFadden met her husband at an Irish club when she was 20 years old. Although the beginning of their relationship was "so much fun," becoming a father to five boys in quick succession took an emotional toll on Mr. McFadden.

> Things didn't work out too well. I think he became jealous of the boys. I think that's what initiated our problems. He was pretty good when they were little. Later, I was afraid he would hurt the boys. I had to call the police a couple of times. And he was extremely jealous of me. He became very abusive, with abusive language. He was a beer drinker. When he drank he was unusually ugly to everyone. Besides, he had a lady friend even before the separation.

Mr. McFadden worked sporadically and lost several jobs due to drinking. He often neglected or refused to pay bills, using the money for drink instead. The McFaddens' home life was financially and emotionally turbulent. Drinking, and the violence that came in its wake, became commonplace. After 24 years of an unhappy marriage, Mrs. McFadden left her husband because of a chance remark made by her eldest son, Paul.

> Paul said to me, 'How much longer are you going to take this?' That was all I needed, a little jolt like that.

Mrs. McFadden's self-esteem was fragile. Staying with an abusive husband seemed safer than forging ahead on her own until her son's comment "woke [her] up." After their separation, Mrs. McFadden harbored no resentment toward her husband. She blames his "mistakes" on his drinking and believes that he inherited his predilection for alcohol from his own father. She stayed in touch with her husband after their separation. In fact, she visited him in the hospital just before he died. "I said, 'I always loved you, Jim McFadden.' 'Oh, heck,' he said, 'I know that.'"

Despite the fact that Mr. McFadden worked sporadically, Mrs. McFadden named the period right after her separation from her husband as the worst financial time in her life. Her primary income came from caring for other people's children.

> He gave support money for the younger children, but it was not really enough. So, the house was always filled with children. Mine and other people's. [Laughter] I loved it.

Mrs. McFadden is "very content" with her present circumstances. Her only daughter, Brigid, "helps out" from time to time with money, gifts, and transportation to and from doctors' appointments. In return, Mrs. McFadden often travels to Brigid's home to care for her two small children while Brigid works. When asked when the best financial time of her life occurred, she answered:

> Well, really and truly, there never was any great time, you know. I never had much.

The McFaddens raised their children in various rented homes in Northwest Philadelphia. One of her sorrows is that she never owned a home. Her greatest sorrow, however, is the suicide of her son, Tommy, at age 28. Mrs. McFadden admits that Tommy suffered a lifelong depression caused by his father's "dislike" of him. Mr. McFadden's "dislike" was exacerbated by his drinking. He would then "try to provoke Tommy to fight." Mrs. Mc-Fadden often had to physically separate father and son. She believes that Tommy's depression triggered his suicide. When asked to recount the story of Tommy's death, Mrs. McFadden recalled her mother's death. "I begged her not to leave me."

Mrs. McFadden then launched into a summary of a recent television show regarding emigrants from Ireland. Finally, after a circuitous tale about a bouquet of flowers that Tommy was going to buy for his girlfriend, Mrs. McFadden finally related that Tommy used the flower money for drugs instead. She then showed a picture of a handsome and smiling young man.

> Here's my sweet lad who's left me, the one who chose to go. [Pause] But I know he's where he wanted to be. He said to me, 'Heaven or hell, whichever gets me, they're getting a good man.'

Mrs. McFadden said that her children, who were "devastated" by their brother's death from a drug overdose, and her child care helped her "get through the terrible years after Tom's death." She admitted that her faith provided her with the most solace during this time. She believes that God's ultimate goodness balanced her greatest sorrow with equally tremendous joy. It granted her what she most values—her family.

> My faith helped me to get through. It helped me to survive what I survived, even with the abuse of Mr. McFadden. My faith helped me turn away from the abuse. It's the only thing I have. God gave me my children. They kept me going. My children were the reason for me to live. And when Tommy died, if I hadn't believed in God, I wouldn't be here. See, when one has a family, they make it all worthwhile. I might be feeling a little depressed sometimes, about the past, you know, but I always manage to get around to looking at the bright side. As far as Jim McFadden is concerned, if I hadn't met him, I wouldn't have had all those wonderful boys. So I thank him for that. And of course my daughter. That's the right way to look at it, don't you think?

Mrs. McFadden believes that her unfailing optimism is a legacy from her grandmother in particular, and from her Irish ancestry in general.

> She [grandmother] was always so gentle. I never heard her raise her voice. She worked so hard and she never complained.

Mrs. McFadden aspired toward certain goals throughout her life—being slender like American girls, taking care of children like Irish girls, and reaching the paradigm of gentleness and hard work that her grandmother embodied. She believes that targeting these physical and emotional plateaus will grant her a reward—the afterlife she envisions.

> I believe in a heaven, I believe I will see Tom again definitely. I feel we will be close in some way although I don't understand what way it will be, whether he will know and I will know . . . . And I'll see my mother. And my father, maybe I'll get to know him.

Mrs. McFadden's conception of heaven includes knowledge and revelation. To see her mother again, to know her father, and to understand why Tommy committed suicide—the issues that saddened and vexed her in this life—will be revealed and resolved in the next.

Mrs. McFadden believes that a dream she had, shortly after the death of a close friend, proves her beliefs about an afterlife.

> I dreamed of a friend, a second mother to Tom whose life was like mine, with her husband I mean. And this friend died right after my dream. I think Tom was trying to reach me somehow, and maybe trying to reach Beth [the friend]. And to tell us everything was all right, and every one is happy. It made me think that heaven is a place where everybody is the same.

Along with seeing heaven as a place of knowledge and revelation, Mrs. McFadden also sees it as the great equalizer—the place where abusive marriages are recompensed, where women with "sturdy" legs are slender and beautiful, where fathers are known, and where lost sons are found and kept.

ISSUES OF DYING AND DEATH

Living "one day at a time," especially for poor respondents, was integral to their feelings, in older age, of independence and well-being. Many women claimed that they "never thought about dying." Although some women admitted that they were "afraid to die alone," others joked that "I won't know what's going on then, they [family members] can do anything they want with me." Several women in the poor Caucasian sample saw death as a time of sleep. After lives of hard work and financial hardship, the thought of eternal rest was welcome.

Many women in the poor African-American sample, although viewing death as the portal to a "better" life, feared the act of dying. Living in a world of nearby, daily and random violence shaped and sharpened fears about *how* they would die. Likewise, experiencing the violent, untimely deaths of their children and grandchildren lent dying a specter of horror.

Many African-American women told harrowing and haunting tales of children's and grandchildren's shortened lives and horrendous deaths.

We present the case of Mrs. Merton, a 78-year-old twice-divorced African-American woman who lives in a cheerful apartment in a subsidized housing facility in South Philadelphia. Mrs. Merton gave birth to 14 children. Three of them died in infancy; 10 are sill living.

Mrs. Merton is heavy set; several of her illnesses, such as heart, leg, and circulation problems, relate to her weight. Mrs. Merton welcomed the interviewer warmly and easily shared intimate details of her life. Despite her emotional and financial hardships, she often punctuated her narrative with jokes.

Mrs. Merton was one of nine children. She and two younger sisters were separated from their parents early in life. After her father suffered a disabling fall and was unable to work, the children were "boarded out."

> I was born at home, the oldest. My mother had nine but she lost three. I was about four when my mother put us out to board because my father took sick and she had to work. And I ate crumbs off the table. I remember that. We used to come home on weekends. But I come back home to stay when I was about ten years old.

Mrs. Merton's father died several years after his fall. She remembers her mother "crying all the time."

Mrs. Merton left school after the sixth grade. Her working life began so early she cannot remember her first job.

> I used to work when I was about ten or eleven. I worked for Irish people on P. Street. That was my second job. I used to go there and wash dishes, scrub floors, put out the trash. The extra money that I made I used to give to my mother. She taught us how to cook, clean, all of that. I worked cleaning theaters, too. I worked at every theater they had on S. Street.

Mrs. Merton became pregnant at age 15 by "Jackie Merton, my first [husband]."

> I didn't know what to do. My older girlfriend was talking turpentine. My mother took me, and his mother, straight to City Hall. They made us get married.

Mrs. Merton gave birth to five children by the age of 19. Mr. Merton became overwhelmed by his responsibilities and eventually succumbed to the economic pressure of his large family.

I used to see him crying all the time. I said, 'What you crying for?' And he said, 'Because I can't take care of you all.' Then he left. He left me when I was carrying the last child. He went home to his mother.

Mrs. Merton also returned to her family home and eventually divorced Jackie Merton. Mrs. Merton met her second husband, Houston, in the early 1940s.

He just come out of the service. He was in France. I knew his sister. We all used to go around together.

Mrs. Merton eventually had her "second set of children" with Houston. She described the "good while" she lived with him as "a nice life." This period of emotional and financial ease was shattered without warning. One night, while Mrs. Merton was at work, Houston quietly left her and the children to live with another woman.

I went back to work. I worked, and then he left. He met somebody. And he just packed up and left. I went looking for him and took all the children. I went to the place he was at. He slammed the door in my face.

Although Mrs. Merton laughed about her memories concerning "when Jackie Merton, my first left me," she quietly detailed how ill she became after Houston "took up with that other woman." Due to a "breakdown," she remained incapacitated for several months after Houston left. She remembers this period as one of the bleakest in her life.

I believed I loved Houston better than the first one [husband]. I knowed more about that. I was forty-some years old when he left me. So I got real sick. I was in the state hospital. I didn't want to live. I tried suicide.

When asked if she still feels sad about her breakup with Houston, she laughed.

Not no more. I used to feel bad. I went to work and I enjoyed myself. I took care of my children. I went to church regular. I bought all new furniture. My life was better after the men. I did a lot of dancing. Now I'm so glad I'm done with that man thing. [Hearty laughter]

In the following decade, Mrs. Merton suffered another severe loss. In 1973 her 39-year-old daughter, Virginia, was poisoned in a bizarre case of mistaken identity.

She [Virginia] had a rough life I believe. Boyfriends wise. They said it was rat poison. A woman done it. But it wasn't meant for her. It was meant for her girlfriend because the woman that done it, Virginia's girlfriend was going with this girl's husband. I wasn't worried about her [Virginia] too much afterward [after her death]. It was all combined together. Her children, what was I going to do with them? They were young. And one girl had two babies. Now, all the time I think of her [Virginia].

It is interesting that after Virginia's death, Mrs. Merton ceased "worrying" about her. She also mentioned that the woman who poisoned Virginia was never "found." "I didn't pursue it. Let bygones be bygones." Like Mrs. Jonas mentioned in Chapter 5, Mrs. Merton refused to look to authorities in the "larger" society to find Virginia's murderer. Blame for her daughter's murder, if placed at all, was situated in the "smaller" society in which she had lived and died.

Her responses suggest that Mrs. Merton believed that Virginia's lifestyle would eventually lead to tragedy. Her fear that she would become responsible for raising Virginia's children and grandchildren (who were living with her at the time of Virginia's death) came to pass. Her preoccupation with a multitude of family crises that also occurred at this time, such as other deaths in the family, her son's clandestine entrance into the military, and financial worries, obstructed her ability to grieve for Virginia. She remembers this period as the saddest time of her life.

Oh, it was terrible. It wasn't long I buried my mother. My mother, and two sisters died in one year. I came all the way down. I was just that sick. I couldn't eat. I drank the beer all the time.

Mrs. Merton's mourning period was forced to be short-lived; in the next year she lost a son-in-law to a drug overdose and two of her children "went to prison" for unnamed offenses. She admitted, however, that in losing Virginia she lost her sole confidant.

Mrs. Merton's coffee table held innumerable family pictures. Each portrait displayed several generations of children, grandchildren, and great-grandchildren. Gazing at the breadth of her fecundity, the interviewer asked what she thought about her family. She answered simply: "There's just so many of them." Mrs. Merton pointed out pictures of smiling grandchildren and greatgrandchildren who had died through murder, drug overdoses, or after contracting AIDS. She waved toward the picture of her greatgrandson, a handsome, 20-something-year-old-man, and said flatly:

He was killed last Mother's Day. He was gay. His friend killed him.

Similar to Mrs. Rose's reaction to her pregnancies, mentioned in Chapter 6, Mrs. Merton also wishes that she had not borne children. When asked what she would do differently in her life if she were able, she answered:

> I wouldn't get married young and I would finish school. I wanted to be a nurse. I didn't mind taking care of the sick. I'd have had me a business. But I had too many children. They talk about abortions, I think I would have had that, too. Church doesn't believe, but I say, let's get it over with. Children kept me from all that. With so many you couldn't get your mind functioning right.

As Mrs. Merton reviews the pictures on her table, she also relives her heartaches. The violent deaths of Virginia and several grandchildren and greatgrandchildren and the destructive lifestyles of other family members might cause her to question her own part in her family's tragedy. She does not appear to question her husbands' roles in their children's lives and deaths. Her antidote to self-blame seems realistic and life-affirming—she does not ask from her children and grandchildren what she knows they are unable to give. Instead, she turns, like Mrs. Warren in Chapter 5, to her ancestors to find proof of her worth. She nourishes her self-esteem by drawing on the uncommon strength she inherited from a long line of independent women.

> I don't like to be asking nobody for nothing. My mother, my grandmother was 95 or 96 when they passed. All worked, and they worked for good families [as domestics]. My aunt raised her daughter in a kitchen in the suburbs.

When asked if she believed in an afterlife, Mrs. Merton shrugged, then revealed that months before her daughter died, she had foreknowledge of the death through a prescient dream. After this confidence, she expressed doubts about an afterlife.

> I used to be a good dreamer. I could see things before they happen. I seen my daughter before she died. She was sitting in a chair and I looked over at her. I said, 'Mmm. I don't think I'm going to have her long.' I never told nobody. But after that [death]? I think you just die. I'm not sure about that. I think your soul just floats on away. I just think when you're gone, you're gone. Ashes to ashes, dust to dust. And that's it.

Mrs. Merton no longer "sees" future deaths through dreams. Perhaps the pain resulting from foreseeing Virginia's death and its actualization causes her to reject supernatural issues. When Mrs. Merton spoke about her own death, she did not envision an afterlife, or any "place" of reunion

with Virginia or other loved ones. Rather, her eschatalogical comments spoke
to a this-worldly aspect of dying.

> I wouldn't want to suffer. I don't think I want nobody to put no life thing
> on me.

Although Mrs. Merton has endured physical and emotional hardship,
remains impoverished, and suffers from several life-threatening illnesses,
she chooses to live in the present, to describe herself as "strong, happy, and
jolly," and to look forward to limited but joyful days ahead. When asked
what she thought the future held for her, she smiled at the early spring sun-
shine pouring into her living room.

> The future don't hold too much for me no more—just a good life! A lot of
> sunshine. I like a day like this.

Although Mrs. Merton judged her life as "hard," she remains impressed
with her own ability to bear her burdens with good humor and thereby overcome their pain.

> Sometimes I think about how I got over all the things that I had to go
> through. You know how? By leaving it backward somewhere and starting
> new. Don't be thinking about it. I'm happy and strong. I'm still strong. And
> I was always jolly. I ain't never was sad. Still ain't.

Although some might construe her cheerful posture as denial, the pa-
rade of family pictures throughout her apartment suggests that she admits
to her family's importance in her life and her sorrow concerning them. Her
pictures are proof of her vast progeny, her acknowledgment of the pain
they've handed her, and her ability to leave that pain "backward somewhere
and start new."

Mrs. Merton challenged the notion of an afterlife. Since traditional
African-American beliefs include an easy transition from this world to the
next through dreams, speaking with the dead, being guided by ancestors,
and dialogue with God, life after death is affirmed by African spirituality.
Following this, Mrs. Merton's uncertain and negative comments concerning an afterlife are significant.

EXPECTATIONS FOR FUTURE GENERATIONS

Regarding finances, most women interviewed, despite their race or financial or social status, spoke of "living within their means" throughout
their lives and reproached future generations for not emulating them. Re-

spondents saw subsequent generations as having more and better opportunities to succeed but as having failed to take advantage of these opportunities. Respondents also decried a lack of similar religious or moral values in their children and grandchildren.

It is important to note that despite the above generalities, women in each of the four groups had different expectations from generations to follow. At this point in the book, we refer back to several of our case studies to illustrate these differing expectations.

For nonpoor Caucasian women, such as Mrs. Quill mentioned in Chapter 3, thoughts and expectations about their children and grandchildren were implicit. Just as this cohort of women expected to do better financially than their parents, respondents tacitly expected their own children to rise even further on the financial and social ladder.

For the African-American nonpoor sample, such as Mrs. Greene and Mrs. Dickson described in Chapter 6, future generations were strongly encouraged to get a good education, to advance financially and socially, and, as Mrs. Greene said, "to make liars out of what all these people say about you." In other words, family support provided the impetus to succeed despite awareness of the continuing obstacle of racism.

The future of the children and grandchildren of respondents in the poor Caucasian sample was harder to predict. Some respondents in this group recognized that education was the path to success and encouraged their children to travel that route. Other women in this sample related that they had "just survived" while raising their children. This struggle allowed little time or know-how to suggest ways in which their children might achieve a "better" life. Many women in this group hoped that their children would find secure, "good-paying" jobs. Security, rather than upward mobility, equaled success.

The poverty of the poor African-American sample often granted a legacy of destruction and despair to future generations. Although some respondents spoke of children and grandchildren who did succeed, such as Mrs. Custer, others, like Mrs. Merton and Mrs. Rose, told harrowing tales of children's and grandchildren's drug use, estrangement, and death.

We present the case of Mrs. Alcott, who exemplifies several of the issues that this chapter addresses, such as spirituality and thoughts about succeeding generations. Mrs. Alcott is a 70-year-old poor Caucasian widow who walks with difficulty and looks older than her years. A stroke that she suffered in 1985 curtailed her continuing desire to "go back to work." Although she realizes that she is not physically able to work, finding a job remains her unfulfilled dream.

> What I'd really like isn't going to happen. I'd love to be able to go back to work somewhere. Of course what I do with this craft stuff is work. See, I'll never be able to get back to work.

Mrs. Alcott lives in a cluttered row home on a narrow street in the Richmond section of Philadelphia. Numerous craft projects, in various stages of completion, conceal the type and age of her furnishings. Every table and chair is covered with Valentine, Easter, Halloween, and Christmas decorations. Mrs. Alcott gives these crafts to friends and family as holiday gifts.

Mrs. Alcott was one of 12 children born to a coal miner and his wife in upstate Pennsylvania.

> I was third from the baby. But we were all close. The older ones helped the younger ones. We didn't have a lot but I think we were more happier than the children are now.

Mrs. Alcott's father lost his job in 1939 and came to Philadelphia to find work at the Navy Yard. The family bought a small house in the Harrowgate section of the city. Mrs. Alcott suffered a variety of illnesses during childhood that caused her to miss school. Despite the physical hardship of this period, Mrs. Alcott holds fond memories of her childhood.

> On Friday when my father got paid, we got a nickel. We would go down to the store and find the candy that you would get the most for a penny and it had to stretch the whole week. I was 16 before I got a brand new coat.

Mrs. Alcott's father passed away at age 55. Her mother died a few years ago at the age of 94. Six siblings, in and near the Philadelphia area, are still living. Mrs. Alcott remains close to all of them.

Mrs. Alcott liked school and was a "good" student. However, repeated absences due to various childhood illnesses made it difficult for her to "keep up" with classwork. Frustrated at "always being behind," she left school at age 16 and found her first job in a candy factory. She met her husband that same year.

> He was in the service. My father brought him home for dinner. At that time people used to bring service people to their homes for dinners. That's how I met him. And that's how my sister met her husband. The two of them came to dinner and were invited back and that's how we met them.

Mr. and Mrs. Alcott married 6 months after they met, and set up housekeeping in North Philadelphia. Lack of "extra" money prohibited Mr. Alcott from pursuing his dream of attending a "school for harness making." Instead, he took a job at the candy factory where Mrs. Alcott worked and remained there for the rest of his life. She described her husband with fondness.

He was easy going and a hard worker. When he got his pay he brought it to me and then I would sit down and bills got taken care of first, then the food. Then what was left, if there was any left—he would take just so much with him.

Mr. Alcott was suddenly stricken with a mysterious illness in the mid-1950s, just before their fifth and next to the last child was born. His illness affected the family emotionally as well as financially. Mrs. Alcott names this period as the worst time in her life.

He would just get paralyzed. At first they said it was MS. When he first came home with a collar on his neck, they [the children] were all crying and some of them were screaming. I said, 'Now look, you're going to have to get used to it because he's got to wear this thing for a while.' After the initial shock, it was all right. We never knew from one day to the next if he would be home or in the hospital. He worked when he could. It was rough on us. Most of the time we were living on 35 dollars a week.

Mr. Alcott was "never really well" physically or emotionally after his initial attack. Mrs. Alcott realized that her husband's inability to work demoralized him.

He never got over the fact that he couldn't get out there and do. It hurt him for me to have to go and him sit home. No matter how I tried to tell him—.

Despite this assault on Mr. Alcott's pride, Mrs. Alcott remembers the family becoming "even closer" after her husband's illness. Following her husband's illness, another tragedy struck. They lost their home when it was firebombed by an unknown perpetrator.

We all felt terrible, but what could we do? There was no reimbursement or anything. We turned it over to the city. We lost everything.

After this loss, the Alcotts "scrimped and saved and got everything together" to buy the small row home in Richmond where she presently lives. It was chosen because of its price, and its proximity to work, school, and public transportation. Mrs. Alcott recalls this period, from the late 1950s until the 1970s, as a "good time" in their lives. Although her husband's illness continued, family joy abounded because "by this time the children were getting married and having babies."

This "good time" in their lives ended abruptly in 1975. Mr. Alcott "took a turn for the worse." While he was hospitalized, their third child and first son, Martin, was killed in a bizarre accident in Texas.

Martin was in the service on the base and he was on a motorcycle and he was leaving the base to pick up his wife and son. I told him his pa was in the hospital. That's why he was going, to get them so he could come up here to see his pa. The fire engine on the base, they run into him. He said they didn't have no lights on. They weren't going to a fire.

Martin remained unconscious for 5 days before his death. Mrs. Alcott had to choose between staying with her sick husband in Philadelphia or going to Texas to be with Martin when he died.

I called my husband's doctor and I said, 'What can I do?' He said, 'Well, I would advise you to stay here because Martin wouldn't know you. He can't talk to you or anything. If you don't visit Barney [husband] he'll know something is wrong.' So that's what I did. Marty lived for five more days, but I had to keep it to myself. Then I told him [husband] when we brought Marty back for the funeral. We all missed him. You never get over it.

Mr. Alcott returned home from the hospital completely disabled. He lived 2 years after his son's death, during which time Mrs. Alcott was his full time caretaker. After his death, Mrs. Alcott subsumed her grief by "going back to work," babysitting for grandchildren, and "taking up crafts" to "keep me busy all the time."

Mrs. Alcott continues to be "always busy." She teaches crafts at the local Baptist church 3 days a week. Although she lives alone, she laughingly revealed that her neighbors call her house "Grand Central Station." Her former son-in-law (her oldest daughter's first husband) stops by often to "do little things around the house." Mrs. Alcott sees her second daughter, who lives next door, four or five times a day. Her youngest son, who lives in the Northeast, visits her once a week. Her oldest daughter, the only child to attend college, lives with her family in Virginia. Mrs. Alcott sees them on holidays.

Financially, Mrs. Alcott is "just getting by." Although her house needs major repairs, she is philosophical about her ability to do them.

Right now there's a lot of repairs I need—the porch, the kitchen . . . . Well, I'd like to be able to fix them, so I save and save and save and when I get the money I fix it.

Despite her financial frustration, Mrs. Alcott loves her home, its "wonderful memories," and the "old neighbors." Although she is saddened by her neighborhood's deterioration, especially in the past 5 years, she remains unperturbed by the mounting crime rate.

There's a big change with drugs and all. But it's all right. I have no problems with anybody.

Mrs. Alcott's salient personality trait is acceptance—of alternative lifestyles as well as for what life hands her. However, her tolerance seems strained by her children's roles as parents. A major theme in Mrs. Alcott's narrative is how differently her own children have raised their children. She perceives radically changed attitudes and values in her grandchildren. Regarding her own children's upbringing, she said:

Mine had good guidance. See, they had to struggle, too. Vera [oldest daughter] went to college. She had to do it on her own. It was what she wanted. Because when my husband was sick it was pretty hard. So now, if they get in a tight bind they can get out of it. But they seem to want to give their children more than they got. That's the trend.

She believes that her grandchildren, because they "get more without seeing where it comes from," move further from the source of struggle, and from the sense of pride and independence that struggle entails. In this, Mrs. Alcott sees hardship as a character builder—a way of discerning one's mettle.

They can do a whole lot more than we were able to do. It all depends on them themselves and whether they accomplish what they should. But I think they get too much nowadays. They're never satisfied is what it is. One [grandchild] went to college. And none of them are wild. But . . .

Mrs. Alcott's disinclination to finish her thought shows ambiguity about her grandchildren's attitudes toward life. Their desire to "make big money" seems to exclude the values that she instilled in her own children. Indeed, Mrs. Alcott does not see her lifelong financial hardship as a negative. When asked to name the happiest time in her life, she answered:

The only thing I can think of is just being able to handle all the situations I've come up against calmly. The way things are you have to more or less guide yourself and build yourself up to the fact that things have to go that way, this way, whatever comes up. I handle it to the best of my knowledge.

Mrs. Alcott's ability to be resourceful and flexible and to work within the circumstances she finds herself remains a source of pride and happiness. She sees past and present deprivation as a challenge to be met and overcome. This perceived talent to "get through the hard times" is intertwined with her description of herself as independent.

I'm content with what I got. I done it all my life. You have your ups and downs in life and it's the way you handle it. Whatever comes up I handle it to the best of my knowledge. Like I'm the type if I need help real bad—I won't ask for it until it's really the last straw because I'll try to figure out a way.

When asked how she feels about her life as a whole, Mrs. Alcott paused a moment, then smiled.

I've enjoyed every bit of it. I feel like I've accomplished something—the fact that I'm still here and the fact that I have a roof over my head and food in my refrigerator, and I'm content. I mean, I've really accomplished a lot considering all the heartaches and hardships I've been through.

The above comment reveals that Mrs. Alcott is most proud of the person she became because of and despite misfortune. For her, hard times "tested" her and evoked qualities that she might not have known she possessed if life had been "easier." Her focus on achievements despite hardship became her life theme and pervaded her narrative. She tempers her greatest regret—that she did not graduate from high school—with an accomplishment.

Not graduating is the one thing I didn't accomplish that I wanted to. That's a loss that I'll never get over. Still, from the sixth to the tenth grade I had to read with my head held way up or I'd get nosebleeds. But I did it until my mother finally took me out of school.

For Mrs. Alcott, adversity continues to provide a major impetus to attempt to reach "new" goals.

When I was a kid the doctor told my mother I wouldn't live to be 16. Now, I'm going to live longer than my mother [94]; I'm going to try. [Laughter]

Mrs. Alcott, a Baptist, considers her religion to be a major source of strength and solace in her life. She believes that personal fortitude works in conjunction with God's blessings to actualize her purpose in life.

I felt like it [faith] was sort of a leaning post. Without the hope and the understanding of it I don't think I could have gotten through all I did. I pray daily. I feel like God's kind of the base on how I been able to cope with all the things that have happened. [Pause] I don't think I would ever give up because I have a very strong constitution about staying alive. I think helping other people is really the base of my life. The main purpose in my life is being able to help my family and help people, do things to enrich their lives.

Throughout her narrative, Mrs Alcott renamed her liabilities, such as illness and tragedy, as accomplishments, such as being strong, calm, and capable, while enduring poor health or the loss of her son. She bequeathed her skill at turning adversity into assets to her children, where she believes it found fruition. She controls the outcome of her life by transforming its loss into self-perceived success.

SUMMARY

A belief about what the future holds is constructed from past and present events and stable or changing self-concepts held throughout life. We conceive of a particular future in order to balance hardship, tie up unresolved issues, or promise an answer to life's mysteries. Generating an end to the life course that logically follows the beginning and middle provides the narrative with integrity.

Mrs. Emil's hope that the afterlife would grant eternal sleep is a reflection of her fear of punishment during her youth and a history of unrelenting hard work. Many women in the poor Caucasian sample preferred sleep or rest to participation in an afterlife. Witness Mrs. Millson's (mentioned in Chapter 4) thoughts about God and the afterlife.

Interviewer: What do you imagine it [the afterlife] to be?

Mrs. Millson: Well, it's hard to imagine where they put all those people. [Laughter] I think God will judge you even though you're an idiot. He will consider the good and the bad. I can't say truthfully that I believe in hell. I think maybe he just puts you aside and just lets you rest. Even if you are worthy God will just let you rest. Rest in peace.

Interviewer: Is that what you want?

Mrs. Millson: Yes. Leave me alone.

Interviewer: Do you think you might want to see God or heaven?

Mrs. Millson: Oh, sure. Just give me a quick look and let me rest.

Mrs. Custer, rather than succumb to despair over perceived failures in this life, believed that she would find spiritual success in the next.

Mrs. Merton chose to focus on the joys of her limited future—her "jolliness" and her ancestors' legacy of a long life, despite her poor health.

The other women discussed in this chapter believed that their hardship was equaled by their good fortune. They believed that the future would offer joys that offset their sorrows. Personal traits, such as strength, self-reliance, and optimism, as well as faith in God's ultimate goodness balanced life scales in their favor. Despite the limiting circumstances of chronic poverty, they remain active players in life's unfolding.

One tightly held belief of most women in this sample is that God is a partner in their lives. Our focus on the religion and spirituality of respondents reflects that these subjects were integral to women's narratives. Many poor women interviewed in our study saw their relationship with God as reciprocal. Their role in the relationship requires a moment-by-moment faith that God intends "good things" for them, both in this life and the next. They believe that these "good things" are revealed through specific answers to prayer, dreams, incidents of good luck, present contentment, and the devotion of their families. Their stance toward God is both humble and assertive. Respondents are not recipients waiting to take God's blessings passively, but active pray-ers to a God they believe hears and concretely answers them.

Continuing on an experiential path of the study of poverty, we turn to Chapter 8. In this chapter we will examine poverty as a moral issue—and whether our respondents internalized and accepted or rejected society's moral vision of poverty.

8

❧

Poverty as a Moral Issue

The word poverty conjures up an array of images: from dilapidated homes on desolate streets to cramped apartments in high-rise subsidized buildings; from aged women whose health problems relate to the jobs they held throughout life to women who see death as a "time of rest" after a lifetime of hard work; outsiders' images of poverty are insiders' worldviews.

Throughout this book, we have seen how poverty creates an environment, affects health status, and engenders a self-concept that colors memories and informs thoughts about the future.

One aspect of poverty is its paradoxes. Although one paradox of poverty was discussed throughout this book, i.e., that women in this study experienced deprivation as not primarily financial, we acknowledge that most readers associate poverty with a lack of economic resources and material goods. In this chapter, we will examine a paradox of poverty that springs from its meaning in American society.

American culture offers the carrot of the American dream—work hard and succeed. American culture places the onus of responsibility on the individual to succeed. Success is usually measured by financial gain or material possessions. This "spirit of capitalism" is not morally neutral. People who don't "make it" are seen as having failed largely through their own fault. This "fault" may be defined as a lack—lack of intelligence, talent, or some other personal trait that, if possessed, would catapult a person to success. This tacit judgment of moral failure confronts those who have worked hard throughout their lives and remain financially impoverished. Their sense of failure may be experienced as both external and internal. Externally devalued by society, they may feel less worthy as individuals by internalizing society's measure of worth. Inability to gain a portion of the rewards that are purportedly open to all implies failure morally as well as materially. Moral failure results in a lack of status as an individual; those who have not succeeded become lumped into a collective monolith called "the

185

poor." This is another paradox of poverty: the society that constructs a class system builds poverty into its structure. Yet it is the individual who is blamed and often accepts blame for being "poor."

In this chapter we will examine the various links between morality and "success." We present the case of Mrs. Gray, a 96-year-old nonpoor Caucasian woman whose account represents two features of the narratives of many nonpoor respondents: (1) choice—their ability to choose one of several desirable options in major arenas of life for women of this cohort, such as marriage or career, and (2) protection—their perception that their families, especially menfolk, continue to protect them from the vagaries of life. These two aspects emerge in Mrs. Gray's narrative as we witness the moral aspect of success—society protects its valued members by both offering them multiple, desirable life choices, then rewards them for their talent in making a choice from the available array.

A caveat is important here. Earlier in the book we described poor women as making active choices throughout their lives. They often seized their choices from a limited number of sometimes not altogether desirable options. Choices were often made in the negative, i.e., a choice to forego a pleasure or do without in order to choose the perceived greater good of independence. Indeed, some poor women made choices based on which alternative was less onerous, such as working as a laundress rather than a domestic or accepting Mother's Assistance rather than work in order to "keep" their children. The second caveat is that Mrs. Gray is not simply nonpoor; she is wealthy. We use her as a case study because she demonstrates the extreme end of our continuum, which shows that nonpoor women enjoy more and different choices than poor women as well as the emotional and physical protection of the men in their family.

Mrs. Gray lives in a large country cottage that is part of an immense retirement community. She came to the cottage shortly after her husband's death 11 years ago. Mrs. Gray, who looks much younger than her 96 years, wore an elegant winter-white dress and understated jewelry. She warmly welcomed the interviewer into her home and offered tea. She began the interview by talking about what her father "thought best for her." A pervasive theme in her narrative is that she fully supported her parents' decisions concerning her life.

> You see, in those days we weren't allowed to go into the kitchen in our homes. There was live-in help. And my father thought if I were to learn to, well, to just take care of a house and then to run it and to do everything necessary that my mother had been through. So I had a training. It was only a few weeks, but we had to go into a house and take all the different positions of being a hostess and a cook and a chambermaid and everything that you

would be in a house. And it made you feel, when you were finally married, nothing seemed difficult, it just seemed part of life.

Mrs. Gray's father primed his daughter to succeed in the role that was open to women of her status and era—to direct the affairs of her home and family. By following his careful plans, Mrs. Gray believes that she enjoyed close to a "perfect" life. When asked to tell her life story, Mrs. Gray smiled.

> Well, I don't know what kind of a story to tell. I was born into a loving Christian family and I had wonderful care and devotion from everybody— parents, grandparents, and greatgrandparents.

Lineage is an important aspect of Mrs. Gray's self-concept. The fact that she knew her grandparents and greatgrandparents helps her to know herself. It also gives her a sense of "belonging" both literally and metaphorically. Mrs. Gray is the oldest of three children born to her father, a Yale man who was "just normal, very nice in every way" and her mother, who was "the same thing." Both of Mrs. Gray's siblings are deceased. Mrs. Gray remembers her childhood as "delightful, very full of pleasant memories." She was raised in the family home in Harrisburg, but because of a certain "restlessness" that emerged in adolescence, she was sent to a private boarding school in New England. She describes her experiences there.

> Oh, it was delightful. We had a lot of outside exercises like hockey. I played center forward and I rode horseback and I don't know what to tell you about it. It was a very good school; still is.

Mrs. Gray's father died after a brief illness when she was 18. She cannot remember grieving for her father. "Of course, I must have been very sad," she added. Her mother soon married a "friend of the family." She reiterated that her mother's choice of a second husband came from a select group of "friends" that the family had known "forever."

> I'd known him for years. He used to be in our home as I grew up and I called him uncle. I wanted my mother to be happy and I was glad for her.

Mrs. Gray met her husband while "wintering" with her grandfather in a suburb of Philadelphia.

> *Mrs. Gray:*   My husband was in a family that was a friend of my family's, to begin with. I heard about him but then I met him just before he went on a ship to be on Admiral S.'s staff

> in London. I didn't know him as a gob [in the Navy, a status lower than officer]; I knew him as an ensign.
>
> *Interviewer:* Did you know when you met him that he would be special in your life?
>
> *Mrs. Gray:* Not particularly, because in those days we didn't, you know, it wasn't necessary to have just one really good person to count on. We were safer in those days. I had an awful lot of friends, really. In my day there was so much protection. My father and my uncles and even my brother were all protecting of females in the family.

Despite Mrs. Gray's "awful lot of friends," she "refused everybody's proposal of marriage all the way up the line" until she met her husband. This comment shows her numerous chances for a "good match." Mrs. Gray also mentioned that her mother "waited" for her father. She strongly identifies with her mother's view of love and marriage and related the similarity between her mother's engagement and her own.

> *Mrs. Gray:* Something just told me to wait, you know. I think it's instinctive with a female, at least it was with me. And with my mother, too—to put it off and put it off until you had a feeling of really being in love.
>
> *Interviewer:* You were in love with your husband?
>
> *Mrs. Gray:* [Adamantly] You had to be in love! I wouldn't allow anybody to be a close friend and be engaged unless I really loved him. You see, some of my girlfriends became engaged soon after their coming out, because it was the thing to do. And that led to so many divorces. I went to a wedding and that bride and groom had a divorce after a few months and I said, 'Mother, what in the world happened?' And I couldn't understand how she could be engaged and yet marry a man that was odd. You see, I didn't have to stay engaged long with him [husband] because we knew the family so well.

For Mrs. Gray, knowing her husband's family ensured that she would not be surprised after marriage by any "oddness." After a short engagement, the couple enjoyed a "beautiful wedding." Their first home was "brand new." Although Mr. and Mrs. Gray were "young and inexperienced" they decided to "go ahead and have a home built." A network of bankers and brokers, who were long-term friends of Mr. and Mrs. Gray's respective families, assured the Grays that their decision to build a home would bring a sound financial return.

We were hesitant about stepping in to buy real estate at this early time in our lives but the trust company knew my grandfather and they knew my husband's uncle very well. They were Civil War veterans and were very good friends and that's how we knew each other.

Mr. and Mrs. Gray raised two sons and a daughter in their home. Mrs. Gray decided "not to have help," since her schooling prepared her for managing all aspects of a "well-run home." Mrs. Gray describes this early period of marriage as "extremely happy." All three children were sent to "terrific" schools and went on to the "best colleges." However, she quickly added that "nobody escapes" misfortune. The Gray's younger son, Kenneth, "a Yale man like his father and grandfather," was killed in an airplane accident when he was 21 years old.

> *Mrs. Gray:* The children were all good pilots. But he [Kenneth] had a date with one of our local people up in Massachusetts. And the morning that he left in his plane, he didn't know that there was a terrible storm coming. I guess when he met it he felt that he could go through it or go around it or something. It happened in the middle of Massachusetts. It was just too much and the plane came down.
>
> *Interviewer:* How did you and your husband cope with such a tragedy?
>
> *Mrs. Gray:* Well, we learned about it and then went right up there to claim his things.

Mrs. Gray could recall the facts concerning her son's death, but not her grief. Of course, Kenneth died close to 50 years ago and the sorrow such a loss engendered may have quieted through the years. Or perhaps Mrs. Gray's upbringing discouraged either giving way to strong emotions or sharing those feelings, especially with a stranger. Whatever, when Mrs. Gray was asked about the saddest time of her life she did not name her son's death. Rather, she recounted the loss of her sister in childbirth, and the relief of knowing that her sister's only child "turned out well." When asked about the happiest time in her life, she definitively named her marriage.

> *Mrs. Gray:* Marrying my husband was the happiest. It was outstanding. Of course it just cast the picture for the rest of my days. He just had all the good qualities. I really could never find fault with him.
>
> *Interviewer:* Is that why you chose him?
>
> *Mrs. Gray:* Oh, I think it had to do with the way my family brought me up. I wouldn't have been happy with certain people. They didn't have the qualities that I admired the most.

Interviewer: What are those qualities?
Mrs. Gray: Well, like coming from a good family and having things in common.
Interviewer: And you learned about those qualities from your family?
Mrs. Gray: I think so. Without realizing it, you had a standard in the back of your mind. The others, I wouldn't have cared to be married to them.

Mrs. Gray emphasized that she had chosen her husband out of several prospective beaus. However, standards learned early in life allowed her to recognize "the most desirable qualities." Material comfort also provided an additional layer of security in her marriage. In this, her life seemed all of a piece—a protective family, good friendships, an outstanding husband—all formed the circle in which Mrs. Gray was happily enclosed.

> Some people go around and travel and they bring back all kinds of artifacts from around the world and they collect and collect. Well, I think that when my husband and I traveled, he didn't want me to pick up any dust catchers and I think our life together was with friends and we had many, many friends. We collected friends.

The Gray's friends were couples like themselves—husbands with good jobs and wives who managed multiple households. Although Mrs. Gray remembers "being busy every minute" in her life, the issue of untapped talents emerged in response to two questions: "Can you name one or two major accomplishments in your life," and "What would you do over or do differently in your life if you could?" Despite Mrs. Gray's "outstanding" marriage, she admitted wondering whether she possessed "potentials that weren't brought out."

Mrs. Gray: I think you have capabilities that you didn't have to ever count on because you were just having a pleasant time. You weren't called upon to use what I'm sure you could have done if you had to. So, I don't know that I ever think about it. Well, I think if I had to live it over again I would make some changes but I don't think they're outstanding.
Interviewer: Can you tell me what they are?
Mrs. Gray: Well I would like to have had a little more ability to do certain things. You see we had our home in Florida for 23 winters and that kept me, in a way, from continuing what I was doing up here. But I felt it important to give my time to my husband and not get too involved down

> there. See, we bought a house and we were just having a very pleasant time motoring and going into the ocean and having a social time.
>
> *Interviewer:* You said you would have liked a little more ability to do certain things. What certain things do you mean?
>
> *Mrs. Gray:* Well, of course I just did volunteer work out of the church or out of the hospital.
>
> *Interviewer:* Are you thinking in terms of a career?
>
> *Mrs. Gray:* Well, maybe that would have been important to me but I felt that what I was doing was all I could do at the time. My husband was quite well and yet I felt he didn't want me to be tied up and not be free to do things when he wanted to go and do things. I felt it important to keep my time quite open.

Mrs. Gray's accomplishments were framed by her gender and her financial and social status. Her successes were the shadows of her husband's achievements, and limited to those of a married, upper-class woman—taking care of her home, traveling, collecting friends, and keeping time "open" for her husband. She reiterated that she has no regrets, but feels only gratitude for the "fortunate" life that she continues to live. Her major fortune centers on having the security of a loving family throughout her life.

> *Mrs. Gray:* I feel mighty fortunate to have such a loving family in the beginning of it and in the end now when I'm towards the end. It's very wonderful. I would be very, very, very sorry for anybody that didn't have it. Do you have a family?
>
> *Interviewer:* No.
>
> *Mrs. Gray:* [Pause] Well, don't worry. The right person will come along.

Mrs. Gray's contentment with her life is linked to a belief that everyone's life is "planned" in advance. Her Calvinist notion of destiny grants an entitlement for the good fortune she enjoys and meaning to the losses she sustained, such as the tragic death of her son. It also precludes feelings of confusion or responsibility for life's inequities.

> *Mrs. Gray:* I believe that if he [son who was killed] had been home in his own bed that was his time.
>
> *Interviewer:* So you believe that there's a plan?
>
> *Mrs. Gray:* I do believe, even before you are born I think there's a plan for you.

Interviewer: Why do you think some people have it very good and
                some people don't have it very good?
Mrs. Gray: I don't think it's in their power. It's been decided. I'm not
              too sure that there's too much control.
Interviewer: Who or what has control?
Mrs. Gray: This is something that's hazy in my mind. Different
              people meet what comes in different ways and I think
              that's pretty much what life is, the way you meet what
              comes. And if you have a solid background, you're car-
              ried through those hard times.

Mrs. Gray's "solid background" could not, of course, keep grief from
her doorstep, nor could it allow her to realize her "potential" in a day when
women's roles were defined by strict social rules. Financial comfort and relational security seemed to buffer many of the slings and arrows of life's
outrageous fortune. In this, Mrs. Gray's "solid background" seemed a soft
padding of protection from life's hardships.

Although poor women may have internalized society's moral judgment
of poverty, they also added a personal moral twist to their own definition
of "being poor." As we mentioned in previous chapters, for poor respondents, feelings of poverty were tied to emotional or relational deprivation.
Women negated their financial impoverishment and emphasized personal
riches by talking about their accomplishments, their happy relationships,
or their strength of character. Following cultural tenets of individualism,
they removed the moral sting from financial hardship by focusing on personal achievement rather than material want. In our culture of inequality,
some women elevated their images of themselves by looking at those who
have even less than they materially, or by contrasting others' negative personality traits with their own positive characteristics.

As we mentioned in Chapter 3, many poor Caucasian women had scant
financial expectations regarding their lives. However, some women, especially those who held youthful hopes for a "better life," were surprised and
embittered by their lifelong poverty. We present the case of Mrs. Stoffer, a
73-year-old poor Caucasian woman who lives in a subsidized apartment
building on the outskirts of Philadelphia. Mrs. Stoffer, at the latter stage of
her life, feels burdened by her early unfulfilled dreams.

Mrs. Stoffer was the eldest of two children born to a working class family
living temporarily in Brooklyn. She was 5 years old when the family moved
to West Philadelphia to make their home in the back of a hardware store
that her father managed. She profoundly regrets her humble beginnings,
and sees her childhood setting as the backdrop that informed her lack of
self-esteem, resentment against her family, and a lifelong desire to find a
"normal" life.

My father was in hardware. So they found a store with three rooms in back of the store and that's where we lived. Until I was 16. And this had a profound effect on me emotionally. We didn't have a bathroom. We had a little room with a toilet in it. Right in the kitchen. Until I was 16 you had to take a bath right there in the kitchen. I was friendly with people who were living in normal kinds of dwellings. I was the odd ball and so this has affected my personality and my behavior that, to this day, affects me—that I was out of it. I never really fit in. I never really belonged. Well, I came from such a troubled household that I thought surely my life was going to be much better and sweeter and less trouble. But, as it turned out, I wasn't capable of fulfilling that because I was too troubled myself. You know, it was like a fantasy, that everything was going to be wonderful.

In Mrs. Stoffer's mind, poverty is a malignant entity that renders its victims "abnormal." She believes that poverty informed her family's dysfunction and scarred her emotionally. She traces her present unhappiness back to her mother's awareness that others "had more." She is convinced that her mother's "cruelty" stemmed from her frustration over "being poor." She described her mother as "bitter and very frustrated because her brother [Mrs. Stoffer's uncle] was a multibillionaire."

Mrs. Stoffer is presently consumed by imagining what she could do with more money. Her desire to have "good" clothes," yet being forced, through impoverishment, to shop at second-hand thrift stores renders her, like her mother, bitter and frustrated. The intertwining of emotional, financial, and relational states are clearly stated in Mrs. Stoffer's narrative.

We weren't close, she [mother] and I. And she didn't really communicate. The only thing I remember her saying to me—that one thing that stands out in my memory—her saying, 'Other people can cross the street and get hit by a bus, why can't I?' She had this death wish. I think she saw that as the only way out. My parents were miserably unhappy. And there was all this fighting and cursing and I was regularly beaten with a strap, a leather strap with a metal buckle. And when a little blood showed, they knew it was time to stop. And I knew that my friends weren't treated this way. That they came from much more healthier, emotionally healthier families where there was much better income.

For Mrs. Stoffer, there is a definite link between material poverty and emotional instability. Although Mrs. Stoffer and her family moved into a "regular" apartment when she was 16, it was "too late." This sense of being thrown off course at an early age is pervasive in Mrs. Stoffer's narrative. It augured her inability to chart a successful life path and informed her pessimistically skewed worldview. Although she considered herself "very bright" as a child and adolescent, and was accepted at a local college, she was "forced," by her family's impoverishment, "to go into business administration." Instead of fulfilling a desire to major in foreign languages, she "had to become a secretary."

> My soul was in a lot of trouble. I was yearning for some kind of normality, which I couldn't latch onto. I couldn't find it. I certainly couldn't find it in my immediate family. And there was nobody that I could relate to. I could never confide in anyone. I was too humiliated with my whole family situation.

Mrs. Stoffer's use of the word "soul" suggests the all-encompassing nature of her suffering. Although she eventually chose another major—music—she "failed a few courses" and did not graduate—something she "heartily regrets." After leaving college, Mrs. Stoffer found several temporary clerical positions which she "hated." Her mother died when she was 21. She does not recall her feelings concerning the loss; she does remember, however, that her mother was "no longer able to help [her]." Mrs. Stoffer's father, whom she "despised," remarried shortly after his wife's death. She described her brother as a "tormentor—he'd start on something and not let up," and is estranged from him. She believes that early alienation from her family paved the way for a lonely and isolated existence.

Mrs. Stoffer mentioned her husband as an afterthought. They met in high school, and continued an on-again, off-again relationship until they married when she was 19 years old. The couple moved into an apartment "outside the city." She quickly realized the mistake of her union and saw her marriage as "doomed."

> I thought I really loved him. I know now that he wasn't the right person for me. He was really a melancholy person. He was bright. He wanted to be a lawyer, but he had no money. And so I think he was beaten emotionally by circumstances. He would start saying something and then just break off in the middle of a sentence as if to say, 'Why bother?'

Mrs. Stoffer circuitously connects her husband's depression to his lack of money. This cements, in her mind, the link between money, success, and happiness. Because of her husband's erratic work history, Mrs. Stoffer continued to hold various secretarial jobs throughout their married life. Eventually, Mrs. Stoffer gave birth to two children, but the family remained in their small suburban apartment. Mr. Stoffer died suddenly from a heart attack after 13 years of marriage. After his death, Mrs. Stoffer felt desperate; worry over emotional and financial security became uppermost in her mind. Overwhelmed by the responsibility of raising two children, she sought the advice of a social worker who recommended that Mrs. Stoffer send her children to live in different "boarding schools." She visited each of them on alternate weekends for 5 years. She explains the reasons that prompted her action:

> I was in good health and I was young. I was 33 when he died and my son was just past 6 and my daughter was almost 11. I was having problems with Clifford [son]. He started gaining weight and when he was about 8 years old he was really obese, he was so fat. And I didn't know what to do about it. And I just wasn't handling things properly. And I was bewildered. I didn't have any family. My mother had died. My brother couldn't be of any help and my father had remarried. I didn't know what to do. I contacted Social Services. I was feeling this desperation. I was so worried. What would happen if I got sick and couldn't work. So the security factor superseded everything else. And I knew that they would be fed and clothed and educated [in the boarding schools].

Mrs. Stoffer admits that she never enjoyed a close relationship with either of her children. She is convinced that physical separation from them as children caused their current emotional distance from her and each other. She also believes that both her son and daughter followed her on their own emotionally troubled paths.

> They're both bright, I would say good-looking people. My son was never married. He's not gay, but because of, uh, of the very difficult past that he had, I don't know that he'll ever get married. My daughter's marriage didn't work out. Both my children have what I consider, well I really don't know what the norm is today for emotional stability, but I would say they have reasonably serious emotional problems. It doesn't stop them from earning a living, but uh, I think in their personal lives it's reflected fairly obviously.

Mrs. Stoffer seems to look at her children from a distance. Although she "sees" their problems, she describes them dispassionately, as though their emotionally troubled lives have little to do with her personally. Indeed, she continues to feel overwhelmed by her own hardship and her inability to alleviate it. Pervasive thoughts about her own unhappiness permit little time to think about others.

Throughout the interview Mrs. Stoffer described her extreme loneliness as "dehumanizing." However, she acknowledges that her standard for companionship is very high; she describes herself as having "a low tolerance level for most people, many things, many situations." When asked about the worst time in her life she named the present.

Mrs. Stoffer: I would say now is probably the worst. What I say is I'm
                  bearing the unbearable. I don't know how I stand it. I just
                  make myself stand it. But it's crazy. It's cruel. It's cruel
                  for a person like myself to have this terrible loneliness
                  imposed on me.
Interviewer: Could it be self-imposed?
Mrs. Stoffer: Who am I going to live with? Who's going to live with
                  me? What am I going to do? Go down the street and grab
                  somebody? And the impact on me [of living alone] has
                  become greater as time goes on.
Interviewer: Why do you think that is?
Mrs. Stoffer: Well, for one thing, I was more involved socially when I
                  was younger. I was also working when I was younger
                  and I also had a better income when I was younger. And
                  I also had more stamina and more hope.

A link between material success (money) and spiritual goods (hope) pervades Mrs. Stoffer's narrative. She understands how she makes this connection in her own mind; she acknowledges that she has "deep insight"
into her troubled psyche. She knows that she is intelligent and is keenly
aware of the "mistakes" of her past. However, past therapy as well as self-
understanding cannot help her find meaning for her life apart from the
equations that money equals happiness and poverty equals misery. When
asked to sum up her life, Mrs. Stoffer considered.

Mrs. Stoffer: Mistakes. Of course everybody makes mistakes. But mine
                  have been possibly more numerous and more serious and
                  more devastating. My life has been anything but the way
                  I wanted it to be and hoped it would be.
Interviewer: Do you feel any responsibility for this?
Mrs. Stoffer: Oh, yeah. Well, I tried to get help, but I don't think I was
                  really helped. I think that the insights I have come by
                  eventually, I did on my own. I never really understood
                  the importance and value of money. Now I have a high
                  regard for money. Had money been more readily avail-
                  able, I think I could have had a somewhat better life, but
                  I think I was too severely scarred by my early childhood
                  and my adolescent years to really be able to deal in a rel-
                  atively normal fashion with life on life's terms. I told
                  you, if I had plenty of money, it would have been great.
                  I'd be so normal and I'd be so wonderful. That's where
                  it's at. The buck.

Mrs. Stoffer believes that family poverty and emotional instability are clearly and profoundly intertwined. She is convinced that within her story, poverty "came first," and effected her emotional troubles, which she then bequeathed to her children. Unhappy decades spent craving a better life soldered the link, in her mind, between material and spiritual contentment.

One of the questions asked in the interview was: "Have you ever had moments when you've felt bad about yourself because you didn't have as much money as other people?" Answers to this question highlight a link between feelings of shame and poverty. As mentioned earlier, most poor women did not equate high income with moral goodness, high self-esteem, or well-being. Respondents focused on their achievements in order to create or safeguard their self-esteem, or used, as their basis for comparison, those who have less, and therefore did not admit to "feeling poor," or "feeling bad" because of their poverty.

Some nonpoor women, however, did admit to negative self-regard earlier in life because of perceived impoverishment. We present the case of Mrs. Bersky, an 82-year-old nonpoor Caucasian woman. Mrs. Bersky describes her entire life as fraught with financial and emotional pressure. Similar to the way she defines her life, her narrative seems frenetic as she jumps back and forth between cognitions, feelings, and time periods. One of four children born in Hungary, Mrs. Bersky and her mother followed her father and three brothers to America when she was 8 years old. The family made their first home in South Philadelphia. She describes her parents this way:

> My father was a sort of reverend. He performed marriages, divorces. He was a cantor. He was a *moile*. He did everything. He was versatile. He was a ladies' man. My mother, she had emotional problems. She drove herself to a nervous breakdown.

When asked to tell the story of her life, Mrs. Bersky chose to tell the story of her first marriage. Her husband, a laborer, graduated from night school with an accounting degree. She thinks of her first marriage as her "real" marriage, the one that "really mattered," because she bore two children. It was during her first marriage that she experienced shame over her perceived poverty.

Mrs. Bersky and her husband raised two daughters in a small home in Northeast Philadelphia. Her husband used the GI Bill to "go to night school and get a better job" as a government employee. Perhaps because the young couple "wanted more from life," she became keenly aware of her financial and social standing relative to neighbors. The emotional

burden of seeing others "who had more" made this early period in her
marriage the "worst time" in her life.

> I had all my friends, my next door neighbor here and my next door neigh-
> bor here, they all joined a swim club. And we couldn't get in at the time. And
> they became quite a bunch and some of them could have bought me and sold
> me 15 times. My neighbor on one side of me, he was an accountant—very fi-
> nancially secure. The other one was a jeweler. They all had cars. I did not have
> a car. They would go places and we couldn't join them. And that hurt me a
> lot. And they formed a clique and like one was a pharmacist. The others were
> in the building business. They were all financially pretty well situated. And
> I couldn't . . . , and I was hurt. And I was hurt plenty of times. They would
> all get in their cars and go places and wouldn't say, 'Join us.' I felt terribly
> hurt. I had these two small children. They wanted to go places and do things
> like that. I couldn't.

Mrs. Bersky's husband died from cancer shortly before his fiftieth birthday. Her mother and brothers helped her financially by paying off her small
home. Mrs. Bersky had other worries; her mother was declining physically
and longed to live with her daughter and grandchildren. Mrs. Bersky's
own depression over her husband's death made this arrangement "impossible." Mrs. Bersky was "forced" to place her mother in a nursing home,
where she lived for 6 years.

> It killed me. I had a house with a room for her and all that. She was in a
> nursing home for 6 years. And I felt very unhappy about it [tearful]. But it
> was a matter of my life, or hers. After my husband died, she always said to
> me, 'When I talk to you I feel fine.' I said, 'Mom, I can't sit and talk to you
> day and night.' Then I had to go to work after he died. His pension was noth-
> ing. Fortunately he worked for the government and they forced employees
> to get insurance equivalent to their salary. But I had this guilt all the time that
> she was in a nursing home. That's the only thing that plagued me to this day.

Mrs. Bersky, like Mrs. Stoffer, linked her present emotional pain to past
financial hardship. If her husband had left her more money she might have
been able to stay home and care for her mother—thus lessening her guilt
over her mother's "forced" placement in a nursing home. However, Mrs.
Bersky received the help from family that Mrs. Stoffer was denied. With the
family home paid off, Mrs. Bersky used her husband's insurance to give
one daughter a wedding and send the other to college. She worked 3 or 4
days a week at various "managerial positions" offered by relatives and
friends. Mrs. Bersky described this period as "difficult" and actively pursued a second marriage in the hope of "finding security" through a hus-

band. Although she dated one man who "strung her along" for 5 years, in 1977 she married her oldest brother's best friend.

> After his wife died, he was besieged on every side with introductions. And one day—he was a good looking man—I said, 'Are you dating yet?' He said, 'No.' I said, 'Well when you start dating, put me on your list.' He said, '[Incredulously] Do you mean it?' I said, 'Yeah.' He said, 'I'm going to put you on the top of the list.'

Unfortunately, her husband's gambling addiction influenced the emotional and financial direction of their marriage. He twice lost his clothing business to gambling debts and filed for bankruptcy in 1982. Six years later he died. Mrs. Bersky did not call her second husband by name. She referred to him sarcastically as "Mr. Big."

> He lost a fortune before me. If I'd have had the money he lost I'd have been a rich woman. By the time he died he didn't have a cent. He didn't leave me a cent. No insurance, nothing.

Although Mrs. Bersky's second husband left her "nothing," she sought help from various relatives and acquaintances to regain her financial footing. Mrs. Bersky's sister, who "dabbled in stocks," advised her on investments. Because she needed "a better job," a business associate invited her to become a partner in his import/export business. Her nephew, a lawyer, loaned her money to buy a condominium with little interest. Her large social network helped her achieve the financial independence that, for her, grants meaning to life. Security remains a priority in Mrs. Bersky's life.

> A person needs money to be independent. It means not having to go to your family or friends for help. It means having a car of my own and driving. If I could no longer take care of myself enough to live independently I don't want to live.

As mentioned above, Mrs. Bersky strongly links notions of emotional contentment with financial independence. She struggled to have a "hands on" experience of the American dream—work hard, "better" yourself, and find happiness. Unfortunately, at least one component in this equation eluded Mrs. Bersky. She cannot remember any outstandingly happy times in her life. She easily recalls her saddest periods—when she watched others reap and enjoy the material rewards of hard work.

> When I was a youngster I took for granted whatever. I figured, this is the way it is. I had a girlfriend who went to dancing school. I used to practice

with her. I never wanted my mother and father to send me to dancing school. They gave me music lessons. The only thing I regretted, I would say is I, we did not have a car. I was married for 16 years before my husband bought a car. That was an unhappy time for me, when all my friends surrounding me all had cars, and then they joined the swim club and we didn't belong and they went places and we couldn't. That was sad for me.

She admits that she "always worried about [her] financial circumstances" and invested wisely. Due to sound investments, she now considers herself "comfortable." Mrs. Bersky's early self-judgment, constructed in the shadow of the achievements of others, remains firmly in place. A sense of comparison, whether of money, possessions, or less tangible goods, pervades her feelings, thoughts, and narrative.

There's a certain vanity in my whole family. I have a feeling that if people knew how old I was—. I have friends that are 15 years younger than I am. They're not aware of it. Well, I've got feelings that if they were [aware] they would probably not have such a close relationship with me. I had a friend that when he found out how old I was, I think that was one of the reasons he dropped me. And I have a feeling that a lot of people are like that. Women are cruel, too. And I was always very conscious of it and I never wanted to divulge my age. [Pause] I'm tired of trying to look younger than I am, but I know it's important.

Besides internalizing American culture's notion of material success, Mrs. Bersky also measured herself according to society's other standards of personal value—youth and beauty. When asked to describe herself as a person, Mrs. Bersky discussed the encompassing nature of her desire to "better herself."

I always wanted things better than I had them. Always. Financially and growing in general. I wouldn't say I was a social climber. But still, I wanted to elevate myself a little more, in the class of people I was with, maybe people who are not necessarily richer than I am but live nicer than I did. More intelligent than the people that I knew.

Unfortunately, the American dream as a package filled with youth, beauty, money, and talent is difficult to possess and maintain, especially for an aging woman. However, Mrs. Bersky also recognizes that standing in the shadow of other's achievements, especially those of her own family, gives her more "room" for success.

Thank God, my first husband was an intelligent man. He never showed it. But basically he was a smart man. And that's what I admired about my sis-

ter. She was worldly wise. She knew what was going on. Even the stock market. I think she knew more than our broker. And my brother, too. And my
daughter, she amazes me. Three times the contestants did not know the Jeopardy answers and she answered them.

Mrs. Bersky admits that she worries about her younger daughter because
her daughter's husband is not successful. She recognizes that women in
her own cohort "needed" husbands to provide them with the tools for financial security, such as earning a good income while married or leaving
them a healthy insurance after death. Mrs. Bersky regularly warns her
younger daughter about her emotional and financial future.

> Her husband is out of work. I says to her, 'Go back to school. GO BACK
> TO SCHOOL!' I see these young women on television, they make something
> of themselves. I says, 'I don't know if your husband will ever make anything
> of himself and you'll have to suffer for it.'

Mrs. Bersky is bequeathing her major themes to her daughters. When
asked what she considered was the main purpose in life, Mrs. Bersky answered definitively:

> To make a—. To grow, grow big and make a decent human being of your-
> self and to achieve your goals. Success—and be a person to be admired by
> people.

Mrs. Bersky's group of reference, which included financially successful people, informed her general discontent throughout her life. She contrasted her lifestyle with neighbors who had more, felt pressure to conform
to their standard of consumerism, and suffered because she could not. Her
eventual grasp of the American dream did not lessen her present pain over
her past difficulty in reaching it.

Many poor African-American women interviewed who were, throughout their lives, distanced from the American dream that Mrs. Bersky
sought showed scant interest in achieving it. When asked the question,
"Has the American dream, i.e., to work your way up to something from
nothing, been part of your life in any way," most poor African-American
women answered in the negative. However, this did not mean that poor
African-American respondents held no notions of success. For many, to
survive in the face of class, gender, and racial discrimination was to succeed. They often wove their dreams within the "crawlspace" that society
allowed them. Although some of their ideas about achievement reflected
the materialistic values of the larger society, they were more often constructed by the women themselves from the mores of the smaller society

in which they lived and worked. In this, accomplishments were drawn from personal resources, such as self-esteem, reputation among family and friends, and personal spirituality. For poor African-American women, moral success or failure had little to do with poverty, but with *themselves,* such as how they treated others, how they carried themselves, and how they stood in relation to God. We present the case of Mrs. Hayworth, who decided, throughout her life, the measure of her own worth. Mrs. Hayworth is an 82-year-old poor African-American woman who resides alone in a large row home in Southwest Philadelphia where she has lived for over 70 years. The walls of her living room are decorated with family portraits drawn by her 86-year-old sister who lives in a nearby nursing home. A large chair placed in front of a bow window gives Mrs. Hayworth clear vantage of the wide, busy street. Beside the chair is an end table filled with medicines, papers, opened and unopened mail, religious tracts, and a well-worn Bible. The tiny area that surrounds this table and chair is Mrs. Hayworth's primary living space.

Mrs. Hayworth is a tall, thin woman who acts and speaks genteelly. When an interview question discomfited her, such as, "What are one or two of the most important things about you as a person?" she laughed shyly but would not answer. Her illnesses, which include leg and vision problems, make her seem frail and keep her housebound. During the interview she had difficulty articulating her responses, which may be due to a stroke she suffered several years ago.

Mrs. Hayworth introduced herself by sharing two important facts about her life: (1) her father was a Baptist minister and founded the church that she still attends, and (2) she worries about mounting unpaid bills accrued from using credit cards to pay for utilities. Mrs. Hayworth's pride in her family of origin and shame in her financial "wrongdoing" were salient themes in her narrative.

Mrs. Hayworth's mother was a widow with five children when she met and married a widower with six children of his own. Together, Mrs. Hayworth's parents had five more children. She described her father as "wonderful, very kind," her mother as "very refined," and her childhood as "glorious." The children were raised in South Philadelphia and moved, when Mrs. Hayworth was "still quite young," to the Southwest Philadelphia home where she still lives. She described herself as a "sickly child" who suffered from many illnesses such as scarlet fever and pneumonia. Despite her illnesses, Mrs. Hayworth remembers her childhood as "lovely. We had rules. After all, we were minister's children." When recalling her parents, she said with deep feeling, "I remember them so well." Mrs. Hayworth often answered an interview question after a long pause and while gazing out of the living room window. One could imagine that she sees, in her mind's eye, scenes from a happy childhood rather than the actual sight of a decaying neighborhood.

Mrs. Hayworth's early social and spiritual values were bred and nurtured by the beliefs of the Baptist Church. She recalls her baptism as one of the most joyous memories of her childhood.

> I didn't get baptized until I was 12 years old. See, in those days when you accepted the Lord you didn't take it as foolishness. The people knew [the answer] when they asked you if you felt like the Lord had forgiven you. Well I didn't feel like I was forgiven until my cousin died. That was very hard because Edna [the cousin] and I had been close. We had a prayer meeting after the funeral and we were all in the living room and I felt that God had forgiven my sins. And then they made arrangements to baptize me.

This anecdote provides us with a window into Mrs. Hayworth's worldview. Her realization of God's forgiveness takes place after her young cousin's death. Perhaps she believes that the suffering endured through grief made her worthy to be baptized. Likewise, the loss of her cousin, described by Mrs. Hayworth as "very hard," becomes emotionally transformed into her rebirth through baptism. Her spiritual notion of self-worth contrasts starkly with Mrs. Stoffer's and Mrs. Bersky's material connotation. Mrs. Hayworth bases value neither on material goods nor financial success, but on spiritual forgiveness and cleansing.

Mrs. Hayworth began to work as a domestic for neighborhood families when she was 12 years old. She also discovered a talent for sewing.

> I started making my father's vestments. Then I started working at [. . .] Department Store, but I fell sick with my back.

Mrs. Hayworth did not enjoy school and left during the eleventh grade with no regrets. After leaving, she tried to find a job in the post office and scored high on their entrance exam. However, physical problems such as fevers and back problems kept her from accepting permanent work. Her employment was therefore sporadic, and mostly confined to day's work, despite her sewing ability and general intelligence.

Mrs. Hayworth was reluctant to speak about her husband and 10-year marriage, which ended in separation in 1951. Neighbors introduced her to her future husband when she was 25 years old. When asked what attracted her to him, she answered:

> I don't know. I didn't know what I was getting into. My mother was sick and I just didn't want to be there [the family home] anymore. They weren't

good years. He had a child. I didn't know that. I found out when she [the child] called. I knew I was in the wrong place.

Although she holds no fond memories of her husband, Mrs. Hayworth did not seek a divorce from him because she had no intention of "meeting anybody else." She sketched a portrait of a shell of a marriage in which both partners looked and traveled in opposite directions. Members of Mrs. Hayworth's family terminated the unhappy union.

Every summer he went down south and I didn't go. It was lonely. But we went to church together. Then he met somebody in the church and they was talking in the seat right behind me. He gambled, too. My aunt and my sister decided I should get out. They moved me out of the house. See, I was sickly. I wasn't strong enough to do anything for myself.

Mrs. Hayworth's unhappy marriage is a source of shame for her. Although she states that she "didn't know what she was getting into," she also admits her part in bringing the shame upon herself by marrying in the first place. She also tries to "forget" about the "unpleasantness" of her life by thinking about "good things."

Most of the bad things I did was my own fault. Even my marriage. I didn't have to get married.

Mrs. Hayworth is willing to take responsibility for her passivity concerning her marriage. This willingness combines her integrity with her regrets. In retrospect, she acknowledges that inaction concerning life's problems *is* a decision in handling those problems. However, she continues to be quiescent concerning issues that presently plague her, such as overdue bills. Her quiescence results in an attitude of surprised embarrassment and stubborn meekness. For example, Mrs. Hayworth is ashamed that she cannot pay her credit card bills. Yet she takes full responsibility for having accrued them and promises not to do it again. While the interviewer was in Mrs. Hayworth's home, several collection agents called. Mrs. Hayworth's demeanor on the phone typified the way that she thought about herself as well as her unpaid bills. To one caller, she said:

You don't have to keep telling me to pay. I know I did wrong and it won't happen again. But the Lord has forgiven me because I have asked him to forgive me.

The above scenario shows that Mrs. Hayworth seeks extrication from her financial problems through a supernatural agent and also reveals her disallowance of disrespect toward her. Her perceived personal worth is based on her closeness to God and her belief in God's ultimate authority over collection agents.

Likewise, the following exchange shows that she believes that because she has proof that God forgave her economic trespasses, the credit card company should do likewise.

Mrs. Hayworth: I've asked the Lord to forgive me for running up the bills. I know I have to go through this thing with the people calling me, but I feel that he's forgiven me for running up the bills.

Interviewer: How do you know the Lord has forgiven you?

Mrs. Hayworth: Because if it wasn't for him I wouldn't be able to function.

Mrs. Hayworth, due to ill health and a retiring personality, feels isolated within her neighborhood. She sees her sister infrequently, is estranged from her only nephew because "he only came here for money and I don't have any, so I don't see him," and is friendly with only one neighbor, an elderly woman who goes grocery shopping for her. She complains that younger people in the neighborhood "wanted to be paid" for doing errands, which she cannot afford. Also, there is a sense that present neighbors do not meet the standard of neighbors remembered from the past.

I'm friendly but I don't know other people's business. We used to have a committee on this street. There were meetings and many attended. People would clean their street. Now they don't. A lot of the people died. It isn't the way it used to be.

For Mrs. Hayworth, change is negative. Although she shyly admitted that she "used to be friendly" as a girl, she now spends most of her day "with God." She passes the day reading the Bible and listening to a Christian radio station. She also counts her blessings.

The Lord has been good to me. I'm so thankful. All the time I think about God and his goodness and his mercy. I mean I'm sitting here. He allows me to walk and talk and speak, and I see. He gets me up in the morning and moving around, and I have something to eat. And I'm able to go to church. People come to get me and take me home. He has done everything for me.

Mrs. Hayworth believes that God is intimately and intricately connected to the personal details of her life. She sees her limited physical mobility as a spiritual gift. A sense of being "managed" by God, from finances to health, distances Mrs. Hayworth from making decisions about her own life and the outcomes that result from those decisions. In some ways, she assumes the role of a third-person observer of her own life, rather than its agent. The above passage also indicates her belief that moral worth results from intimacy with God. Her worthiness grants self-esteem and a sense of contentment even though she is anxious about her financial situation.

Mrs. Hayworth often reflected on times' past with a sad wistfulness. Indeed, the most significant people in her life are dead and its most joyous events are over. When asked what she believed the future held for her, she answered:

> Not very much. I'm at the place now where the sun is going down. Do you know what I mean? But everything is in the Lord's hands as far as I'm concerned. [Pause] I never could come to a place when I didn't think of having a mother. To think that I got to 80, that was really a surprise to me. I didn't think I'd live so long.

In some ways, Mrs. Hayworth seems surprised and overwhelmed by her entire life. The intense grief that she still feels for her mother, dead now for over 40 years, combined with amazement about her own longevity produce feelings of both loneliness and gratitude in Mrs. Hayworth. Although she is perplexed about God's reason for allowing her to live, she is convinced her life has meaning. When asked what she believed is the main purpose in life, she answered:

> I don't know why God keeps me going. For some purpose, but I don't know what it is. I guess to do good, that's all I can think of. Of course, I wouldn't want to be here if I can't help in some way. So I guess my purpose is giving, just giving.

Mrs. Hayworth's belief that God loves her and has forgiven her for accruing utility bills proves, in her mind, her value as a human being. In this, her financial poverty, reflected in her inability to pay her bills, actually becomes a springboard for her self-esteem and sense of moral worth. Her closeness to the ultimate source of all good gifts (God) grants her a paradoxical view of herself as spiritually strong though financially and physically weakened.

SUMMARY

American society's creation and sanction of class, gender, and racial preferences, prevalent especially in the era when respondents were being raised, systemically cements the moral component of poverty within society's institutions. Poverty dons its strongest moral tone as a concept that is intricately linked to all experiential domains, such as self-concept, regrets and hopes, opinions about others, and thoughts about God. The women in our study added their own moral meaning to poverty through their complex personal histories, expectations about the future, cultural ideals, and spiritual beliefs. In this, although the women who experience "objective" poverty cannot be removed from the culture that actually imputes its moral meaning, they can and do subjectively decide what determines poverty or privilege within the smaller sphere of their own lives. They may do this in at least three ways: (1) internalize society's measure of poverty, and extricate themselves from it by working within the system, (2) agree to society's measure of success, feel incapable of working within the system for whatever reason, and therefore despair over not reaching it, or (3) create new definitions of moral worth and success.

For example, Mrs. Gray, Mrs. Bersky, and Mrs. Stoffer all internalized society's ethos—which links morality and success. The narratives of all three women highlight the notion that personal and financial worth is linked. Mrs. Gray's idea of success matched her external circumstances, creating, for her "a solid background" in which she thrived emotionally and materially. Mrs. Bersky, believing that without financial security her worth as a person would be diminished, worked hard to make her financial circumstances secure enough to grant her limited emotional contentment. Mrs. Stoffer's despair resulted from like-minded thinking. Her life seemed a sad addendum to the cliché "money buys happiness." Mrs. Hayworth, however, defined personal value, success, and happiness differently from the above respondents. Her sense of moral worth was linked not to finances, but to a personal relationship with a powerful and forgiving God.

We turn now to Chapter 9, which deals with how respondents valued looking back over their lives as they constructed their life story and imbued it with a retrospective meaning.

9

The Value of Retrospection

The value of telling your life story, especially in older age, is manifold. By recounting life events and retrospectively imbuing them with meaning, respondents weave their lives into a meaningful whole. In this, the past is measured through the lens of the present. For example, if present circumstances and relationships seem satisfactory, the life course makes sense—even hardship fits into a purposeful totality. Through the life story respondents show not only the value of looking back at life, but the value to self and others of having lived.

This chapter has a connection with all preceding chapters, in that all chapters used the framework of case studies. We placed respondents' salient remarks within a particular chapter in order to invest them with a "thick description" (Geertz, 1973). Chapter 9 has a special link with Chapter 2, Subjective and Objective Poverty, because it both elucidates the past, of which the respondent is still the subject, and elaborates the objective events of the past. It also shows how respondents look at the past teleologically, granting the circumstances of life, even its hardship, a purpose that becomes clear with age and "true" with the telling of the life story.

As mentioned earlier, meaning is often made clear through a chronological unfolding of life's events. This sense of a beginning, middle, and projected end allows narrators to explain "how things got to be this way," and to project a future based on information from the past. Some respondents are unable or unwilling to share painful details of their lives, or they prefer to forget the circumstances of which those details were a part. These gaps, which occur at crucial points in the life story, offer a window into the women's worldview.

As respondents allow their life story to unfold, we examine the actors who play significant parts, exploring whether the women themselves are the heroines or whether another character occupies center stage throughout the narrative.

In this chapter, we will also examine the "package" that women present of themselves. Life stories become crystallized in older age, tightly bound by assimilating new events and information about the self into an already existing totality. The crystallization of the life story in older age is tied to its integrity. Present conflict over past experiences requires both a scrutiny of the past and a redefinition of the self in order to realize that the self has been transformed, i.e., "I am not the woman I was." Despair may result from an inability to find new information that redefines a shamed self-concept.

Some respondents tell their life story with a liberal use of metaphor. We therefore add to the trove of subjective experience the use of metaphor in narration. For our purposes, we are defining metaphor as a symbol that represents, stands in for, or suggests something else. In this book, the "something else" is the self.

Although all respondents complied with our request to "tell the story of your life," some recalled their pasts with joy and others admitted that retrospection engenders pain. Some women shunned recollection of certain times or events in their lives. Painful memories made looking at the past a selective activity. We introduce Mrs. Guterez, who happily recounted her early childhood and preferred to focus on the present, but chose to skirt the memories of her recent past and the losses she encountered there.

Mrs. Guterez is an 85-year-old poor Caucasian widow who gave birth to five children, three of whom are living. She looks younger than her years; skillfully applied make-up and a bright, fashionable sweater add to her youthful appearance. She asked to be interviewed at a local senior center so that the interviewer would not come to her home. "The neighbors will want to know who you are and it's none of their business," she explained.

Mrs. Guterez is the second oldest of nine children who were born and raised in South Philadelphia to parents who had emigrated from Spain. She is proud of her Spanish heritage and spoke fondly of her childhood.

> It was lovely. We only talked Spanish in my house. No English. My mother was fabulous. There was no mom like my mom. Some moms are good but my mom was a mom . . . . She was so good. My father worked in a fishing place. 'Oh, pop, you smell of fish,' I used to tell him. My father was very temperamental. We all were. That's why nobody in my family married Spanish, I mean not my kids or grandkids. See, our tempers are too bad. They'd be killing each other. [Laughter]

Mrs. Guterez began her narrative by telling the story of her 49-year-old daughter's death, which occurred 4 years previously. Rene was married only a year when she discovered that she had an incurable cancer.

> Rene was sick for two and a half years. But she never saw me cry. I would say to her, 'God don't want bad people like you.' I went to see her the night before she died. I said, 'How you doing, babe?' She didn't know that I knew.

After this comment, Mrs. Guterez launched into a record of other family deaths. She listed their ages and recounted in detail the death of her first-born infant, the aroma of coffee brewing the day her father died, and the color of the dress her mother was wearing when she passed away. When asked about her feelings concerning these deaths, she paused, then explained why she feels angry with Rene's husband, Joe. A week after Rene died Mrs. Guterez called Joe's home, "just to talk." A woman describing herself as "Joe's girlfriend" answered.

'Why you son of a bitch,' I said to him, 'you couldn't wait long enough until my little girl's soul rested in heaven. But don't worry, her soul is resting in heaven and your soul is never going to rest. You're going to pay for this.' I never heard from him since.

During the interview, when Mrs. Guterez was asked "how she felt" about a sad or unpleasant story that she initiated, she changed the subject to recall a distant happy event, to recount facts rather than feelings, or to tell another story in which her primary emotion was anger. Choosing her tale as well as the emotion pervading it allowed Mrs. Guterez to control what she felt during the interview. After her remarks about Joe, Mrs. Guterez recounted, with a smile of pride, her history of hard work.

I only went to school 'til I was 16. I had to go to work for my mother because we had no money and I had to go to work in a candy factory. And I worked at the railroad as mail girl. And I used to clean the windows and clean the floors.

Mrs. Guterez painted a fun-filled picture of her young adulthood. She described herself as "very pretty" and much sought after by neighborhood boys. Mrs. Guterez met her first husband, a cook at a Spanish club, when she was 20 years old. They married a year later. She remembers this time of her life as "fabulous."

He played the violin. He was brilliant. And he was so handsome. I was in shows at the Spanish club. I had a fabulous, fabulous life then. I was Miss Spain.

After two "lovely" years, her marriage turned sour due to her husband's philandering. Four children were born to the couple during their 8 years together. Rene, the last child, was born after Mrs. Guterez' first husband left his family. Mrs. Guterez nonchalantly described her unfaithful husband and their broken marriage.

He was a good man until he met that woman. He stayed out one night and my son asked me where he went. Then he said, 'I found somebody else.'

And I said, 'Okay.' Just like that. Then he joined the service and he wouldn't give me no support. [Pause] But I had a good family. All I had to do was say something and they were right there.

Although Mrs. Guterez named the period after her husband left as the worst financial time in her life, she insisted that she was emotionally unmoved by his leaving. Her children, she said, were also unaffected by their father's departure from their home and their lives. She emphasized that they suffered no ill effects from his desertion; in fact they knew "even as kids" that their life was "better without him."

'Go ahead, go.' I said. 'If you found a better life, go ahead.' They [the children] weren't upset. They knew. My oldest son said, 'Look, he didn't want us, mom, that's okay with us. We'll stick together.' And we did. And they all went to school and graduated and everything.

Although the children lost contact with their father, he attempted to see them late in his life. Mrs. Guterez' oldest son, Albert, then 18, reluctantly agreed to see him when he learned his father was ill. They had not communicated for over 10 years.

They all said no [to seeing their father]. But later, when he got very very sick with cancer my son went to see him. He said to him, 'Albert, I was nasty to your mother. I was rotten to your mother. And that's what I'm paying for now. You have a good mother. Don't ever let her go.'

Perhaps Mrs. Guterez had, for many years, longed to hear her husband's admission of guilt. She was therefore vindicated by his deathbed confession. By stating that he unequivocally acknowledged his mistake and accepted his illness as punishment, she neatly ties up the loose ends of her first marriage and puts closure on this chapter of her life. When asked what she thought about her husband's remorse, she shrugged.

I thought he was telling the truth. He died the next day. But I never forgave him. He left me with nothing.

Mrs. Guterez spoke with fondness of her second husband, a man she had known "all her life." He was an electrician who boarded in her parents' home prior to their marriage. When asked about her decision to marry Mr. Guterez, a man 12 years her senior, she replied:

He was good to me. I didn't love him but I got to like him because he was giving my kids a home. He said. 'I've got a good job. I'll keep your kids.' He loved my little girl [Rene] like she was his. She called him daddy.

Their marriage of 15 years ended with Mr. Guterez' death from cancer. One of the dreams that Mrs. Guterez held for her first marriage came true in her second—owning a home. She is proud of the South Philadelphia row home that she and Mr. Guterez bought over 40 years ago and in which she still lives. She often "robbed Peter to pay Paul" to "get a down payment together." Despite hard times financially, they were able to make mortgage payments because of her careful management. Her skill as a financial manager engendered lifelong self-esteem and a strong sense of independence. When asked who handled the money in the Guterez home, Mrs. Guterez laughed.

> I managed the money. I got the house. I'm still handling the money. I don't need nobody. I can make it on my own. Even now, if I want to buy something I wait. I might do without something first. [Pause] You can be poor and be independent.

Mrs. Guterez is proud to "deny" herself rather than be dependent on anyone. Her pride hinges on her ability to choose; she chooses to "do without" and be independent rather than "ask anybody for anything." When asked what she thinks about when she thinks of her life as a whole, Mrs. Guterez answered:

> I just thank God I'm here. I have $600 in the bank. I have no money, but I don't care. As long as I have enough to feed me. Once in a while I go to a casino. I used to wonder what was going to happen to me when I get old like my mother, how will I manage? Now I sit back. I have food. I have a freezer. I have can goods. I don't owe nobody nothing. When I go to bed at night I say, I'll wear the blue blouse and the blue pants and the blue shoes tomorrow. I plan what I'm going to wear for the next day. And what color nail polish.

Mrs. Guterez' sense of independence relating to choice extends to cognitive and emotional arenas. She decides how she will arrange her memories—which ones she will call to mind and which she will banish to her unconscious. She also chooses how she will "feel" about and handle her problematic relationships with her children and grandchildren. She is distressed that her son Albert, now 63, has been married and divorced three times. "I think that's crazy," she commented. Her relationship with her middle daughter, Carmen, now 60, has "always" been troublesome.

> She moved away from us. She had a little boy, Fred. She left him with us and she got married. And then she left her husband and moved back with us. Then she disappeared. We raised all three of her kids. Fred belongs to one man; Matt to another and Lynn belongs to another. Fred was about 6 years

old when she walked out. I never knew where she got to. From the time he was six until he was 18. I raised him all those years. To this day she won't tell me where she was. She's had more boyfriends than I have hairs on my head. Right now she's wrapped up in a cocoon with this man she's living with. I can't talk to her. She's not sensitive. Rene was the only one . . .

Although Mrs. Guterez raised all three of Carmen's children, she is, by her choice, estranged from two of them. She disapproves of their life-styles—Matt is on drugs and refuses to get help with his addiction; Lynn, the mother of one child, is again pregnant and remains unmarried. Although both contact her regularly, she refuses to allow them into her home until they "set themselves straight." She admits to being "pretty close" to Fred. All three grandchildren have lost contact with their mother, Carmen.

Mrs. Guterez' children, grandchildren, and greatgrandchildren are an important part of her narrative. Her displeasure with them is rooted in how she sees herself—she is the model for how to maneuver through the ups and downs in life.

> Like I said, I'm outspoken. I like things straight. And if it's not straight, forget it. I love all my kids but they should do what's right, not just what they want to do.

Mrs. Guterez pleasure in "having things straight" includes a notion of justice. Her first husband's acknowledgment of guilt concerning their marriage seemed proper. Even his final sufferings had a certain propriety—behaving badly deserves punishment. She therefore hopes that Rene's husband Joe will learn through a "little bit of punishment" the error of having an affair so soon after Rene's death.

> I don't wish him no illness or bad luck. But I want him to be punished a little bit to let him know that what he did was wrong. Like take away his job or if he wants to buy a car, don't let him buy the car.

Her sense of punitiveness toward Joe is modeled on God's perceived attribute of revenge. This idiosyncratic notion of a divine power bent on retribution is reminiscent of Mrs. Sheck's (in Chapter 2) hope that her recalcitrant son would "get it paid back to him one way or another." Mrs. Guterez, like Mrs. Thorne, also mentioned in Chapter 2, questions who God targeted by "giving" Rene cancer. She believes that it was she, rather than her daughter, who was God's focus for punishment.

> 'Look God,' I used to say, 'I know she's not going to get better, so why are you keeping her on this earth to punish me?'

Mrs. Guterez often told anecdotes about casino trips, gossiped about other seniors from the center, or described current knitting projects after being asked a question about her children or grandchildren. Living "in the present" protected her against the memories that might undermine her daily battle against sorrow. Her ability to shield herself against the erosion of grief seemed a lesson learned and perfected throughout life. By focusing on the minutiae of moment by moment she defended herself against the trauma of decades of disappointment and loss.

Mrs. Guterez' best defense, however, was her cherished memories—her family of origin, Rene in good health, and the distant past. Indeed, Mrs. Guterez seemed to find her greatest solace in her recollection of childhood. She meshed the simple pleasures of the past with her belief in an afterlife. This melding granted her a sense of closure about her life; it allowed her to view life's journey as a straight, uncomplicated route from childhood to death.

> I want to be cremated and throw my ashes in Penn Treaty Park. I used to go there when I was five years old. We used to go there on a boat. My mother would bring sandwiches. Monday, Wednesday, Friday, we clean. Tuesday, Thursday, Saturday, we go to Soupy Island in Penn Treaty Park. Oh, I liked that place. I want to go back.

SELF AS PACKAGE

Respondents disclosed themselves in many ways. How they dressed for the interview, the order of the room in which the interview took place, the display of family pictures and awards—all were part of women's narratives. Respondents' discussion of how they looked or "carried" themselves and their interest in new clothes, fixing their hair, and wearing make-up were also integral to women's self-disclosure. Concern with personal appearance and control over one's surroundings remain, in older age, links to independence, self-esteem, and a message to others of perceived self-worth.

Respondents sometimes presented themselves through a personal ideology, i.e., an organizing principle around which they wove a worldview. Like a recurring theme, a personal ideology knits the events of life into a meaningful totality of emotions and values. Unlike a recurring theme, personal ideology sometimes replaces self-knowledge and precludes flexibility in thinking, i.e., it disallows a change of mind and scorns others' dissimilar values. It offers a picture of the world in black and white. Straight lines permit respondents to see their lives as well-ordered and their views as well-defined.

We present Mrs. Desoto, who responded to late-life despair by zealously defending her opinions on various subjects. She organized her thoughts around a sense of propriety, and maintained strict control over which events in her past she allowed herself to recall.

Mrs. Desoto is a 71-year-old poor Caucasian woman who looks middle age. She lives in a tidy, bright apartment in a suburban subsidized housing community. Although she married and divorced two times after she was widowed at age 27, she uses her first husband's surname and calls herself a widow. Her first marriage yielded two children, Pat, now aged 45, who never married and lives "somewhere in Europe and belongs to a cult," and Greg, aged 41, who lives nearby with his family. She named her only grandson as the person closest to her, although she sees him "only at holidays." When asked to tell the story of her life, Mrs. Desoto began:

> Good or bad? My life hasn't been very good from the beginning. I had a very hard childhood. I had an older brother and sister who were very important to my parents. My mother was a lover of beauty and I wasn't beautiful. I was reminded of this all my life. I was the one that was not wanted. I was told by her I wasn't wanted. I can't remember my father. I think he was away a lot. Even when he was home he never interfered.

Mrs. Desoto endured physical and sexual abuse as a child and recalled her family's dysfunction. Her brother tried repeatedly to rape her when she was a teenager. She believes that the only reason he failed was because of "my loud mouth." Her brother often beat her; she, as well as the rest of the family, were "scared to death" of him. She never told her parents of the attempted rapes; she believes that they either would have "blamed" her or would have been powerless to stop him.

> He even hit her [mother]. They used to fight a lot. I remember many times getting up in the middle of the night and running after the milkman, asking him to get the police. [Pause] She [mother] didn't love him, but what's the word I'm looking for? She used to drag me to his hang out to beg him to come home. I can see him [brother] standing with his foot up on the wall and she [mother] was saying, 'Please, Frankie, please come home.' And he came home. I was so embarrassed. [Pause] It almost seemed as if she looked on him as a lover instead of a son.

Mrs. Desoto's troubles continued. She was raped at age 18 by three "friends" of a boy she dated at the time. She told no one of the incident and remains proud of her "self-control" in keeping past and present problems to herself. Although she is friendly with several of her neighbors, she admits that no one knows about her past or current hardship.

Despite her problematic feelings about her parents, Mrs. Desoto "did the right thing" when they became "old and ill." She cleaned the family home, prepared meals, and eventually paid for their funerals. She could not remember precisely when her mother died, but recalled only that "nobody was there. Nobody came to my mother's funeral except my son and I." When asked what her mother was like as a person, she responded after a long pause. "I don't know. I just don't know what kind of a person she was."

Mrs. Desoto's father died in 1955, which was the last time that she saw her brother and sister; to this day she does not know if they are "dead or alive."

Mrs. Desoto left high school in the tenth grade to work at "whatever—mostly waitressing—just to get out of the house." She subsequently moved to a rooming house in South Philadelphia. She sought refuge from her memories by partying nightly. She describes herself as a 21-year-old alcoholic when she met Luke, an 18-year-old sailor, in a bar on Delaware Avenue. They married a year later. Mrs. Desoto believes that marriage and motherhood cured her alcoholism.

The best financial time in Mrs. Desoto's life was also the happiest emotionally—the short period when she was married to her first husband and raising their children. When asked to describe her husband, she answered:

> He really loved me. I think that he was the one and only person who ever truly loved me. After we got married I drank very little.

After only 6 years of marriage, Mr. Desoto, a mechanic, was killed in an accident at work when he was 25. Their daughter was 5 years old and their son was 18 months. Mrs. Desoto named the day her husband died as the saddest of her life, and the subsequent year after his death as one of her bleakest periods.

> The day my husband was killed—that was the saddest in my life. Everything changed. We had just bought a house. And he was making good money at the end. One of the biggest tragedies was how people treated me. People said, 'Don't cry.' So I didn't cry. To this day I can't cry. I may get filled up, but I can't cry.

Due to her intense grief and her inability to "let it out," she "blacked out" the first year of widowhood. She returned to waitressing after her husband's death. Her major regrets about her life are her subsequent marriages. She remarried 2 years after her first husband's death, divorced her second husband after a year, married her third husband shortly after, and divorced him within 6 months. She summed up her two brief marriages in a short statement of remorse.

I should never have remarried, but life just went on. I got married and divorced, then I just jumped right back in. I was not in love with the third; the
second was horrible; the third was worse.

Mrs. Desoto paid off her home with her husband's life insurance, saved
"enough" to send her children to college, and instilled in them her own
drive for success. Although she never finished high school, Mrs. Desoto
earned a GED at age 50, received a diploma in medical assisting at age 51,
then earned a certificate as an occupational therapist a year later. She eventually was hired as a medical assistant. However, her boss's gradual plan
to "get rid of her" tainted her sense of achievement.

When I first started [in the doctor's office] I was treated with the utmost respect. I did everything in that office. But then it changed. [Pause] I remember another woman who was there for 7 years, an older woman. She wasn't
treated very well. Then when I got older, I got the same treatment. There is
absolute discrimination for an older woman. The last 5 years I hated it. For
the last 2 years I got no raises. It was demeaning.

Mrs. Desoto named the day she retired as the happiest of her life. Shortly
after retirement she moved into her current apartment. Although she anticipated "having things easier," she is disappointed by the high cost of
living, even in a subsidized housing complex. When asked about the hardest time of her life financially, she considered.

It's a toss up between right now and the year before I retired because my
rent went up so much. Now, food gets cut first because that's the only thing
that can be cut. That and going cold. You can't cut other things.

Mrs. Desoto believes that her lack of money negatively affects her relationship with her son. She is convinced that like herself, her son is disappointed by her poverty. Because of the unease she feels with her son and
daughter-in-law, she decided to spend last Christmas Day with a friend.
Perhaps her desire "to be rich" is as much a yearning for closeness with her
son as for financial well-being. When asked to describe him, she answered
cryptically.

If I had more money my son would be over here every week. I think he's
very disappointed that I'm poor. [Pause] He would do anything for me, but
I have to ask him, and sometimes he lies to make things easier for himself.
See, there's no warmth there. When I go there [to her son's home] it's very
strained. My son and grandson watch football. If I try to get into a conversation with my daughter-in-law she leaves the room. [Pause] But I have let

it go. Not made peace, but accepted it. Still, I would love to be a really rich person.

Mrs. Desoto's daughter, now a missionary in Europe, joined a small religious group while a junior in college, over 25 years ago. When asked if she had been close with her daughter before she joined the group, Mrs. Desoto replied:

> It was not a normal closeness. As I look back on it, I was not a really good mother. I never cuddled the children. We just didn't do that [cuddle] in those days. But I guess she loved me until she got into that cult. Then she totally alienated herself from a mother–daughter relationship. She stopped coming home. After she joined, she went to a girlfriend's house which was two blocks away from where we lived and she never even called me. And that was the end of mother and daughter.

Although Mrs. Desoto "usually" hears from Pat every 2 or 3 months, it has been 6 months since she last received a letter from her daughter. Even though they are physically and emotionally estranged, she is proud of Pat and integrates her daughter's success into her own sense of achievement. When Mrs. Desoto was asked to name *her* accomplishments, she answered:

> Pat was the first one on either side of the family to graduate from high school. The first one to graduate from college. And now she's getting a Ph.D.

Mrs. Desoto admits that she would like to forget about the past. Although she acknowledges that forgetting is difficult, she is convinced that reminiscing is far worse. Thinking about her unhappy childhood and the incidents that led to her children's estrangement robs her of peace. She believes that her personal history bears out her wisdom in "suppressing everything all my life, never giving way to my emotions." After she retired, she suffered a clinical depression. For her, depression resulted from "too much thinking."

> I never think. If I find myself doing that I stop because I would like for the rest of my life to have a little peace. That was one time [after retirement] I allowed myself to think about things. And that's what happens. I went into a severe depression. She [the therapist] really didn't help me. I mean she didn't change anything. I think if I had steeled myself as I had done all my life I could have done it on my own.

Sharing her feelings with a therapist proved to be useless, just as "thinking about things" portended disaster. This shows the crux of Mrs. Desoto's ideology—to be independent and manage her immediate environment,

she must control herself and forego introspection. Her "straight" path includes a strict propriety. She arms herself against the disarray of living by
prescribing appropriate conduct for herself and others.

> I believe you should dress properly and speak properly. You should keep
> your home properly. And don't ever lie to me.

Mrs. Desoto extends her sense of propriety to how she believes God
should act. As a born-again Christian, Mrs. Desoto describes herself as
"very religious." She believes that God's law is integrated into the very
structure of her personality in order to make sure that she acts appropri-
ately. God is therefore manifested in her life in concrete, worldly, and primarily negative ways.

> He [God] wasn't appreciating my going to bingo. It was gambling and
> that's why I never won. He fixed the buttons so that my card wouldn't win.
> [Pause] It may be that he [God] gave me that phobia about bridges to keep
> me from going down to Atlantic City to gamble. He wouldn't run the bus off
> the road, but he would just make sure I didn't win, and he would make the
> phobia about bridges worse.

The notion of a personal, rather petty God who dislikes gambling and
frightened Mrs. Desoto into abstaining from this vice fits into her view of
appropriate behavior for both God (as an authority figure) and herself (as
a believer). Her stringent requirement of how others should act leaves little
room for error or even humor. Indeed, one of the reasons that she left the
Catholic Church was the off-handed remark of a priest. She believes that
the degeneration of authority figures, like priests, portends general disaster for America.

> *Mrs. Desoto:* One day my son came home from school and said, we
> asked Father So and So why he wore pointed shoes. He
> answered, 'To kill the cockroaches in the corners.' I
> thought that was terrible. That was the beginning of the
> end for me.
> *Interviewer:* I'm not sure I understand.
> *Mrs. Desoto:* [Surprised] It [the answer] was beneath him. It was not
> an appropriate answer for a priest. It was not dignified.
> See, we don't revere anybody anymore. No one has au-
> thority now. I see this country going to hell and quickly.

Mrs. Desoto believes that the country's rapid descent has been hastened
by blurred gender roles. The fact that mothers work outside the home

augurs the disintegration of the family. She addressed the female interviewer with an unwavering stare.

> To me there was nothing greater than keeping the house clean and taking care of my children. Women who work are not happy. [Pointedly] You are not happy. Women are not happy with what they have today.

Despite her implacable stance on certain issues, other questions caused Mrs. Desoto to pause with confusion or lack of comprehension. When asked to name one or two important things about herself as a person, she replied haltingly and after a long pause.

> You've got me there. I can't think of anything. That's the first time anybody's ever asked me that. It just astounds me that I don't know myself well enough to describe myself to anybody. [Pause] My daughter once compared me to a steam engine. You just plow right ahead.

Earlier in the interview, Mrs. Desoto was unable to describe her mother. Perhaps because her boundaries were so brutally violated during her abusive childhood, Mrs. Desoto built especially impenetrable ones later in life. Her mental stanchions censor her memories and her self-knowledge. Although Mrs. Desoto continues to improve herself intellectually by reading avidly and auditing courses, she avoids introspection. Her strong opinion on matters of etiquette equals her lack of self-description. Strict rules of propriety keep her life ordered, controlled, solitary, and with little hope. When asked what she believed the future held for her, she answered:

> Nothing more than I have right now. I'm not contented, but there isn't much I can do about it. [Pause] I fear dying alone. I would like someone to be with me. I would love to see my daughter once before I died.

CHARACTERS IN THE STORY

Although most respondents were the heroines of their life story, other characters also occupied center stage. Ironically, many of these central characters were either dead or estranged from the women. However, their emotional importance in the women's lives magnified their ability to hurt or heal the women from the distance of place, time, or even death. For example, Mrs. Clarkson, mentioned in Chapter 3, was consumed by thoughts of her deceased husband and her role in his suicide. Mrs. Sheck, discussed in Chapter 2, and Mrs. Desoto, mentioned above, agonized over the estrangement of their children. These off-stage characters negatively influenced the women's quality of life in the present through the unresolved issues they represented.

For many poor African-American women, God was a central character in the life story. Several African-American respondents named God as "the person closest to me." To emphasize the spirituality of African-American women is not to portray them as unidimensional; rather it is to acknowledge that, in our sample, elderly African-American women living in poverty described God as the person or entity who was most present to them on a daily basis, who most strongly influenced their self-view and their behavior toward themselves and others, and who filled the role, often lacking in the women's lives, of a long-standing partner and confidant. God was in some ways an alter-ego of the women—the power that leveraged their relative "powerlessness" in this world.

We introduce Mrs. Billings as a respondent who views God as a main character in her life story. She is a 73-year-old poor African-American divorcee who lives in a finely furnished apartment in a subsidized housing facility.

Mrs. Billings was one of three sisters born to a family of sharecroppers in Virginia. The family moved to the Hunting Park section of Philadelphia when she was 3 years old.

> I'm going to tell you the truth. My father was a lovely man. I love him to death, but he wasn't a good provider. My mother worked day and night for her kids. He wasn't one to run out in the street or nothing like that, but he just couldn't give up his money. Mom was the one that saw we had this and that. My father thought as long as you have the table set you don't need nothing else.

Mrs. Billings' parents separated when their daughters were grown. However, the family members remained close; they always lived within a three block radius of one another. At one point, Mrs. Billings lived with her father. Her mother moved in with another daughter and her family.

> It was a hurting day, the day she [mother] told me she was going to leave [my father]. She called me sister. She said, 'I'm going, sister.' We knew that one day that would happen because she was a hard working person and she liked nice things. We knew it would happen and we almost relished it. See, we wanted a good life for mom and for ourselves. My sisters married nice men who gave them nice homes. I never had the opportunity.

Mrs. Billings admitted that she, like her mother and sister, cared about possessing "nice things" and living a "respectable" life and had dreams of "doing well." When she met her husband, she thought her dreams would materialize. Reality hit Mrs. Billings immediately after her wedding.

> I liked him [husband] right away. He was a tall gentleman and I think he was good-looking, handsome really, and he dressed very well. Well, he got that way about him. Bull. He was full of bull. That's what he really was. When I told my mother I was getting married she wouldn't have any parts of it, because she said he didn't treat me right. Papa said, 'Oh, let her go on.' Well, we got married on a Saturday and I bought myself a nice little aqua two piece dress and a brown straw hat. I did look nice. My mother was heartbroken. She wouldn't give me her blessing but my father was all gung ho. But I'm telling you now, the next day, that Sunday morning I knew I made a mistake. Oh, girl, what are you in for? See we went to live with the Billings [husband's family]. I just had an eerie feeling that I wasn't wanted. I felt like I was an alien, like so alone, yet not that far from my mother. It was the loneliness, the emptiness. And that I didn't belong. When my mother came to visit me, she said, 'Sister, you look so sad.'

Mrs. Billings' Sunday morning prescience about her marriage came to pass. Loneliness, poverty, and humiliation were more present companions than her husband. Mr. Billings' gambling debts forced the couple into dire straits. Living with her in-laws added to her anguish. Even the birth of their only son did not alleviate her longing to "go home."

> He never made a place for me. The one place he did make for me, my God, that was a little rat-infested place. He said we'll stay here until we do better but he never made preparations to do better. In fact, every Friday he said to me, 'Take your ring to the pawn shop.' The man knew me because he knew every Friday I'd be up there to get my wedding band pawned. And every Monday I'd take his suit to the pawn shop. That was a ritual every week.

Mrs. Billings left the Billings' home prior to her third wedding anniversary. She is certain that her husband did not suffer the loss of his wife and son.

> I don't think he paid any mind. I don't think he was even at home. It was a Saturday morning when it just struck me all of a sudden. Time to move on. And I called my mother. I said, 'Can I come home?' So I came home that day, a Saturday with a baby in my arms and the clothes on my back. And with a bushel basket that they used to put vegetables in. That was for the clothes the baby had. I didn't have anything.

Mrs. Billings remembers this period of her life as exceedingly bleak. She received no support from her husband and finally stopped asking for it.

She then related a series of events in which her in-laws would "steal" her
son. She tired of trying to "steal him back." These stressful incidents cul-
minated in her "giving" her son to her husband's family when Norbert was
"just about six or seven years old." When the interviewer commented on
the pain that this must have caused her, she replied:

> Oh, I almost died. See, they let him do anything he wanted to. They were
> that type of family. I said to him, 'You want to leave mama?' And he said,
> 'Yeah.' My mother said, 'Sister, you're not giving him up, but to give him a
> better life, better conditions than what we had.' See, my mother couldn't see
> me keeping him because the Billings stole him a couple of times. My mother
> would be down the avenue or the street, and then she would say, 'I wonder
> where the baby is. Oh, the Billings took him.' Now I got to go down there and
> my mother would do the fighting. I'm not a fighter. And she would have to
> get him and say. 'Don't take him any more without letting sister know.' So to
> get all that out of the way my mother said, 'He'll have a better life down at
> the Billings.' They just doted on him.

When asked how often she saw her son after the Billings "took" him,
she answered, "I'd run into him, but I didn't go to their house. But he still
came to our church." After his infancy, Mrs. Billings never shared a home
with her son.

It was hard to connect Mrs. Billings present feeling—she often punctuated her story with laughter—to the events that she relayed. However,
after a pause Mrs. Billings said softly:

> It was a terrible experience. The only reason he was down at the Billings
> was my mother and she was such a good person I know she wouldn't tell me
> nothing if it wasn't for his own good.

Mrs. Billings distanced herself from the loss of her son. By reiterating
that her mother encouraged her to "give him to the Billings," Mrs. Billings
put the onus of responsibility for his loss on her mother's concern for her
as well as for the need to give Norbert a good life. When asked if she ever
regretted her decision, she answered adamantly.

> No. No, indeed not. He had a better life there. They lived a different life-
> style from me. She [mother-in-law] never had to work. My mother knew the
> Billings and how they lived a nice life, had a nice home. So she said, 'Sister,
> it's too much for you to do.' And they cared for my son because they didn't
> have too many other grandchildren. My mother said let him go down there
> and they will give him a better life because we didn't have the comforts of
> some people's home. We had outdoor plumbing.

At the time of the interview, Mrs. Billings had problems with her eyes; an unnamed virus renders them "tired" and unable to focus. Therefore, Mrs. Billings told the above narrative with eyes half-closed and averted. Perhaps she was refusing to "see" this incident in her memory. A network of conflicting emotions permeated her narrative. Her desire to have a better life for her son found fruition when he moved in with the Billings. However, the price that she paid for her son's "good" life was perhaps more than she could afford. Poverty for Mrs. Billings was the loss of her son, for which she still pays with her painful memories.

The year following Norbert's move to the Billings' home posed extra hardships for Mrs. Billings. Her mother, aged 48, died after a brief bout with cancer. Mrs. Billings suffered a major depression. Grief over her mother's death was especially acute; she had always looked to her mother to provide counsel for her indecision.

> When I got myself to feeling better I went to work. I stayed with my father until I was 35 years old and then I went out on my own. My father was good to me. He would bring food for me every Friday. I got myself a nice apartment. I always wanted to better myself.

Mrs. Billings strongly commiserates with the plight of single working women who try to improve their situation. She once thought that by remarrying she could better her financial circumstances. While working as a sales person she intended to marry a second time but found out that her fiancé had "two or three women." She assured the interviewer that although she was disappointed, she now believes she was better off without him.

> I still see him now and then, and I just look at him like he was one of them pieces of wood. He means nothing. See, most girls I know, if they have anything now, they got that on their own. No man helped them to get it.

Mrs. Billings is an expert on self-improvement and optimism; she looks for, and finds, the "silver lining" in life's gloomiest events. She lived alone for the rest of her life and eventually bought a home, which she considers one of her major accomplishments. When asked how Norbert's life unfolded, Mrs. Billings paused, then replied:

> He got a scholarship which he did not use. He wanted to be with the crowd and he said no [to the scholarship]. He's sorry today. After he came out of the service he worked for the [. . .] company. Some of these things are very unpleasant. He worked; he was doing well. And I thought everything was fine. And one day it came on the radio about this man held up a truck driver. And the name was Norbert Billings. Someone called me and said, 'Is that Norbert?'

I said, 'I hope not.' But it was. Now he got out of that because the judge said, 'You did not have a record, you been in the service. What in the world possessed you to hold up a truck?' He had a gun. It didn't have no bullets in it, but the old man driving, he passed away. It scared him to death. They put him on five years probation. That was a heartache. I didn't want to believe it but a fact is a fact. It was in the newspaper. I think he [Norbert] stole that from me [the newspaper]. I keep things so you can reflect back some times whether it's good or bad.

Mrs. Billings admits that self-insight includes acknowledging "negative" events. Although she willingly reveals her various "bad times," she makes it clear that there is no dearth of "good things in life." Her "good things" hinge on her "upbeat" personality, which is a legacy from her mother, and her faith in God. Her mother and God are central characters in her life story. She names her mother's influence as integral to her positive personal characteristics, such as independence, an emphasis on "carrying yourself well," pride that she has survived hardship, and an optimistic view of the future.

I feel very good about myself that I have this independent attitude. It just does something to me. I have a strong sense of pride because I come from that type of family. I also come from a giving mother. My girlfriend says, 'You strong. Don't you never tell nobody you weak. Because a weak person could never have survived what you went through.' I used to think of myself as weak. But I know I'm not. But you really have to fight and you can't give up. If you give up you will not survive. I'm going to make it; I'm going to do it. This is going to be the case.

Mrs. Billings describes herself as "blessed" despite her physical and emotional sufferings. Although she receives food stamps and reimbursement for utility bills, she contributes to several charities and various churches. She views generosity as the appropriate response in her reciprocal relationship with God.

Mrs. Billings: That's where I think I get my blessings from. I don't have it but I do. I want to be able to give something to God. I mean he keeps me going and he's been good to me and I think I should be able to do that.
Interviewer: How has God been good to you?
Mrs. Billings: Well, I have life. And I have a place to live that's comfortable. And I believe he will help me with my eyes. [Pause] You got to have faith. I have faith that my eyes are going to get better, that I'm going to be able to see

like I did see. It may not ever occur. But I have to believe
that it is even though it's taking a lengthy time. They
[doctors] don't know the solution to it; they don't know
nothing about it. But through my faith it will get better.

Mrs. Billings believes that she will be able to "see" only through her
faith. She also admits that she has long petitioned God for healing and acknowledges that her eyesight might never be restored. She is convinced
that human (doctors) intervention is useless. She is certain that the onus of
responsibility for healing rests on her faith. To demonstrate proof of faith's
power in her life, she recounted a "miracle" that occurred when she and
her son were most needful.

We were living at my father's and the baby was just an infant. I nursed
him but he needed some milk and I didn't have a penny in the house and my
father was at work. I said the baby is going to wake up and there was snow
on the ground and the store was around the corner. And somebody knocked
on the window and said, 'How's the baby?' I said, 'Oh, he's asleep.' It was a
neighbor. He said, 'Here's a dollar, go get the baby some ice cream.' Soon as
that person turned the corner, I put on my coat. I think the baby had woke up
then. I sped around that corner; I prayed the whole time 'til I got that milk.
But I had the faith. I always nursed him, but evidently he nursed it all out.
And if you don't eat you won't have none yourself. I had a lot of faith then.
I had to. Cause I have had some knocks in my life. You have to have faith because I don't think—. If you don't have faith, I don't think that the incident
or whatever will never happen. It will never happen if you don't have the
faith. Part of what happens is your believing it will happen.

In this, Mrs. Billings' faith is prior to God's assistance. God, as a character in her life story, is ever waiting in the wings to respond. She is empowered, through her personal sense of responsibility *and* her faith to do
her part, which is to pray and believe she will be answered. The following
is Mrs. Billings answer to the question: "Can you name one or two major
accomplishments in your life?"

Mrs. Billings: I accomplished a better awareness of the power of God;
                    of what God can actually do for you if you believe.
Interviewer: How did you accomplish that?
Mrs. Billings: I think with certain situations happening in my life and
                    how I overcame some of the obstacles, it had to be a
                    higher being than man.
Interviewer: Can you give me an example?
Mrs. Billings: I lost my job in '82 and I wasn't really ready to retire and

my compensation ran out. I had no income. I prayed and I thought some way, some how, you will make it to keep this house, my only house, or wherever you will go you'll be able to make it. You have to be 62 to get in here. And I wasn't quite 60 when I lost my job. So those two years were hard but I made it. I lost the house but as soon as I saw this [apartment] I fell in love with it. I'm very happy here. He'll take care of you. Besides, I can't call on mama, so I guess I call on God more.

Mrs. Billings highlights her own significance in her relationship with God. God's power is made manifest through her belief. She also seems to see God as a concrete, mundane, and personal replacement for her deceased mother. God must now stand where her mother stood—ready and willing to help her with difficult life events. Several of Mrs. Billings' major life decisions, such as "giving" Norbert to the Billings, were made at her mother's suggestion. Now, God assumes the role that her mother once held—knowing what is best for her and advising her of it.

METAPHORS

Telling a life story lends a testimonial flavor to recounting life. Some respondents use the vehicle of metaphor as a means to present an integrated life story. A strong, unifying metaphor becomes the frame in which life circumstances are securely set as well as a tool to gather the disappointments that threaten to unravel a life. We present Mrs. McDouglas, whose all-pervasive metaphor is a backdrop for major life events and the measure she uses to evaluate herself.

Mrs. McDouglas is a 96-year-old poor Caucasian widow who lives in the Fishtown section of Philadelphia. The front of Mrs. McDouglas' home, now boarded and covered by graffiti, was the family grocery store. It was opened in 1900 by her grandmother, later owned by her mother, and finally owned and operated by Mrs. McDouglas and her husband. She closed the store in 1979 because she "just got tired."

Mrs. McDouglas' home is the back of the store. It consists of an unheated dining room, where the interview took place on a drizzly February morning, a large kitchen, and an "upstairs." One of the three upstairs rooms is her "winter living room because it's warm." Her dining furniture, dark and bulky, is reminiscent of the 1920s. Tiny white and green tiles, fashionable during the 1940s, line the kitchen walls. The entrance to the vacant grocery store is through a bolted glass door in the dining room. Only shadows of boxes are seen through the smoky glass, and an eerie sense of time warp emanates from the darkness. Mrs. McDouglas enters the store "once in a while" to retrieve "papers and things" that are stored there.

Mrs. McDouglas is small, thin, with a slightly stooped stance and a gentle manner. Although she had a "bad night" and hadn't slept much, she insisted on keeping the appointment with the interviewer. Mrs. McDouglas was born in 1899 in her parents' home in Kensington. Her family eventually moved into the store, where she and her younger sister were raised. She left school when she was 14 years old to work in a hosiery factory. Because of asthma, she quit her job, stayed home, and helped in the store. Her adeptness at managing the store allowed her mother some needed time off.

> When I was 18 my mother was able to go to the seashore for a couple weeks and I took care of the store. That store was my life right from the beginning.

While Mrs. McDouglas was still a youngster her parents divorced. She quickly lost all contact with her father and learned that "he was killed" some years later, but did not remember the circumstances. "It was all so long ago," she explained. Mrs. McDouglas recalls her youth as pleasant and "just normal." It consisted of working in the store, enjoying a close relationship with her mother and sister, and busying herself with a host of customers and friends.

Mrs. McDouglas met her husband at a Halloween party when she was 23 years old. Their decision to live behind the store augured well for them financially.

> My mother was very good to us. Of course she owned the store and she made a fairly good living out of it. So we all enjoyed a good living. See, I always had the store, and we always had plenty to eat.

Mrs. McDouglas inherited the store from her mother in 1950, after her death. The McDouglas children were "pretty well grown" by then, but still living at home. Mr. McDouglas, a truck driver, helped out in the store after hours by doing heavy work, such as unloading cartons and lifting boxes. Mrs. McDouglas painted a portrait of her husband as a quiet, hard-working, and agreeable man. She believes their marriage was "good." She recalled, with the hint of a smile, the only request her husband ever made of her.

> After my mother died he [husband] wanted me to sell the store and live like regular people. See, because the store came first. But I couldn't. I depended on the store. [Pause] But he was a very good man. He used to give me his whole pay.

The McDouglas' two children, Ellen and John, were raised much the way she had been raised—behind the store—even attending the same schools that she attended as a girl. Both children eventually moved away from the neighborhood and now live in the suburbs of Philadelphia. Mr. McDouglas died in 1970 from a heart attack. Mrs. McDouglas' life changed little after her children moved and her husband died. The store became "more important" in her life.

Although Mrs. McDouglas can remember when her neighborhood was a series of farms, the grim changes she witnesses in her neighborhood, such as drug use, unemployment, and crime, do not frighten her. Her children would like her to move. However, she is convinced that because of *their* problems, she must maintain her independence in her own home. Ellen, 66, is married and seriously ill with a respiratory ailment. John, now 62 and divorced, is raising his granddaughter. Mrs. McDouglas sees her children infrequently.

> If I got sick Ellen couldn't take care of me. Of course maybe if she would ask me to come to live with her, I might. John doesn't have any place for me to go either. Besides, I'd hate to depend on them and I wouldn't want to disrupt their lives. I've talked to a lot of people who have given up their homes to live with their children. Every one of them advised me not to do it. I don't know what's going to happen to me in the end. I guess I'm going to have to go in some retirement home or . . . . I don't want to do it. I want to do what I'm doing now.

No clear picture of Mrs. McDouglas' relationship with her children emerged through her narrative. What did seem clear is that her children are not integral to her sense of satisfaction about life. Indeed, she admits that she is "almost never home." She visits a senior center daily, borrows library books "religiously," and on Saturday evenings dates a gentleman friend.

> The last movie we saw was "Babe." I just loved it. But he's not the marrying kind. We're just friends.

When asked to describe herself, Mrs. McDouglas listed attributes that she cultivated because of the store.

> I'm friendly, which is important when you have a business. When you're in the store you have to be pleasant to everybody. You have to put your best face forward. Also, I'm independent. I think I'm independent because I always ran the store, talking to people and being congenial, and that gives you a sense of confidence.

Mrs. McDouglas' mirror, as well as the lens through which she views the world, is the store. It was the site of her vocation, as well as the setting in which she found and refined a social identity. She summed up the store's importance in her life when she related how she had been robbed at gun point while she was working in the store during the late 1960s.

> *Interviewer:*   Did that make you want to get rid of the store?
> *Mrs. McDouglas:*   Oh, no. [With a chuckle] That store was my life, really.

Mrs. McDouglas was recently the subject of a neighborhood newspaper article that announced her ninety-sixth birthday. The article ended with a quote from Mrs. McDouglas: "Life is what you make it." When the interviewer commented on this remark, Mrs. McDouglas added:

> And working very hard in that store. I used to be open from 7 in the morning until 7 at night.

The store provided Mrs. McDouglas with the major fodder for summing up 96 years of life. Her spirituality was also rooted and nurtured in the store, and in the ethical decisions she was forced to make there. For example, she continued to extend credit to profligate customers.

> They never paid me back. Sometimes I'd never see them again and sometimes they'd walk right by me on the street like it never happened. But I don't think the worst of everybody. I don't have any enemies that I couldn't forgive.

Mrs. McDouglas lives squarely in the present and anticipates future joys, such as learning how to play pool. Although her daughter's health, neighborhood crime, and the disintegration of her property are problems that vex her, she waxed philosophical on these issues. For example, when commenting on the graffiti that covers every inch of her beloved store, she chuckled.

> I'd like to paint it but I know it will be a wonderful spot for them to do it all over again.

She admits that she seldom thinks of the past and has no desire to re-work her mistakes or recount her regrets. She infrequently worries about the future.

> I like to think about now. When I can't sleep I keep on thinking about what I'm going to do when I get old, but only when I can't sleep.

At age 96, the above comment is both poignant and stunning. Mrs. Mc-Douglas does not yet think of herself as old. Instead, she enjoys "one day at a time" and hopes to continue the path of busyness, congeniality, and optimism on which the "store" placed her over 80 years ago.

SUMMARY

The value of retrospection is the value of choice. In this, independence remains an important component in the women's stories, from what they chose to do with their limited finances, as well as what parts of the past they chose to look back on and share in the interview.

Mrs. Guterez decided which incidents, events, and emotions she would recall and mention, and how she would react to them. Likewise, Mrs. Desoto chose an alternative but equally active route regarding retrospection— she chose "never" to think about the past because her memories engendered pain. Mrs. Billings looked squarely at the "good" and "bad" in her life and chose to emphasize her active, powerful relationship with God and the importance of faith in calling forth God's blessings.

The value of retrospection, while being a matter of choice, is intricately tied to our expectations about life. Both Mrs. Guterez and Mrs. Desoto probably expected more emotional sustenance at this stage of their lives, especially from their children. Mrs. Guterez outlived her beloved daughter and Mrs. Desoto is estranged, in different ways, from both of her children. Mrs. Billings, early on, disconnected her sense of contentment from the unfolding of her son's life. In the latter stage of life, Mrs. Billings is happy to finally "have nice things" and "live respectably." Her surprised reaction to her present ease also speaks to the issue of race regarding women's expectations.

Mrs. McDouglas' busy, happy daily life is built on a past that was similar—busy because of the store and pleasant because it exceeded her expectations both financially and emotionally. Her pleasure at succeeding at "outside" work speaks to the sense of personal development and self-confidence that women of her cohort gained from "working in the world."

Our final chapter, The Conclusion, offers a summary of the findings of our research.

10

&

Conclusion

W e acknowledge that any study of the "poor" has political assumptions and implications. If the prime purpose of research is to eliminate poverty, studies on the economy are more significant than data on the lifestyles of impoverished women. Our path follows Gans' (1970:153) suggestion that if research on the "poor" as individuals hopes to reflect their diverse cultural and personality elements, it must record their "aspirations, to see where they exist [and] how strongly they are held." However, aspirations themselves are complex, and can act both as a lens to view the world and a tool to maneuver one's way through it. We therefore examined the earlier and continuing expectations of women living in poverty as an important gauge of their self-concept and worldview.

At least three conclusions can be reached from our research. First, because of the concerns by and about an aging population, the material welfare of the women interviewed improved as they aged. Supplemental Security Income, Disability Insurance, Medicare and Medicaid, and housing, food, and energy assistance greatly improved the quality of their lives. Because of this governmental aid, most women in our "poor" groups altered earlier definitions—which included abuse, hunger, and homelessness—of poverty. Present definitions of poverty were linked to what was expected from life, what was achieved, as well as to current emotional and relational contentment or dissatisfaction.

Second, financial hardship in older age did not mean that an elder considered herself "poor." Although admitting to "having it hard" throughout their lives, poor women equated poverty with emotional, familial, or relational deprivation. As mentioned earlier, we termed this "renaming" the paradox of poverty in order to reflect women's rejection of traditional cultural and historical definitions of poverty. Also, although respondents may have conceived of the circumstances of their lives as related to the "larger" world of economic, political, and social conditions, their "being poor" was embedded in the everyday web of the "smaller" world in which

233

they lived. For example, on the whole there was little insight into the macro-economy that constructed "the poor" as a class status in American society. However, women had scrutinized and often tried to enlarge the boundaries of their microeconomy by any means possible, such as taking an extra job or "making soup from one onion." Their intimate portrait of poverty shows a miniaturization not only of their satisfaction, but of their discontent as well (Rubinstein, 1991).

An inability to plan for the future, often ascribed to the poor, may have been the case early in women's lives due to the limits society placed on women, especially on poor women, and most especially on poor women of color. In the latter stage of their lives, however, women took pride in the active choices they made concerning the daily minutiae of their lives, such as choosing, because of limited finances, to forego dinner and have dessert instead. In this, they acquired the sense of control over their lives that informs high self-esteem.

Third, our research shows, in a profound way, the salience of women's faith. It might be said that their experience of God is also miniaturized. It is concrete, personal, and integrated into the mundane events of everyday life. However, this belies Merton's [1996 (1956):82] view that "familiarity [with God] has destroyed all sense of the reality of God's *Tremendum Mysterium*." For most poor women interviewed, their experience of God was as expectant in silence, as nuanced in conversation, as varied in intimacy, and as well-honed in acceptance as any bond between partners of long-standing who remain mystified by each other. Women's faith was their primary coping mechanism, as well as their main route in seeking emotional, spiritual, *and* financial support. To ignore older women's experience of God is to diminish an all-encompassing reality in their lives.

SUBJECTIVE AND OBJECTIVE POVERTY

In telling their life story, women looked at their pasts in both subjective and objective ways. As an object, the past could be unearthed, i.e., opened not only to investigation but to re-creation. However, stepping into the past, like stepping into Heraclitus' river, changed it. Women experienced new emotions by "retelling" past events. In this, women easily waded in and out of subjective and objective notions of poverty *and* of their lives. They actually entered the nitty gritty of memory, examined what they stored there, and emerged with an organizing story in hand.

From this, our book might be seen as a collection of random autobiographies, unique narratives of women that cannot be generalized to any larger population. However, if women's stories do not define their generation, they do, like literature, grant a "truth" by offering a window into a small section of a certain society at a particular time.

We offer a shift in perspective by viewing history from the vantage of disenfranchised women. Like snapshots from someone else's album, women's narratives show a different slice of history. Their narratives selected a subjective "scene" from their personal pasts. They removed the unessential from the longer, broader, and more detailed "objective" panorama, and enshrined their version by telling the story they chose to tell (Wiener & Rosenthal, 1993).

Through our research we learned about the "larger" world's breadth of social injustice—its tentacles reach destructively into subsequent generations. We also learned that women mine their strength in the face of adversity in various ways, especially through an experience of God bred and nourished within their "smaller" world. By telling their stories, women became active in their personal history (Gutierez, 1987), and joined the cacophony of long-silenced voices.

FUTURE RESEARCH

As we noted throughout this book, the political and social events of the "larger" world profoundly influenced individual development (Stewart, 1994). Growing and struggling through the Depression and at least one world war etched personal and public concepts of poverty, sacrifice, and security into respondents' worldviews. We, as researchers, wonder about the offspring of the women who "scrimped, saved, and worked hard" to ensure a "better life" for their children. Certainly, the concept of poverty will be different for generations—the "sandwich" generation that is now in its sixties, and more especially the baby-boomers—who follow. A lower threshold both for "what poor is" and for present sacrifice for future rewards will alter both the subjective and objective definitions of poverty.

We end our book with a hope that researchers in the future will ask our generation to tell our life stories (Hoffman, 1999). The prosperity of the 1950s, the Vietnam War, civil rights and women's movements, feminism, womanism, political assassinations and scandals, and differing cultural definitions of "truth," morality, and spirituality will be the "larger" backdrop against which we frame the "smaller" stories of our emotional dreams and financial goals, retrospective expectations, perceived accomplishments, and our experience of God.

References

Abel-Smith, Brian, & Townsend, Peter. 1972. "The poor and the poorest." In *Poverty: Selected readings*. Jack L. Roach & Janet K. Roach, eds. Pp. 138–150. Baltimore, MD: Penguin Books.

Bentz, Marilyn. 1997. "Beyond ethics: Science, friendship, and privacy." In *Indians and anthropologists: Vine Deloria, Jr., and the critique of anthropology*. Thomas Biolsi & Larry J. Zimmerman, eds. Pp. 120–132. Tucson, AR: The University of Arizona Press.

Black, Helen K. 1997a. "Perception of privilege." Paper presented at the 50th annual meeting of The Gerontological Society of America, Cincinnati, OH.

Black, Helen K. 1997b. "Spirituality intersecting at the crossroad of gender, aging and identity." Paper presented at the 50th annual meeting of The Gerontological Society of America, Cincinnati, OH.

Blank, Rebecca M. 1992. *Do justice: Linking Christian faith and modern economic life*. Cleveland, OH: United Church Press.

Bound, J., Duncan, G., Laren, D., & Oleinick, G. 1991. "Poverty dynamics in widowhood." *Journal of Gerontology, 46*, S115–S134.

Bower, Anne. 1996. "The Next step: Poor and non-poor elderly women's attitudes toward job-related advancement." Paper presented at the 49th annual meeting of The Gerontological Society of America, Washington, DC.

Brubaker, Pam. 1994. *Women don't count: The challenge of women's poverty to Christian ethics*. Atlanta, GA: Scholars Press.

Burkhauser, R., & Duncan, G. 1988. "Life events, public policy and the economic vulnerability of children and the elderly." In *The vulnerable*. J. Palmer, ed. Pp. 55–88. Washington, DC: Urban Institute Press.

Cannon, Katie. 1997. Personal correspondence, March 17.

Chatters, L., & Jackson, J. 1989. "Quality of life and subjective well being among black Americans." In *Black adult development and aging*. R. Jones, ed. Pp. 191–214. Berkeley: Henry & Cobb.

Clark, W. 1988. *Old and poor*. Lexington, KY: Lexington Books.

Coe, R. 1988. "A longitudinal examination of poverty in the elderly years." *Gerontologist, 28*, 540–544.

Coughlin, T., Liu, K., & McBride, T. 1992. "Severely disabled elderly persons with financially catastrophic health care expenses." *Gerontologist, 32*, 391–403.

Crystal, S., & Beck, P. 1992. "A room of one's own: The SRO and the single elderly." *Gerontologist, 32*, 684–692.

Crystal, S., Shea, D., & Krishnaswami, S. 1992. "Educational attainment, occupational history and stratification: Determinants of later life economic outcomes." *Journal of Gerontology, 47,* S213–S221.

Davis, K., Grant, P., & Rowland, D. 1992. "Alone and poor: The plight of elderly women." In *Gender and aging.* L. Glasse and J. Hendricks, eds. Pp. 79–90. Amityville, NY: Baywood.

Dodge, Hiroko H. 1996. *Poverty transitions among elderly widows.* New York: Garland.

Facio, Elisa. 1993. "Ethnography as personal experience." *In Race and ethnicity in research methods.* John H. Stanfield II & Rutledge M. Dennis, eds. Pp. 75–91. Newbury Park, CA: Sage.

Ford, A., Haug, M., Roy, A., Jones, P., & Folmar, S. 1992. "New cohorts of urban elders: Are they in trouble?" *Journal of Gerontology, 47,* S297–303.

Fraser, Nancy. 1997. *Justice interruptus.* New York: Routledge.

Frazier, E. Franklin. 1962. *The black bourgeoisie.* New York: Free Press.

Funkenstein, Amos. 1993. "The incomprehensible catastrophe: Memory and narrative." In *The narrative study of lives,* Vol. 1. Ruthellen Josselson & Amia Lieblich, eds. Pp. 21 –29. Newbury Park, CA: Sage.

Gans, Herbert J. 1970. "Poverty and culture: Some basic questions about methods of studying life-styles of the poor." In *The concept of poverty.* Peter Townsend, ed. Pp. 146–164. New York: American Elsevier.

Geertz, Clifford. 1973. *The interpretation of cultures.* New York: Basic Books.

Gergen, Mary M., & Gergen, Kenneth J. 1993. "Narratives of the gendered body in popular autobiography." In *The narrative study of lives,* Vol. 1. Ruthellen Josselson & Amia Lieblich, eds. Pp. 191–218. Newbury Park, CA: Sage.

Grant, J. 1989. "Womanist theology: Black women's experience as a source for doing theology, with special reference to Christology." In *African American religious studies.* G. Wilmore, ed. Pp. 208–227. Durham, NC: Duke University Press.

Gubrium, Jaber F. 1993. *Speaking of life.* New York: Aldine de Gruyter.

Gubrium, Jaber F., & Holstein, James A. 1997. *The new language of qualitative method.* New York: Oxford University Press.

Gutierez, Gustavo. 1987. *On Job: God-talk and the suffering of the innocent.* Translated from the Spanish by Matthew J. O'Connell. Maryknoll, NY: Orbis.

Harrington, Michael. 1965. *The politics of poverty.* New York: League for Industrial Democracy.

Hess, B. 1995. "Poverty." In *Encyclopedia of aging.* G. Maddox, ed. Pp. 748–751. New York: Springer.

Hoffman, Christine. 1999. Personal correspondence of February 12.

Holden, K., Burkheiser, R., & Myers, D. 1986. "Income transition at older stages of life." *Gerontologist, 64,* 292–297.

Jackson, J., Chatters, L., & Taylor, R. 1993. *Aging in black America.* Newbury Park, CA: Sage.

Jones, John D. 1990. *Poverty and the human condition.* Lewiston, NY: Edwin Mellon.

Jordan, Bill. 1996. *A theory of poverty and social exclusion.* Cambridge, MA: Blackwell.

Josselson, Ruthellen. 1993. "A narrative introduction." In *The narrative study of lives,* Vol. 1. Ruthellen Josselson & Amia Lieblich, eds. Pp. ix–xii. Newbury Park, CA: Sage.

Kaufman, Sharon. 1986. *The ageless self.* Madison, WI: University of Wisconsin Press.

King, Deborah. 1988. "Multiple jeopardy, multiple consciousness." *Signs, 14,* 42–72.

King, Martin Luther. 1964. *Poverty*. Nobel Lecture. New York: Harper & Row.

Lloyd, Cynthia B. 1994. *Household structure and poverty: What are the connections?* The Population Council, Research Division, working papers, no. 74. New York: The Population Council.

Mencher, Samuel. 1972. "The problem of measuring poverty." In *Poverty: Selected readings*. Jack L. Roach & Janet K. Roach, eds. Pp. 71–85. Baltimore, MD: Penguin.

Merton, Thomas. 1996 (1956). *A Search for solitude: The journals of Thomas Merton*, Vol. 3, 1952–1960. Lawrence S. Cunningham, ed. San Francisco: Harper.

Mitchell, H. 1975. *Black belief*. New York: Harper & Row.

Moon, M. 1988. "The economic situation of older Americans." *Annual Revue of Gerontology, 8*, 102–131.

Pargament, Kenneth I. 1997. *The psychology of religion and coping*. New York: Guilford.

The President's Commission in Income Maintenance Programs. 1972. "Poverty amid plenty: The American paradox." In *Poverty: Selected readings*. Jack L. Roach & Janet K. Roach, eds. Pp. 109–121. Baltimore, MD: Penguin.

Roach, Jack L., & Roach, Janet K. 1972. "Introduction." In *Poverty: Selected readings*. Jack L. Roach & Janet K. Roach, eds. Pp. 9–39. Baltimore, MD: Penguin.

Rosenthal, Gabriele. 1993. "Reconstruction of life stories: Principles of selection in generating stories for narrative biographical interviews." In *The narrative study of lives*, Vol. 1. Ruthellen Josselson & Amia Lieblich, eds. Pp. 59–91. Newbury Park, CA: Sage.

Rubinstein, Robert L. 1989. "Home environments of older people." *Journal of Gerontology, 44*, S45–55.

Rubinstein, Robert L. 1991. "The miniaturization of satisfaction among frail elders living alone." Paper presented at the 44th annual meeting of The Gerontological Society of America, San Francisco, CA.

Rubinstein, Robert L. 1992. "Anthropological methods in gerontological research: Entering the world of meaning." *Journal of Aging Studies, 6*, 57–66.

Rubinstein, Robert L. 1996. "Biographic perspectives on hardship: Lifetime poverty in old age." Paper presented at the 49th annual meeting of The Gerontological Society of America, Washington, DC.

Ruggles, P. 1987. *The economic status of low income elderly*. Washington, DC: The Urban Institute.

Ruggles, P., & Moon, M. 1986. *Poverty rates for the elderly and non-elderly under alternative definitions of income*. Washington, DC: The Urban Institute.

Schiller, Bradley R. 1989. *The economics of poverty and discrimination*. Englewood Cliffs, NJ: Prentice Hall.

Smeeding, T. 1986. "Nonmoney income and the elderly: The case of the 'tweeners." *Journal of Political Analysis and Management, 5*, 707–724.

Smeeding, T. 1990. "Economic status of the elderly." In *Handbook of aging and the social sciences*. R. Binstock & L. George, eds. Pp. 362–382. New York: Academic Press.

Stewart, Abigal J. 1994. "The women's movement and women's lives: Linking individual development and social events." In *The narrative study of lives: Exploring idenity and gender*, Vol. 2. Amia Lieblich & Ruthellen Josselson, eds. Pp. 230–250. Thousand Oaks, CA: Sage.

Townsend, Peter. 1970. "Introduction." In *The concept of poverty*. Peter Townsend, ed. Pp. ix–xi. New York: American Elsevier.

Villiers Foundation. 1987. *On the other side of easy street*. Washington, DC.

Weber, Max. 1996 (1930). *The Protestant ethic and the spirit of capitalism*. Los Angeles, CA: Roxbury.

Widdershoven, Guy A.M. 1993. "The story of life: Hermeneutic perspectives on the relationship between narrative and life history." In *The narrative study of lives*, Vol. 1. Ruthellen Josselson & Amia Lieblich, eds. Pp. 1–20. Newbury Park, CA: Sage.

Wiener, Wendy J., & Rosenthal, George C. 1993. "A moment's monument: The psychology of keeping a diary." In *The narrative study of lives*, Vol. 1. Ruthellen Josselson & Amia Lieblich, eds. Pp. 30–58. Newbury Park, CA: Sage.

Zimmerman, Larry J. 1997. "Anthropology and responses to the reburial issue." In *Indians and anthropologists: Vine Deloria, Jr., and the critique of anthropology*. Thomas Biolsi and Larry J. Zimmerman, eds. Pp. 92–112. Tucson, AR: The University of Arizona Press.

Index

Accomplishments
  as coping strategy, 113–118
  expectations and, 64–70
African American women, 60 (see also
  Class)
Afterlife, 161–166
Age issues, 7–9
Alcott, Mrs., 177–183
Awareness of class, 135–139

Bernini, Mrs., 83–85
Bersky, Mrs., 197–202, 207
Billings, Mrs., 222–228
Billson, Mrs., 81–83
Bowser, Mrs., 92–96
Butcher, Mrs., 26–32

Caucasian women, 60, 192 (see also
  Class)
Characters in story, 209, 221–228
Clarkson, Mrs., 63–64, 221
Class (see also Self-concept and class)
  awareness of, 135–139
  expectations and, 60–62
  theoretical description and issues of,
    7–9
Cleveland, Mrs., 55–57
Coles, Ms., 58–60
Coping strategies and techniques
  accomplishments, 113–118
  generativity, 97–107
  overview, 14–15, 97
  spirituality, 107–113
  summary, 118–119
Corner, Mrs., 60–62
Culture, American, 185

Cummings, Mrs., 113–119, 154
Curston, Mrs., 144–149
Custer, Mrs., 78–81, 96, 165–166, 183

Davies, Mrs., 161–165
Death, issues of, 166–171
Depression, Great, 86, 121
DeSoto, Mrs., 215–222
Dickson, Mrs., 135–139, 148–149, 177
Dying, issues of, 166–171

Eldredge, Mrs., 155–161
Emil, Mrs., 151–154, 183
Expectations
  accomplishments in light of, 64–70
  class and, 60–62
  family and, legacy of, 47–57
  financial, 192
  for future, personal, 176–183
  gender and, 57–60
  limitations and, perceived, 62–64
  overview, 13, 47
  summary, 70–71

Family, legacy of, 47–57
Financial expectations, 192
Findings, summary of
  future research and, 235
  overview, 17, 233–234
  subjective and objective poverty
    and, 234–235
Future research, 235
Future, thoughts of personal
  afterlife, 161–166
  dying and death, 171–176
  expectations for, 176–183

Future, thoughts of persona *(continued)*
    overview, 15–16, 151–155
    paranormal experiences, 166–171
    spirituality, 155–160
    summary, 183–184

Gender
    expectations and, 57–60
    theoretical description and issues of,
        7–9
Generativity as coping strategy, 97–107
God, experiences with, 9–10
Gray, Mrs., 186–192, 207
Greene, Mrs., 122–126, 130, 148–149
Grosso, Mrs., 74–75
Guterez, Mrs., 210–215, 232

Harrington, Michael, 11
Hayworth, Mrs., 202–206

Independence, 73, 86–89
Interviewees *(see specific names)*

Jonas, Mrs., 107–113, 118, 130

Life story, 74–83, 210
Limitations, expectations shaped by
    perceived, 62–64

McDouglas, Mrs., 228–232
McFadden, Mrs., 167–171
McKenna, Mrs., 52–55
Mary, Miss, 126–131
Merton, Mrs., 172–176, 183
Metaphors, 228–232
Methods of study
    conceptual framework, 3–4
    format, 5–6
    procedure, 5
    respondents, 4–5
Meyer, Mrs., 89–92, 96
Millson, Mrs., 86–89, 183
Moon, M., 10
Moral issue of poverty
    overview, 16, 185–206
    summary, 206–207

Narrative issues, 6–7

Paranormal experiences, 166–171
Pargament, Kenneth I., 155
Pierson, Mrs., 131–135, 148
Potts, Mrs., 49–52, 57
Poverty *(see also* Coping strategies and
        techniques; Subjective and objec-
        tive poverty)
    background of, 10–12
    as moral issue, 16, 185–207
    perception of, 131–135
    "rediscovery" of American, 11
Privilege, perception of, 122–131

Quaid, Mrs., 65–70
Quill, Mrs., 47–49, 56–57, 139, 177

Race issues, 7–9
"Rediscovery" of American poverty,
    11
Retrospection
    characters in story, 209, 221–228
    life story, 210
    metaphors, 228–232
    overview, 16–17, 209–215
    self as package, 209–210, 215–221
    subjective and objective poverty
        and, 209
    summary, 232
Rose, Mrs., 140–144
Ruggles, P., 10

Self as package, 209–210, 215–221
Self-concept and class
    awareness of class and, 135–139
    interview, 144–148
    overview, 15, 121–122
    poverty and, perception of, 131–135
    privilege and, perception of, 122–131
    social forces and, 139–144
    summary, 148–149
Self-presentation
    independence, 73, 86–89
    life story and, 74–83

overview, 13–14, 73
summary, 96
temporal focus, 73, 89–95
themes, overview of, 83–85
Sheck, Mrs., 21–26, 221
Simmons, Mrs., 103–107
Social class (*see* Class)
Social forces, 139–144
Spirituality
  as coping strategy, 107–113
  future and, thoughts of personal,
    155–160
Stoffer, Mrs., 192–197, 207
Subjective and objective poverty
  Butcher and (Mrs.), 26–32
  concept, 19–20
  findings and, 234–235
  overview, 12–13, 19–21
  retrospection and, 209
  Sheck and (Mrs.), 21–26
  summary, 45–46

Thorne and (Mrs.), 32–37
Winter and (Mrs.), 37–45
Supplemental Security Income, 20–21

Temporal focus, 73, 89–95
Theoretical description
  age issues, 7–9
  background of poverty, 10–12
  class issues, 7–9
  gender issues, 7–9
  God, experiences of, 9–10
  methods, 3–6
  narrative issues, 6–7
  overview, 1–3, 12
  race issues, 7–9
Thorne, Mrs., 32–37
Tweeners, 11

Warren, Mrs., 97–103, 118
Wexler, Mrs., 75–78, 96
Winter, Mrs., 37–45